South Asian Migration to Gulf Countries

T0360903

South Asians constitute the largest expatriate population in the Gulf Cooperation Council (GCC) countries. Their contribution in the socio-economic, technological and educational development of GCC nations is immense. This book offers one of the first systematic analyses of South Asia–Gulf migration dynamics and its varied impact on countries such as India, Nepal, Bangladesh, Pakistan and Sri Lanka. It deals with public policy, socio-economic mobility, remittance policy, global financial crisis and labour issues. Bringing together essays from contributors from around the world, the volume reveals not only the multi-dimensionality of the migration process between the two regions, but also the diversity and the underlying unity of the South Asian countries.

This book will be invaluable to scholars and students of migration studies, development studies and sociology as well as policymakers, administrators, academics and non-governmental organisations in the field.

Prakash C. Jain is Senior Fellow at the Indian Council of Social Science Research and affiliated to the Centre for Comparative Politics & Political Theory, School of International Studies, Jawaharlal Nehru University, New Delhi.

Ginu Zacharia Oommen is Junior Fellow at the Nehru Memorial Museum and Library, Teen Murti House, New Delhi.

South Asian Migration to Gulf Countries

History, policies, development

Edited by
Prakash C. Jain and
Ginu Zacharia Oommen

Routledge
Taylor & Francis Group

LONDON AND NEW YORK

First published 2016 by Routledge

2 Park Square, Milton Park, Abingdon, Oxfordshire OX14 4RN
711 Third Avenue, New York, NY 10017

Routledge is an imprint of the Taylor & Francis Group, an informa business

First issued in paperback 2017

British Library Cataloguing-in-Publication Data
A catalogue record for this book is available from the British Library

Library of Congress Cataloging-in-Publication Data
A catalog record has been requested for this book

ISBN: 978-1-138-89894-3 (hbk)
ISBN: 978-0-8153-7604-0 (pbk)

Typeset in Sabon
by Apex CoVantage, LLC

Contents

Figures

Tables

Boxes

Acknowledgements

We take this opportunity to express our sincere thanks to all the contributors without whose cooperation and support this volume would not have been completed and taken the shape it did. We also extend our gratitude to Dr Rohan D'Souza and Professor Irudaya Rajan for their earnest and generous advice towards the publication of this anthology. Finally, our heartfelt appreciation to the entire Routledge team for their meticulous efforts and hard work in making this project a great success.

Prakash C. Jain
Ginu Zacharia Oommen

Abbreviations

ARAMCO	Arabian American Oil Company
BAPCO	Bahrain Petroleum Company
BHRS	Bangladesh Household Remittance Survey
BMET	Bureau of Manpower, Employment and Training
CDS	Centre for Development Studies
DFID	Department for International Development
EMB	Emigration Management Bill
FDI	Foreign Direct Investment
GCC	Gulf Cooperation Council
GDP	Gross Domestic Product
IOM	International Organization for Migration
ICWF	Indian Community Welfare Fund
IMF	International Monetary Fund
KOC	Kuwait Oil Company
KSA	Kingdom of Saudi Arabia
LAS	League of Arab States
MGPSY	Mahatma Gandhi Pravasi Suraksha Yojana
MOIA	Ministry of Overseas Indian Affairs
MRC	Migration Resource Centre
MTO	Money Transfer Operator
NELM	New Economics of Labour Migration
NGO	Non-governmental Organisation
NRI	Non-resident Indian
NWFP	North West Frontier Province
OECD	Organisation for Economic Co-operation and Development
OPEC	Organization of Petroleum Exporting Countries
OWRC	Overseas Workers Resource Centre

PDQ	Petroleum Development Qatar
PPS	Probability Proportional to Size
SAARC	South Asian Association for Regional Cooperation
UAE	United Arab Emirates
UN	United Nations

Contributors

Rita Afsar is a sociologist at the Bangladesh Institute of Development Studies, Dhaka, and visiting professor at the University of Western Australia. Her research focuses on Bangladeshi migrant labour, urbanisation and urban poverty.

Andrzej Kapiszewski was a renowned Polish sociologist and was Professor at the Jagiellonian University in Krakow. He was Polish Ambassador to the United Arab Emirates and Qatar and wrote extensively on migrant labour.

G.M. Arif is a demographer, and currently he is Joint Director at the Pakistan Institute of Development Studies, Islamabad. He has been member of various government commissions and study groups on poverty reduction and migration.

Michele Ruth Gamburd is Professor and Chair, Anthropology Department at the Portland State University, USA. She is the author of *The Kitchen Spoon's Handle: Transnationalism and Sri Lanka's Migrant Housemaids*.

Zakir Hussain is Research Fellow at the Indian Council of World Affairs, New Delhi. He completed his doctorate on India's economic relations with the GCC countries in the post-1990 period.

Prakash C. Jain is Senior Fellow at the Indian Council for Social Sciences Research (ICSSR). He was until recently Professor (sociology) at the School of International Studies, Jawaharlal Nehru University, New Delhi. The author of *Racial Discrimination against Overseas Indians: A Class Analysis* (1990), *Indians* *in South Africa: Political Economy of Race Relations* (1999), *Population and Society in West Asia: Essays in Comparative Demography* (2001), and *Non-Resident Indian Entrepreneurs in the United Arab Emirates* (2010), Dr Jain has to his credit a number of articles published in reputed journals.

Kundan Kumar is a doctoral candidate at the Centre for West Asian Studies, School of International Studies, Jawaharlal Nehru University. He has recently co-edited a book titled *Indian Trade Diaspora in the Arabian Peninsula*. He is currently working on issues of inter-Asia movement, migration and displacement of Indians, with special emphasis on the British colonial times.

D. Narayana is Professor at the Centre for Development Studies, Thiruvananthapuram, Kerala. He was a Fulbright Fellow at Harvard and visiting professor at the University of Montreal.

Ginu Zacharia Oommen is Junior Fellow at the Nehru Memorial Museum and Library, New Delhi. Prior to this, he was Hermès Postdoctoral Fellow at MIGRINTER, University of Poitiers, France, and Associate Fellow at Foundation Maison des Sciences de l'homme, Paris. His major publications include *Ethnicity, Marginality and Identity: The Jews of Cochin in Israel* (2011). He has done fieldwork on Indian immigrants in Israel, Palestine, Kuwait and France.

Marie Percot is an anthropologist and is associated with *the Laboratoire d' AnthropologieUrbaine/Institut Interdisciplinaire d' Anthropologie du Contemporain* (EHESS) in Paris, France. She worked extensively on the anthropology of labour and has edited three books on migration.

Md Mizanur Rahman is Senior Research Fellow at the Institute of South Asian Studies, National University of Singapore. Dr Rahman's areas of expertise include international labour migration, diaspora engagement, migrant businesses, immigrant integration, migration and development, migration policy and remittances.

S. Irudaya Rajan is Chair Professor, Ministry of Overseas Indian Affairs, Research Unit on International Migration at the Centre for Development Studies, Thiruvananthapuram, Kerala. He has coordinated several major migration surveys and has published extensively in both national and international journals. He is the author and editor of various books on Indian migration.

Philippe Venier is a geographer and Assistant Professor at MIGRINTER, University de Poitiers, France. His current research focuses on Keralite migrants in the Gulf countries.

Neha Wadhawan is Postdoctoral Fellow in the Research Unit on International Migration at the Centre for Development Studies, Thiruvananthapuram, Kerala. She has completed her doctorate on the migration of Nepalese to the Gulf countries.

Introduction

Prakash C. Jain and Ginu Zacharia Oommen

In the contemporary globalised world, migration and flow of people across the world is an inevitable phenomenon. Some idea of this can be had from the fact that each year over 200 million people migrate globally from one country to another in search of gainful employment. International migration generally involves movement of people from low-income countries to high-income countries. During the past few decades, the Persian Gulf region has been one such area which has witnessed tremendous economic development due to its oil economy. This oil boom in the Gulf countries has attracted a large number of workers from around the world. South Asians constitute an important segment of this labour force.

The terms South Asia and South Asian are of recent vintage, coined and used more by Western academics and numerous international agencies in order to categorize countries, inhabitants and diasporic communities from the Indian subcontinent settled in different parts of the world. The term South Asian has undergone a long and evolutionary transformation from subcontinental immigrants being called 'Hindoos', 'East Indians', 'Asian Indians', 'Pakistanis', and 'Bangladeshis' to 'South Asians'. The term is widely prevalent and understood by academics and policymakers of the subcontinent. At the same time, these terms are also increasingly gaining ground in the field of migration and diaspora studies. Classificatory usage apart, South Asian countries also share a number of socio-economic, cultural and religious characteristics including levels of poverty, inequality, corruption, ethnic conflicts, modernization, and development. Notwithstanding the historicity of outmigration from the subcontinent, it is for the reasons of these similarities that a massive South Asian migration has been taking place to the Gulf countries. The brief account of the South Asian outmigration in modern times would further put the Gulf migration phenomenon into proper perspective.

Migration from the Indian subcontinent overseas began with the export of indentured, contract or 'coolie' labour in the 1830s when, following the abolition of slavery in the British Empire, labour was needed to work on the sugar, rice and rubber plantations in various British colonies. Until the Second World War Indians migrated mainly as *indentured* labourers to British Guiana, Trinidad, Surinam (then a Dutch colony), South Africa, Fiji, Mauritius, Reunion Island (then a French colony) (Tinker 1974; Jain 1990), and as *kangani* or *maistry* labourers to Burma, Malaya, Singapore, and Ceylon (Sri Lanka) (Mahajani 1960; Arasaratnam 1970). Indian traders also migrated to Fiji, Kenya, Uganda, Tanzania, and South Africa (Mangat 1969; Jain 1990). Such migration, however, was proportionately very small. This form of emigration is known as 'free' or 'passage' emigration – the nomenclature being derived from the fact that the emigrants paid their own passage and were free in all respects.

Following the Second World War, migration from the Indian subcontinent to the advanced industrialised countries of Europe and North America had also begun to gain momentum. The post-war economic expansion in these countries created heavy demand for skilled labour and professionals. Simultaneously, immigration laws were also relaxed in Canada and the United States (US). This form of overseas migration of skilled and educated personnel, popularly known as 'brain drain', thus resulted in the formation of sizeable Indian and Pakistani communities in Britain, Canada, the US, Australia, and New Zealand (Helweg 1987; Helweg and Helweg 1990; High Level Committee, 2001). Along with this form of migration, which still is very active these days due to the migration of information technology (IT) professionals, labour migration to the Gulf countries had also been taking place since at least the mid-1970s (Jain 2003). In 1971, with the formation of Bangladesh, international migration accelerated, particularly to Western Europe, North America and the Asia-Pacific region and, subsequently, to the Persian Gulf countries.

Although migration from Sri Lanka, especially of Tamil minorities, had been going on to some of the South East Asian countries since the early colonial period, the internal political turmoil, particularly the Sinhalese-Tamil ethnic conflict, had intensified overseas labour migration in the late 1970s to countries of the Organisation for Economic Cooperation and Development (OECD) and Gulf Cooperation Council (GCC). In the case of Nepal, the migratory process had started during the colonial period, whereby a small number of Nepalese migrated mainly as soldiers in the British army. Additionally, they also migrated as tea plantation workers to the tea estates in India which were largely owned by British companies. Moreover, in the 1990s, political instability, unemployment and poverty had compelled a large outflow of migrants from Nepal to the GCC countries, particularly as domestic workers, cooks, waiters, security personnel, and nurses.

Thus, historically, five distinctive patterns of emigration can be broadly identified in the South Asian region: (*i*) indentured labour emigration; (*ii*) kangani/maistry labour emigration; (*iii*) 'passage' or 'free' migration; (*iv*) 'brain drain' type or voluntary emigration to the metropolitan countries of Europe, North America and Oceania; and (*v*) labour migration to West Asia including the Gulf countries. While the first three forms of migration were colonial phenomena, the last two are the result of the inherent contradiction of postcolonial socio-economic developments in South Asian countries (Jain 1990). This volume focuses on the last form of migration mentioned above.

South Asia's trade relations with the Persian Gulf region date back to the period of the Indus Valley Civilization. A number of small colonies of Gujarati banias dotted the region as early as the 9th century CE. Archaeological evidence in the form of a Hindu temple's ruins at Qalhat in Oman is available from the 16th century onwards, suggesting the presence of Indians. By the 17th and 18th centuries, such settlements were common throughout the region, particularly in present-day Iran, Iraq, Oman, Yemen, Bahrain, and Saudi Arabia. British colonization of the Gulf region as well as the Indian subcontinent in the 19th century further helped in consolidating the settlement of Indians (as merchants, bankers, pearl financiers, importers and exporters, customs farmers, contractors, and government officials) in the Gulf countries.

The emergence of Gulf countries as oil exporting economies since the early 1970s, and developmental activities throughout the region, further changed the size and complexion of the South Asian labour community in the region as well as of the trading, entrepreneurial and professional communities. Today, the South Asian labour community is a vibrant community without which Gulf economies perhaps would not survive (see Jain and Kumar 2012).

The story of South Asian labour immigration into the Gulf region is neither as old nor as intriguing as that of the trading community. It is about a century-old phenomenon, dating back to the early 20th century when oil began to be discovered and explored in the region (Seccombe and Lawless 1986). As a result of the oil export economy since the 1970s, the Gulf countries have emerged as the prime destination for immigrant manpower from across the world, of which South Asians have undoubtedly become the predominant group. Two major events were particularly helpful in this process: (*i*) the intensification of globalisation since the 1990s which accelerated developmental activities and the demand for immigrant manpower in the Gulf states and (*ii*) the withdrawal of Yemeni and Palestinian labour from Saudi Arabia and other Gulf countries on account of Iraq's invasion of Kuwait in the wake of their support to Iraq. Both these factors were instrumental in rendering numeric primacy to South Asians in the Gulf countries. Thus the proportion of the Arabian expatriate population which was 72 per cent in the 1970s was reduced to 31 per cent in the late 1990s (Kapiszewski 2006). Certain characteristic features of South Asian manpower, namely docility, political neutrality, flexibility, willingness to work at marginal wage differentials, and capacity to work hard also helped in this process.

Currently, nearly 9.5 million South Asian expatriates are working in various sectors of the GCC region (Rajan and Narayana 2012). The large numbers of South Asian migrants in the GCC countries undoubtedly have a significant impact on the economic, social, cultural, and political milieu of these countries. However, there is very little quantitative information on these migrants, leaving large knowledge gaps with regard to the extent and type of influences that migrants have on the GCC countries and also the influence of the migration experience on the migrants themselves. This anthology attempts to understand the multifaceted nuances and dynamics of this unique migratory phenomenon.

This volume is divided into three parts. Part I deals with comparative and theoretical issues, whereas Part II and Part III focus on two major substantive themes, namely migration dynamics and the impact of migration respectively. The division is only heuristic as some chapters cover a little of all the themes.

International migration is a complex process involving constituent elements such as motivation and decision to migrate; knowledge and choice of destination; dealing with recruitment agents and/or networking with family members, kin or friends already abroad; arranging for the requisite finance; and, finally, getting the passport, visa and other paperwork necessary for eventual migration. These aspects can be summarised using the concept of 'migration dynamics', which mainly focuses on the causes and wherewithal of migration in the sending country/region.

Likewise, the impact of migration is a multifarious phenomenon – with implications for both the sending as well as the receiving country/region in terms of demographics, sociopolitical system, economic development, educational and occupational mobility, and way of life and value system. In the context of the sending country/region, the impact of migration is often understood in terms of economic remittances, on the one hand, and sociocultural remittances, on the other. While the former occurs through the transfer of money and gifts, the latter is done by the migrants themselves through their changed world view and way of life. Philanthropy directed towards the sending region by the migrants should be considered a hyphenated by-product or activity of the two forms of remittances mentioned above. Migration to the Gulf being temporary and circular in nature, return migration and rehabilitation of returnees have also emerged as important issues in most South Asian countries.

Ginu Zacharia Oommen, in Chapter 1, explores the multifaceted nuances of the 'South Asia-Gulf migration corridor' and also attempts to unearth the future prospects and major challenges. At present, in the Gulf region, South Asian expatriates number around 9 million, of which Indians constitute the largest group, followed by Pakistanis and Bangladeshis. Surprisingly, the recent global economic crisis, nationalisation policies, job cuts, anti-immigrant policies of the GCC governments, socio-spatial isolation of the expatriates, and ethnic/racial discrimination have not been able to dent the flow of migrants from the South Asian region. The strategic and economic effects of Asianisation of migrant workers in GCC countries, particularly its impact in terms of migration and remittances, are undoubtedly an important aspect in the context of the emerging Gulf-South Asia relations. The South Asia region, especially India, receives the largest amount of remittances ($23 billion) and those from the GCC form the major external financial flow for these developing nations. This chapter also discusses remittance behaviour, the changing gender roles of immigrants, social-spatial mobility, strategic interests of both South Asia and GCC Countries, migrants' perception and the interaction between nationals and non-nationals.

In addition to South Asian labour there is also a significant number of manpower from South East Asian countries. The 'Asianisation' of migrant labour in the Gulf is the outcome of the 'preference and choice' of the receiving governments due to various economic-political considerations. Though the composition of migrant workers has been shifting in the GCC, a consistent and significant shift from Arab workers to Asians had taken place ever since the late 1970s, mainly to safeguard the political interests of the oil-rich monarchies. Chapter 2 (Andrzej Kapiszewski) explores the intrinsic issues, population dilemmas, policy challenges and socio-economic implications of the Asian migrant workers in the host society. The Asian community has made a remarkable contribution to the socio-economic and cultural development of the GCC countries and has become the dominant workforce in the economy of the region. The large influx of foreign workers has 'posed security, socio-economic and cultural threats to the local population' and therefore the receiving governments have had to promulgate certain policies to restrict the inflow of excessive migrants and also to control the activities of the expatriates. Kapiszewski cautions that, in the future, migration would remain a complex issue in the GCC region between the profit-driven private sector and the state apparatus due to the growing unemployment of the natives, security issues and the undesirable cultural influence of the migrants. Nevertheless, Kapiszewski predicts that owing to various factors like unique royal culture, stereotype images towards certain job sectors, restrictions on native women in the workforce, and the unwelcoming attitude towards non-GCC Arab labour, Asians will continue to dominate the workforce.

Kundan Kumar, in Chapter 3, provides a historical perspective on migratory movements from the Indian subcontinent to the Persian Gulf countries. He highlights the existence of Indian settlements and merchant guilds in Aden and other Gulf ports prior to the discovery of oil. During the 19th century, the industrialisation process, pearl trading, haj, and the requirement of skilled workers in the ports had prompted the flow of Indians to the Persian Gulf region. These included ordinary artisans, masons, technicians, clerks, and administrative personnel, etc., largely to support the British colonial apparatus in the region. Kundan argues that colonial powers used 'Indian subjects' as treasured resources to sustain and operate communications, educational institutions, health care systems, bureaucracy, postal services, and so on. Later, in the 1930s, almost all major Western oil companies like Kuwait Oil Company (KOC), Arabian-American Oil Company (ARMACO) and Petroleum Development Qatar (PDQ) employed a substantial number of labourers from the subcontinent, and a recruiting office was established in Surat for this purpose. Moreover, the British had encouraged and favoured the conscription of Indians in the industrial and development sectors over workers from neighbouring Arab countries. Thus, by the late 1950s, Indian and Pakistani migrant workers constituted the largest workforce in many Gulf countries, particularly in Kuwait and Bahrain. Kundan makes the point that the contemporary large-scale migration of workers to GCC countries from India is not an isolated event connected to the oil boom of the 1970s, as it dates back to colonial policies and historic trade linkages.

Zakir Hussain, in Chapter 4, attempts to explore the multilayered reasons for the eventual Asianisation of migration to GCC countries. Hussain argues that massive developmental activities forced the oil-rich monarchies to follow an 'open door' demographic policy, encouraging large-scale of migration from outside the region. The neighbouring Arab countries had failed to provide a suitable and skilled workforce to the region. However, the labour market in the GCC is vertically divided into public and private sectors and a large numbers of expatriate workers have been accommodated in the private sector with relatively low wages and fewer facilities compared to the native workers who are employed in the public sector. Thus, Hussain argues that the job market is not egalitarian in nature and that the wage differential is quite high between the expatriates and the natives. In spite of this, and including the recent economic recession and the radical decline of oil production, the inflow of migrant labour to the GCC countries hasn't reduced. However, various domestic factors, such as high unemployment among the natives, economic burdens due to the Gulf Wars, increase in female participation in the labour market, and the Arab Spring, have forced many GCC countries to introduce restrictive policies towards migration (e.g., the implementation of the Nitaqat Law) and active enrolment of natives in the private sector. Thus, the flow of migration from South Asia to GCC countries in the future might be hampered due to the domestic compulsions and restrictive policies of the host countries.

Chapter 5 by Prakash C. Jain highlights the fact that although Indian labour migration to the Gulf countries began with the emergence of the oil industry in the Gulf region during the early years of the 20th century, the process only gained momentum with the oil price boom of 1973–74. Since then, with minor fluctuations, the upward trend of Indian labour migration continued unabated and has resulted in drastic changes in the size and complexion of the Indian expatriate population in the Gulf. This is so in spite of the fact that the Gulf countries have been pursuing a policy of indigenisation with regard to labour recruitment for over three decades now. Against this background, this chapter focuses on the major aspects of migration dynamics of Indian labour to the Gulf countries. These include studying circular and return migration, the socio-economic characteristics of the migrants, and volume and strength of migrants.

A very large majority of the population living in the United Arab Emirates (UAE) is foreign workers, particularly of Indian origin. Philippe Venier, in Chapter 6, discusses the socio-spatial mobility and migratory strategies of highly skilled/professional Keralite workers in the UAE. Venier notes that immigrants from the state of Kerala are the most important visible and dynamic expatriate community. In the Gulf countries, migration is temporary and linked with a working contract. However, Venier argues that this notion of migration being temporary is now questioned by a minority of Keralites who consider emigration to be an opportunity to live with their family in the host country and stay on longer as expatriates. Various factors are at the root of these new migratory strategies: a numerically strong and long-established Keralite community, a set of laws facilitating family reunification and entrepreneurial initiatives, and new migration projects related to socio-economic changes in the country of origin. The spatial trends in the UAE show that longer settlements of some migrants are linked to the globalisation and 'metropolisation' processes occurring in the UAE. Chapter 6 also reveals the variability in economic development between various UAE cities and its connection with the settlement patterns of Kerala immigrants.

Bangladesh is a late entrant into the GCC job market connected to its wounded separation from Pakistan and its turbulent relations with the Islamic world. However, since 1976, nearly 6 million Bangladeshi workers have migrated to the GCC region and Bangladesh has emerged as one of the top ten remittances-recipient countries in the world. The astounding exodus of migrant workers to the GCC countries and the multifaceted dynamics of the migratory process have been studied by Rita Afsar in Chapter 7. Amongst other factors, unemployment, poverty, climatic disasters, uneven development, and debt are some of the reasons for the large outflow of male-dominated migration to GCC countries, particularly to Saudi Arabia and the UAE. Afsar undertakes an in-depth analysis of the burden of migrant families prior to the migration and argues that both 'pull and push' factors have been significantly influenced by the idea of 'Bhalo visa' (one that would yield better work opportunities and higher incomes), despite the high cost involved.

Nepali migration to GCC countries is a recent phenomenon as India has always been a traditional destination for migrant workers from Nepal. Since time immemorial, Nepalese have been living and working in India and vice versa. The Indian census data for the years 1961, 1971, 1981, and 1991 record about half a million Nepalese migrants to India (Dutta 2005). Political instability, a repressive monarchy, the Maoist insurgency, and extended political movements are some of the factors that have prompted large-scale migration of Nepalese outside the Himalayan region. Neha Wadhawan, in Chapter 8, examines the migratory process of Nepalese workers to the GCC countries, the flow of remittances, and the impact of this process on Nepalese society. This chapter is an empirical/ethnographic study and it analyses the gendered nature of the migration. Wadhawan argues that the migration of women to the GCC region has increased substantially despite the implementation of restrictive legislations in Nepal. At the same time, the ban on the migration of women domestic workers and the patriarchal approach of the government agencies has forced women to rely on illegal channels and spurious recruiting agencies. However, despite the challenges, the GCC region holds greater appeal and hope among the downtrodden sections of society, and the migration of both men and women has been continuing uninterruptedly from Nepal.

Md Mizanur Rahman, in Chapter 9, discusses the risks, challenges, trials, cheatings by the recruiting agencies, and huge economic burden that migrants undertake during the migration process from their home country. This is a unique study which highlights the hidden and painful stories of migrant workers and the risk taken by the 'transnationally split' migrant families in their expedition to reach the 'dream land', Gulf, through the anthropological research on Bangladeshi migrant workers in Saudi Arabia. Rahman highlights the dreadful risks and implications of the 'Kafala system' (sponsorship system) and exposes the darker side of the 'visa trade' and its potential impact of the economic structure of the family. The exploitation of the recruiting agencies and the helplessness of the governments of the home countries of the migrants in curtailing the powerful recruitment private lobby are two issues that are being raised at various high-level meetings on migrant workers. This chapter also unearths the uneven management of remittances in the migrant households and Rahman points out that migration does not necessarily contribute to capital accumulation. He also explains how the spurious recruitment process, visa trading, harsh working conditions, the autocratic nature of the Kafala system, and the high visa cost undermine the stability and economic structures of the migrant families. Therefore, both sending and receiving countries have to deliberate upon the plight of migrants more seriously and formulate policies that safeguard the rights of the migrant workers.

In Chapter 10, Michele Ruth Gamburd analyses the sociocultural and migration dynamics of Sri Lankan women domestic workers in the GCC region. Though the prolonged ethnic conflicts, political instability and unemployment are some of the major factors that have prompted an outward flow of migrant workers, the interesting point is that female migrants have outnumbered male migrants in the case of Sri Lanka. Unlike other South Asian countries, the women have assumed the role of breadwinners and entered into the 'care industry' of GCC countries on a massive scale since the 1990s. Gamburd notes further that the unprecedented and voluminous flow of remittances from the GCC countries was a great wherewithal for the conflict-ridden and ailing Sri Lankan economy as the migrant workers to the GCC countries constitute a foremost share of the total migrant workers from the island. Gamburd argues that the working conditions of women migrant workers in the GCC countries are quite alarming as there is hardly any law to safeguard labour rights, abuse and isolation of maids who are working in households. The social consequences of female migration to GCC countries is quite significant as it has altered the patriarchal norms, gender roles, family settings, and class structure of Sri Lankan society. Moreover, the economic dependency on women migrants has fortified the authority and position of women in the family and has also affected the class hierarchies of the Gulf pockets (places with large concentration of Gulf migrants) to a great extent.

Women's migration to GCC countries, particularly of nurses, has not received adequate attention in migration studies. Chapter 11 (Marie Percot) offers an ethnographic study on the subject. The large demand for paramedics and nurses in GCC countries has miraculously removed the stigma attached to the nursing profession and in the contemporary context this kind of migration is considered to be a major avenue for social mobility and prosperity. Percot argues that for young women a nursing degree is not a mere academic degree but a passport to move up the social ladder as well as to escape from the patriarchal and social hierarchy of society. The 'exceedingly affluent Gulf nurse' is in high demand in the 'matrimonial market' and this has perhaps altered the gender equations of migrant households. Percot notes how 'feminine networks' play a crucial role in nursing migration and how the oil-rich Gulf countries continue to be the main destination for qualified nurses and paramedics. The migration of nurses brings significant changes in social mobility, migratory opportunities, social status, and saving patterns of migrant households.

G. M. Arif, in Chapter 12, highlights the positive impact of Gulf migration from Pakistan and confirms the fact that remittances have contributed immensely in the socio-economic mobility of migrant families. The poverty-stricken rural areas were uplifted in an unprecedented manner due to the voluminous flow of remittances from the Gulf region and the social networks have enabled the poor to reach the Gulf with relatively lesser cost. Arif argues that the remittances have increased consumerism among migrant households and that a major share was spent on housing, food, education, purchase of land, and on health care. There is a visible occupation shift for return migrants. The diverse occupational experience attained abroad and the capital earned in the host society has induced return migrants with a spirit of entrepreneurship, with most of them preferring self-employment/own business to their previous occupation. Thus Arif indicates that return migrants inadvertently promote entrepreneurship in society and thereby help households to sustain and maintain continuity in the economic structure. This chapter concludes with an appeal for the extension of migration opportunities to the poorer regions of Pakistan and also for affordable recruitment services in the backward regions of the country.

S. Irudaya Rajan and D. Narayana, in Chapter 13, examine the implications of global recession in GCC countries and its impact on migrant workers. The authors argue that the vast trade surplus and diversification of oil wealth of the oil-rich monarchies have helped the GCC countries to overcome the global recession. Moreover it has reduced the negative impact of recession in terms of large-scale retrenchment, massive wage cuts and decline of outward remittances. Rajan and Narayana observe that the economic recession did have a marginal impact on the South Asian migrant workers as the return flow of South Asians from the GCC region was less than 5 per cent. At the same time, the inflow of migrant workers to the GCC region from South Asia during the recession period continued without any drastic reduction as was expected by policymakers. More importantly, based on field survey, both Rajan and Narayana argue that the flow of remittances to the migrant household in South Asia has not been reduced and that the consumption patterns have also continued to remain steady during the period 2008–09. The chapter concludes that with the quick recovery of the economy in 2010 both the outflow of labour from South Asia and the inflow of remittances from the GCC region have been maintained uninterruptedly.

Migration dynamics in South Asian countries is not a smooth process. Bureaucracy and red tape are two major hurdles in the smooth functioning of this process. In the case of India, for example, getting a passport and obtaining emigration clearance from the Protector General of Emigrants (PGE), arranging for a work visa from the employer and attestation of the same by the Indian mission in the country of destination (in the case of unskilled workers), etc., are generally time-consuming activities. At the individual level, arranging the requisite funds for meeting expenses involved in migration, which is often done through bank loans and or mortgaging/selling property/land, is also not conducive to smooth functioning of migration dynamics. Fraudulent recruitment agents, some of whom are not registered with the PGE, create additional problems. Some of these problems can easily be overcome by widely disseminating information about migration procedures in the sending country/region of South Asia. In this connection, regional cooperation is required which can be effected by creating a body like the South Asian Migration Commission under the aegis of the South Asian Association for Regional Cooperation (SAARC) to regulate migration from South Asia (Soban 2011).

The contributions to this volume focus on select aspects of South Asian migration to the Gulf and its impact on the sending countries. Return migration and rehabilitation, for example, are two major areas of migration dynamics that need to be discussed in detail in different South Asian contexts. Migration dynamics is not complete without taking into account the diasporic life or diasporic experience of emigrants in destination countries. Although in the case of Gulf countries the diasporic experience for most migrant workers is short and temporary, it is vital nonetheless. It is vital for the comprehension of the whole migration process. The diasporic experience of an emigrant community or an expatriate group focuses not only on their settlement patterns and economic, political and sociocultural status in the host country, but also on their smooth integration into it. In other words, expatriate communities must enjoy full human rights and should not be discriminated against in any manner. As most chapters in this volume reveal, this has not been so. South Asian expatriates, particularly unskilled labour and women workers, suffer from a number of disabilities in the Gulf countries, all of which need to be rectified. Some of these problems could be addressed by taking into account the initiatives taken through the Colombo Process and Abu Dhabi Dialogue.

References

Allen, Jr, Calvin. 1981. 'The Indian Merchant Community of Masqat', *Bulletin of the School of Oriental and African Studies*, 44(1): 39–51.

Arasaratnam, S. 1970. *Indians in Malaysia and Singapore*. Bombay: Oxford University Press.

Dutta, Pradipa. 2005. 'Feminisation of Nepali Migration to India', Paper Submitted at the IUSSP XXV International Conference, Tours, France, 18–23 July, 2005. http://iussp2005.princeton.edu/papers/50047.

Helweg, A. W. 1987. *Sikhs in England: The Development of Migrant Community*. Delhi: Oxford University Press.

Helweg, A. W. and Usha M. Helweg. 1990. *An Immigrant Success Story: East Indians in America*. Delhi: Oxford University Press.

High Level Committee, Ministry of External Affairs, Government of India, High Level Committee Report on the Indian Diaspora, Ministry of External Affairs, Government of India, New Delhi, 2001.

Jain, Prakash C. 1990. *Racial Discrimination against Overseas Indians: A Class Analysis*. Delhi: Concept Publishing Company.

Jain, Prakash C. and Kundan Kumar. 2012. *Indian Trade Diaspora in the Arabian Peninsula*. New Delhi: New Academic Publishers.

Kapiszewski, Andrzej. 2006. 'Arab Versus Asian Migrant Workers in the GCC Countries', United Nations Expert Group Meeting on International Migration and Development in the Arab Region, Population Division, Beirut, United Nations Secretariat, 22 May.

Mahajani, Usha. 1960. *The Role of Indian Minorities in Burma and Malaysia*. Bombay: Vora and Co.

Mangat, J. S. 1969. *A History of Asians in East Africa*. Oxford: Clarendon Press.

Rajan, S. Irudaya and D. Narayana. 2012. 'The Financial Crisis in the Gulf and its Impact on South Asian Migration', in Ibrahim Sirkeci, Jeffrey H. Cohen and Dilip Ratha (eds), *Migration and Remittances during the Global Financial Crisis and Beyond*. Washington DC: World Bank.

Seccombe, I. J. and R. I. Lawless. 1986. ' "Foreign Workers Dependence in the Gulf and the International Oil Companies 1910–50', *International Migration Review*, 20(3): 548–74.

Soban, Faorroq. 2011. 'South Asia Migrant Commission', in Saman Kelegama et al. (eds), *Migration, Remittances and Development in South Asia*, pp. 3–10. New Delhi: Sage Publications.

Tinker, Hugh. 1974. *A New System of Slavery: The Export of Indian Labour Overseas, 1830–1920*. London: Oxford University Press.

Part I

Comparative and theoretical issues

1

South Asian migration to the GCC countries

Emerging trends and challenges[1]

Ginu Zacharia Oommen

South Asia's long historical and cultural links with the Gulf date back to ancient times when West Asian ports were a key element in maritime trade. The discovery of oil and the economic rise of the Gulf Cooperation Council (GCC) countries attracted a huge influx of migrant workers from South Asian countries, particularly India, to the Gulf. At present, out of 15 million expatriates in the Gulf region, South Asians constitute around 9.5 million (Ozaki 2012). Of these, Indians are the largest group. The historical linkages, colonial domination, religious and cultural proximity, poverty, unemployment, political instability and insurgency in the South Asian countries are some of the factors that have led to this large influx to GCC countries. Kapiszewski (2006) argues that in the international milieu, West Asia has always been a major destination for labour migration, particularly the GCC countries. In Gulf countries, migrants constitute one-third of the total population.

In the 19th century, the British administration recruited skilled workers from the Indian subcontinent to the Gulf region in clerical and secretarial positions for the smooth functioning of the colonial administration (Jain 2006). Later, with the development of the oil industry, it created an additional need for workers in clerical jobs as well as skilled and semi-skilled manual occupations. As the local labour of the region was scarce, or had limited experience in industrial employment, oil companies were obliged to import large numbers of foreign workers in these categories. The South Asia region, especially India, receives the largest amount of remittances, particularly from the Gulf. Remittances from GCC countries form the major external financial flow for these countries. Seccombe and Lawless (1986) noted that the British administration promoted the migration of Indian workers to the newly established oil fields and they also blocked the inflow of Arab workers from the neighbouring Arab countries.

The strategic and economic implications of 'Asianisation' in terms of migration and remittance flow is quite important for both the sending and receiving countries, as India alone received US$23 billion in 2012 from the GCC region (Ozaki 2012). The South Asian community has made a remarkable contribution to the socio-economic progress and cultural development of the GCC countries. Interestingly, the 'Asianisation' of migrant labour in the Gulf is the outcome of the 'preference and choice' of the receiving governments due to various economic-political considerations. Though the composition of migrant workers has been shifting in GCC countries, a consistent and significant shift from Arab workers to Asians workers has taken place, ever since the late 1970s, mainly to safeguard the political interests of the oil-rich monarchies (Kapiszewski 2006). The initial domination of Arab workers from the neighbouring non-GCC countries started to decline in the mid-1970s, while, on the other hand, the inflow of South Asian workers increased significantly, which defended both the strategic and economic interests of the Gulf region. Moreover, the Asian migrant workers are considered to be relatively less expensive, diligent, submissive, and least interested in local politics. The flow of migrant workers from Asia, particularly South Asia, had given stiff competition to workers from West Asia (Silva and Naufal 2012). In the last three decades, GCC countries have massively recruited maximum workers from India, Pakistan, Bangladesh, Sri Lanka, and Nepal (Kapiszewski 2006). Thus the South Asian community has become the dominant workforce in the economy of the region. Table 1.1 indicates the unparalleled flow of South Asian migrant workers to the GCC region, from 1,069,761 in 2005 to 1,530,222 in 2008.

Surprisingly, the global economic crisis, job cuts, Arabisation policies of the GCC governments, and socio-spatial isolation of the expatriates has not reduced the steady flow of migrants from the Asian region, nor has it created a 'reverse migration' back to the sending countries. Irudaya Rajan, in "The Financial Crisis in the Gulf and its Impact on South Asian Migration and Remittances" notes that only 5 per cent of the migrant labourers returned to South Asia during the economic crisis (Rajan and Narayana 2012). The GCC government's frequent appeal for the 'localisation of jobs' has not

Table 1.1 Outflow of migrant workers from South Asia to the Gulf, 2005–09

Year	India	Pakistan	Bangladesh	Nepal	Sri Lanka
2005	454,628	127,810	207,089	88,230	192,004
2006	618,286	172,837	307,620	128,306	170,049
2007	770,510	278,631	483,757	182,870	188,365
2008	818,315	419,842	643,424	169,510	215,793
2009	592,299	407,077	N.A.	152,272	226,299
2010	610,409	350,147	286,975	168,302	229,352
2011	603,159	448,060	460,179	240,852	222,052
2012	722,139	628,452	457,590	274,221	247,356

Source: Rajan and Narayana (2012) "The Financial Crisis in the Gulf and its impact on South Asia Migration", in Ibrahim Sirkeci, Jeffrey H Cohen and Dilip Ratha (eds.) *Migration and Remittances during the Global Financial Crisis and Beyond*, The World Bank, Washington, DC; MOIA Annual Reports-2012; SLBFE (2013); BMET (2013); Department of Foreign Employment, Government of Nepal (2012).

been fully implemented by the workforce due to the non-availability of a well-qualified workforce from the native population.

The recent decision of the Saudi Arabian government to strictly implement *Nitaqat* or the nationalisation of the workforce could be an unexpected setback in the free flow of migration to the Gulf region (*The Hindu* 2013). The majority of expatriate workers in GCC countries are largely from South Asian countries. In 2009, the share of Asians in the workforce in Qatar, Bahrain and the United Arab Emirates (UAE) was around 80 per cent, while Asians constituted 60 per cent of the workforce in Saudi Arabia (*Migration News* 2012). The global financial crisis partially affected migrant workers as the GCC countries had high reserves accumulated which they had earned during the oil price hike and they invested this capital in infrastructure projects during this period. Thus reverse migration to the South Asian region was less (Rajan and Narayana 2012). Moreover, the local population is facing either a skill-mismatch in the job market or the current educational system in the Gulf region is inadequate to produce an efficient and skilful workforce.

This chapter explores new trends in the 'South Asia-Gulf migration industry'. This particular aspect has not been given much attention in the relevant literature, despite the emergence of the 'South Asia-Gulf Corridor' as an important epicentre of transnational migration with greater opportunities, prospects and challenges.

Migration history and trends

Part I

Trade relations between the Indian subcontinent and the Arab region as the West Asian was very strong, and ports were the epicentre of Indo-Mediterranean trade (Jain 2006). However, the historical contributions of the Semitic communities in the Indo-Mediterranean trade, cultural and religious interface have not figured prominently in South Asian studies. Jain, in his studies on the Indian Merchant communities, highlights the presence of vibrant Indian merchant communities in the Persian Gulf towns during the British Raj (ibid.). India's trade in the Mediterranean region was fostered by the presence of Indian business settlements across the Persian Gulf. By the beginning of the 20th century, the Indian merchant community had a significant role in the internal trade of Oman and the UAE (Allen 1981). In 1929, Indian goods constituted 72.47 per cent of the total imports of Bahrain (Fuccaro 2009). However, with the independence of the Gulf countries, the influence of the Indian merchant communities started receding in favour of native trading communities. The skilled Indian workers played a key role in running the colonial administration in the GCC region and Indians were the 'preferred' workforce of the British (Seccombe and Lawless 1986). In the post-Second World War period, a large number of Indians were recruited in postal services, communications, police, and in various colonial administrative sectors (Jain 2006).

Seccombe and Lawless point out that in 1939, Indians accounted for nearly 94.3 per cent of the total clerical and technical employees and 91.1 per cent of the total artisans employed in Bahrain Petroleum Company, a leading oil company (ibid.). By 1950, the large oil companies in the Gulf employed nearly 8,000 immigrants from the Indian subcontinent (Claude 1999). A majority of these migrants are reportedly known to have originated in Kerala and other south Indian provinces. Most of them – even the highly educated professionals – are on contract and, therefore, are not allowed to settle permanently in these countries. Later, the large-scale extraction of oil and the subsequent economic rise of the GCC countries in the late 1960s inspired a huge flow of migrant workers from India to the Gulf region. Thus, in 1970–71, there were only 50,000 Indians in the region. This figure rose to 150,000 in 1975 and 1.5 million in 1991 (Natarajan 2013). Presently, the Indian population in the Gulf region is estimated at about 5.5 million (MOIA 2012). Indian communities in the Gulf countries predominantly consist of skilled, low-skilled and semi-skilled workers; technical, supervisory and managerial personnel; professionals and sub-professionals; and entrepreneurs/businesspersons.

The state of Kerala continues to be the largest migrant-sending state, followed by Andhra Pradesh, Uttar Pradesh and Bihar (Rajan and Zacharia 2012). Out of a total 6 million migrant workers who migrated internationally during 2000–10, 85 per cent joined the workforce of the oil-rich countries in the Persian Gulf (Ozaki 2012). While the construction boom of the 1970s led to the employment migration to the Gulf countries, globalisation and the IT boom of the 1990s have accelerated mutual trade and investment in both regions. Statistics show that the flow of migrant workers from India to the GCC countries was never quite fast in the late 1970s. By the mid-1980s, even this flow had lessened, although by the beginning of the 1990s the flow of migrants had accelerated once again. It declined drastically in the late 1990s, but once again peaked in mid-2000 (Jain 2008). Table 1.2 shows how since 2001 there has been a significant upsurge in the flow of migrant workers from India to the GCC countries. It went from 223,668 in 2001 to 818,315 in 2008. However, due to recession, the flow of migrants declined slightly during 2009–11, but bounced back again to 722,139 in 2012. Table 1.2 also shows that the unexpected upward flow of migrants to the UAE during 2002–08 was reduced drastically in the later period, and Saudi Arabia has emerged as the favoured destination. In 2012, nearly 375,503 Indians migrated to Saudi Arabia, while only 141,138 had moved to the UAE.

Pakistani migration to GCC countries started with the oil boom in the late 1970s, and out of nearly 4 million Pakistani diaspora, the Gulf region hosts around 3 million immigrants (Arif 2009). The economic turmoil which followed the partition of the subcontinent in 1947 and 1971, combined with issues relating to poverty, religious affiliation, geographical proximity, and a volatile political situation led to a large outflow of migrants to the GCC countries. The major destinations for the Pakistanis are the UAE and Saudi Arabia, though the numbers fluctuate from time to time. A patriarchal approach, coupled with the Pakistani government's restrictive rules towards female migration, has lowered the flow of women migrant workers. As a result, the majority of expatriates from Pakistan are males. Migration from Pakistan to the GCC countries is

Table 1.2 Indian migration to GCC countries, 2001–12

Year	Bahrain	Kuwait	Oman	Qatar	Saudi Arabia	UAE	Total
2001	16,382	39,751	30,985	13,829	78,048	53,673	232,668
2002	20,807	48,549	41,209	12,596	99,453	95,034	317,648
2003	24,778	54,434	36,816	14,251	121,431	143,804	395,514
2004	22,980	52,064	33,275	16,325	123,522	175,262	423,428
2005	30,060	39,124	40,931	50,222	99,879	194,412	454,628
2006	37,688	47,449	67,992	76,324	134,059	254,774	618,286
2007	29,966	48,467	95462	88,483	195,437	312,695	770,510
2008	31,924	35,562	89,659	82,937	228,406	349,827	818,315
2009	17,541	42,091	74,963	46,292	281,110	130,302	592,299
2010	15,101	37,667	105,807	45,752	275,172	130,910	610,409
2011	14,323	45,149	73,819	41,710	289,297	138,861	603,159
2012	20,150	55,868	84,384	63,096	375,503	141,138	722,139

Source: Ministry of Labour (2003, 2004 and 2005) and MOIA (2011, 2012 and 2013).

not properly represented across the country as a majority of the migrants to the Gulf are from Punjab province followed by Khyber Pakhtunkhwa, formerly known as North West Frontier Province (NWFP) and, to a lesser extent, Sindh (ibid.). Migration to the GCC countries reached peaked between 1970 and the mid-1980s. It slowed down in the 1990s, but bounced back again in the 2000s. In 2004, nearly 1.89 million Pakistani workers were in the Gulf region. Nearly 50 per cent of the Pakistani workers belong to the unskilled category, followed by 36 per cent of skilled workers (Thimothy and Sasikumar 2012). Remittances from these countries play a significant role in poverty alleviation and the socio-economic development of Pakistan (ibid. 2009). Table 1.1 shows the upward flow of Pakistani migrant workers to GCC counties, from 127,810 in 2005 to 172,837 in 2006, 278,631 in 2007 and 407,007 in 2009.

Bangladesh is among the top 10 remittances-recipient countries in the world. The partition of Bangladesh from Pakistan in 1971 and its proximity with India had negatively affected the image of Bangladesh in the GCC region. Therefore, migration from Bangladesh, too, started late compared to other South Asian countries. Interestingly, the country which started with modest migration of 6,087 in 1976 has reached an astonishing figure of 4.75 million in 2009 (BMET 2010). At present, a majority of Bangladeshi migrants are stationed in the GCC region. Rita Afsar (2009) highlights the migration of 6 million Bangladeshis to the GCC region between 1976 and 2012. Moreover, Saudi Arabia has emerged as the most-favoured destination for Bangladeshi migrants. Between 2000 and 2011, US$21.42 billion was remitted from Saudi Arabia alone to Bangladesh. Out of total 7.13 million Bangladeshis who migrated abroad between 1976 and 2010, nearly 2.58 million moved to Saudi Arabia (Rahman 2012). In 2009, Bangladesh received US$10.8 billion in remittances, and the majority was received from GCC countries (ibid.). The vast majority of Bangladeshi workers are unskilled and semi-skilled, and female migration is relatively better compared to Pakistan. Table 1.1 indicates the unmatched flow of migrant workers from Bangladesh to the GCC region, from 207,089 in 2005 to 483,757 in 2007 and 643,342 in 2008. In 2011, the total number of migrant workers from Bangladesh was nearly 5 million. Of them, 80 per cent migrated to the GCC countries, with 40 per cent to the UAE alone (Ozaki 2012).

Political turmoil, Maoist insurgency, natural calamity, and political instability are some of the reasons behind the recent upsurge of Nepalese workers to various parts of the world. Nepal's migratory history dates back to colonial times when a large number of Nepalese were recruited in the British army and in the tea estates owned by the colonial powers (Sharma 2012). Massive poverty and social inequality are considered to be the main reasons for the large exodus (Dixit 2013). Migration to the GCC countries is a rather recent phenomenon which started in the 1990s. In 2008–09, out of a population of 30 million, around 5 million Nepalese were living abroad, and one-third of the Nepalese workers migrated to the GCC countries (Mohapatra, Ratha and Silwal 2012; Sharma 2012). In 2001, nearly 200,000 Nepalese were living in the GCC region (Graner and Ganesh 2003). In 2010, a majority of the males had migrated to the UAE and Saudi Arabia, while the females migrated to Kuwait and the UAE (NIDS 2010). According to a United Nations (UN) report, in 2011 nearly 2.7 million Nepalese, which included 2 million documented and around 700,000 undocumented people, were working in the GCC countries (*The Himalayan Times* 2013). Remittances are an important factor in the economy of Nepal. In 2010, the country received US$3 billion as remittances (Mohapatra, Ratha and Silwal 2012). Table 1.1 reveals the incredible rise in Nepalese migration from a mere 88,230 in 2005 to 169,510 in 2008. According to the available sources, in 2010, of the total migrants from Nepal, 32.4 per cent migrated to

Malaysia, 28.7 per cent to Qatar, 19.81 per cent to Saudi Arabia, and 12.68 per cent to the UAE (Sharma 2012).

Sri Lanka, the island country of South Asia, was a victim of ethnic conflict and violent bloodshed for nearly three decades. The recent acceleration of migration to the Gulf is attributed to the political turmoil in Sri Lanka. Table 1.1 displays the uninterrupted and steep flow of Sri Lankan migrant workers to the GCC countries from 192,004 in 2005 to 170,049 in 2006, 188,365 in 2007, 215,793 in 2008 and 226,229 in 2009. In 2009, out of 1 million migrant workers from Sri Lanka, 82 per cent were working in Saudi Arabia, the UAE, Qatar, and Malaysia. Moreover, Saudi Arabia alone accommodates 31 per cent of the total Sri Lankan migrant workers who went abroad in 2009 (Ozaki 2012). Despite its high ranking in the human development index, Sri Lanka has a very high unemployment rate. Though initial Sri Lankan migration to GCC countries was male-dominated, by the late 1990s female migration had increased substantially. In 2011, out of the total migrants, nearly 48 per cent were women (Gamburd 2010).

Part II

The Nitaqat Labour Law

The decision of the Government of Saudi Arabia to implement the Nitaqat Labour Law is a matter of great concern in South Asia. In the post-economic recession period, more than 54.7 per cent of South Asian workers were stationed in Saudi Arabia. In 2012, out of a total of 722,139 Indians who migrated to the Gulf, 375,503 immigrated to Saudi Arabia (MOIA 2012). Thus the decision of Saudi Arabia that one out of every five employees in business establishment will have to be a Saudi national, is leading to displacement and deportation of thousands of Asian migrant workers from the country. A more worrisome point is the stamping of the 'entry ban' on the passports of migrant workers and the 'deporting route' of the Saudi government rather than the normal exit passage. The Government of India is negotiating with the Saudi government to avoid deportation of migrant workers and the marking of the entry ban on their documents.

Based on level of compliance, the Saudi government has categorised local business establishments into four groups: Blue, Green, Yellow, and Red. The Blue and Green businesses have the highest localisation ratios, Yellow falls in the intermediate range, and is Red the least compliant. While Blue and Green establishments are being rewarded and Yellow is given more time to implement changes, companies in the Red zone are under pressure to comply with the Nitaqat Law (Ramachandran 2013).

The largest expatriate group working in the private sector is the Indians. According to the labour ministry of Saudi Arabia, nearly 6.5 million foreign workers are employed in the private sector. The process of unemployment and deportation has created anxiety among the thousands of migrant households in India. Saudi Arabia has declared nearly 30,000 Pakistanis as illegal immigrants and more are likely to face deportation (*The Economic Times* 2013). In 2004, too, the Saudi government has tried to impose naturalisation policies but failed miserably due to various domestic factors. The percentage of natives that Nitaqat requires firms to employ varies from 6 per cent for construction jobs to 30 per cent for oil and gas extraction, to over 50 per cent for banks and financial institutions (for firms with under 500 employees). The natives are quite unwilling to assume the blue collar jobs that are available in the construction sector and manufacturing industry, and are unwilling to work as assistants, domestic workers, hotel boys and so on. However, migration experts like Irudaya Rajan are of the opinion that the impact of Nitaqat Law could be very minimal, and that 'just as these policies had no impact for the last twenty years, I expect there will be no impact this time too' (Basheer 2013).

Already domestic workers from Sri Lanka and the Philippines are exempted from the Nitaqat Law due to the unwillingness of natives to work in these areas. At the same time, the financial, banking, information technology (IT), health, education, and corporate sectors would also face severe difficulties due to the unavailability of an efficient and competitive workforce from the native population. Due to pressure from the sending countries, Saudi Arabia deferred the implementation of the Nitaqat Law until 3 July 2013, allowing illegal migrants to leave the country through normal passage rather than face a jail term or entry ban (ibid.). According to official statistics, nearly 90,000 Indians have returned home from Saudi Arabia (*The Indian Express* 2013).

The Kuwaiti crackdown on those working with an expired visa a month after the implementation of the new Nitaqat Law by Saudi Arabia has further aggravated the misery of migrant workers. The hundreds of emigrant workers, mostly from India, Pakistan and

Bangladesh, employed on domestic visas who are engaged in blue collar jobs have been arrested for violating the visa norms in Kuwait (Sananda Kumar 2013). Most of the workers prefer a domestic visa as it is relatively cheap and costs between 300 and 400 dinars, while the work visa is exorbitant. A sizeable number of Indian migrant workers, especially from Kerala, have been arrested and deported to Delhi. The Nitaqat Law and the curbing of migrants in Kuwait would adversely affect the migration flow from South Asia to the GCC region in the future.

Migratory process, cost and social networks

The channel of migration is a vital factor in the migratory process. Migrants use various networks to reach destination countries. The three main channels of migration are social networks or the informal channel, recruiting agencies and government channels. In the context of South Asian migration, social networks play a significant role in the massive migration of the labour force from remote areas to the unknown oil-rich monarchies. The social networks comprise family, friends and relatives and they are the prime source of information regarding destination countries, and also a vital link to the destination countries (Shah 2000).

The 'Gulf returnees' contribute positively to the dissemination of information, providing information on the job opportunities available, and linking prospective migrants to the unknown destination countries. An all-India survey conducted by Centre for Development Studies (CDS) shows that 85 per cent of Indian migrants relied on social networks, 13.5 per cent on private recruiting agencies and a mere 0.5 per cent on government channels to migrate to the GCC countries (Rajan and Narayana 2012). Interestingly, migrants trust, and rely more on, friends and relatives and they also depend on social networks to adjust in the destination countries.

Presently, the cost of a visa is extremely high compared to previous years and social networks do play a crucial role in reducing the cost of migration. The minimum cost of migration in India through a recruiting agency is nearly US$2000, while the cost is nearly half when the migration is through social networks (ibid.).

In some cases, though social networks provide the initial information, the final implementation of migration, such as arranging the visa, tickets and choosing the job, is done by private recruiting agencies. Unfortunately, spurious recruiting agencies are on the increase in South Asia, and there are innumerable cases of fraudulent practices and cheating by these agencies (Oishi 2005; Shah 2000). In recent times, the overseas ministries of the sending countries are relatively more active in providing information on legal procedures, and also about cautioning the public on fraudulent practices. For instance, the Ministry of Overseas Indian Affairs (MOIA) frequently advertises on the procedures, laws and other crucial legal aspects related to migration and only those recruiting agencies that are approved by MOIA are allowed to recruit workers abroad. Numerous scholars have pointed out that prospective migrants either pawn land/property or take loans at higher interest rates to meet the financial expenditure for visa and other migration-related expenses (Gamburd 2010; Rajan and Narayana 2012). Due to the precarious nature of domestic compulsions and unemployment in the South Asian region, most poor migrants are ready to take the high risk of migrating to an alien land with the cost of huge loans (Afsar 2009). During my field research in Kuwait, I observed an enormous portion of migrants' incomes being channelised towards repaying the loan.

Rita Afsar, in her research on Bangladeshi immigrants, points out that 75 per cent of the respondents relied on social networks as these provide them with first-hand information on job opportunities, the socio-political conditions of the destination countries and also the challenges and fraudulent practices (ibid.). The inability of the respective sending governments to regulate the migration process had given rise to spurious recruiting agencies across the subcontinent. Visa rackets, smuggling and human trafficking are rampant due to inadequate monitoring by the government agencies. Interestingly, Nasra Shah, in her research on the South Asian male migrants in Kuwait, highlights how crucial personal networks are for migration, and how these networks are directly linked to the duration of the migrant's stay, stability, economic success and job satisfaction. Nasra argues that the migrants who came to the destination countries through personal networks are more successful than those who relied on the government or recruiting agencies. The recent global economic crisis did not cause a flow of returning migrants back to the home countries. For their sustained stay in other countries, one of the oft-cited factors is the support provided by social networks. In the eventuality of job loss, the migrants made use of relatives and friends in the destination countries and stayed back looking for newer opportunities rather than returning to the home countries. Thieme (2006) argues that the migration of Nepalese workers has been sustained and supported by the strong social networks among the immigrants.

Migration of women to GCC countries

South Asian migration to GCC countries is predominantly a male phenomenon. The relatively limited participation of women as a migrating workforce is attributed largely to the prevalence of patriarchy in the sending countries. According to an Asian Development Bank (ADB) report, women migrants constitute nearly 15 per cent of the total migrant workers from South Asia (Ozaki 2012). Not surprisingly, studies on Asian women migrant workers have received less attention both in the academic world and at the policy level. 'Migration of Women from South Asia to the Gulf' by Thimothy and Sasikumar (2012), 'Indian Nurses in Persian Gulf' (Percot 2006) and 'Sri Lankan Migration to the Gulf: Female Bread Winners' (Gamburd 2010) are some of the notable academic works in this regard. In the context of international labour migration, a majority of the women workers are from South Asia-Southeast Asia, and most are engaged in low-skilled and semi-skilled jobs (Baldwin-Edwards 2011).

The oil boom of the 1960s in the Gulf countries lowered the participation of nationals in the workforce and brought a new form of 'royal sheikh culture' which heightened the demand for maids and domestic workers. South Asian women are mostly employed as teachers, paramedics, nurses, assistants, workers in manufacturing and entertainment, and as maids and domestic workers in the care industry (Ozaki 2012). Gamburd (2010) noted that the 'army of house maids' represents the feminization of migration in South Asia. Historically, there are three streams of women's migration from South Asia – first, to the GCC region; second, to Brunei, Singapore and Hong Kong; and finally to countries like the United States of America (USA), Canada and Europe of the Organisation for Economic Co-operation and Development (OECD) (Thimothy and Sasikumar 2012). The first two streams consisted of low-skilled and semi-skilled workers, while migratory flow towards OECD countries consisted of mostly skilled workers and professionals. Initially women workers migrated from India, Pakistan and Bangladesh, but by the year 2000, Sri Lankan women migrants had emerged as the largest group in the GCC region. In 2009, 52 per cent of the total migrant workers from Sri Lanka were women, and the majority migrated to the GCC countries, especially to the UAE and Kuwait (SLBFE 2011). Sri Lanka has a long tradition of participation of women in plantation work, garment factories and the tea industry. Therefore, it was easier for both state and society to accept the large-scale migration of Sri Lankan women in search of livelihood.

The factors that prompted the migration of South Asian women were mainly poverty, hunger, debt, an oppressive social system, marital discord, alcoholism of the spouse, the aspiration for a better life and so on (Gamburd 2010). In India, Kerala, Andhra Pradesh, and Maharashtra are the major states from which maximum women workers migrate to the GCC region (Rajan and Sukendaran 2010). At the same time, Kerala has a high level of female migration, and a majority of the Indian nurses working in the GCC region are from here (Percot 2006). Percot points out that in Kerala a nursing degree serves more as a 'passport' to move towards a better life in the Western world; it offers more freedom and an opportunity to escape from the shackles of a patriarchal social system. The socio-economic mobility of certain communities in Kerala is greatly attributed to the nursing profession. The South Asian countries, except Sri Lanka, have approached women's migration within the framework of patriarchy with restrictive policies and irrational conditions. The strict policies of the sending countries have heightened irregular migration and forced the women to choose the risky channels to migrate (Bindulakshmi 2010).

Most South Asian countries have temporarily banned the migration of women and have imposed age restrictions on women migrants, which unequivocally hamper the economic mobility and livelihood of the women to a great extent. India prohibits women below 30 years of age to migrate aboard, while for Pakistan it is 35, for Nepal it is 18, for Sri Lanka it is 21, and for Bangladesh it is 25. Women migrant workers are often victims of patriarchy in both sending and receiving countries (Kabeer 2007). Sexual abuse, harassment at the workplace and long working hours without proper payment are quite rampant in the GCC countries. The recent Malayalam movie *Gaddama* reveals the harsh realities of the lives of maids and domestic workers from Asian countries in the oil-rich monarchies (Manoramaonline.com 2011). Nepal banned the migration of women workers in 1998 due to the mysterious death of a Nepali domestic worker in Kuwait and later revoked the ban in 2003. Gamburd (2010) noted that in Sri Lanka a large section of women migrant workers were married; they had reshaped patriarchal norms and assumed the role of 'breadwinners' of the family. However, the precarious issues related to women migrants have received less attention and more women-friendly policies need to be formulated by both the sending and the receiving countries in the future.

Economic and occupational profile of the South Asian migrants

The oil boom in the late 1960s followed by an unprecedented carousel of infrastructure development has attracted millions of migrant workers to the GCC region. Most of the migrant workers in the beginning were from the Arab region, India and Pakistan. In the beginning, a majority of the workers were engaged in the construction sector and the oil industry, particularly oil refineries. However, the establishment of hospitals in the region by the Americans, particularly in Kuwait, also prompted the migration of paramedics, mostly male nurses in the late 1950s. Nearly 50 per cent of the workforce in the GCC region is employed in manufacturing, trade and construction. However, in Kuwait and Saudi Arabia a large number of people are also working in public administration and defence (Rajan and Narayana 2012). The GCC countries are the largest recipients of the international migrant workforce as the expatriates constitute 43 per cent of their total population (Fargues 2011). The startling demographic imbalance still continues in the region as nearly 80 per cent of the total population of both Qatar and the UAE are comprised of foreign workers (ibid.).

In the 1990s, demand shifted in favour of the care industry, paramedics and IT professionals but the major demand for labour hasn't declined either. Since the 1990s, the participation of the indigenous population in the workforce, especially the youth, has increased dramatically although a major chunk of the indigenous workforce is employed in government and public sectors mainly due to the fact that remuneration and facilities are inexplicably better in these sectors. Consequently, the service sector, construction and manufacturing sectors, health and education sectors, and low-paying jobs (e.g., security guards, assistants and domestic workers) are predominantly filled with expatriates, especially migrant workers from Asia (Baldwin-Edwards 2011). Though GCC countries have initiated numerous policies to restrict labour immigrants, non-participation of GCC nationals in the service and other low-paying sectors has increased the intake of migrant workers rather than decrease labour flow. The covert and overt restriction of local female participation in the workforce and lack of skilled and competent personnel amongst the nationals has further increased the dependence of oil-rich monarchies on expatriate workers.

Table 1.3 Nationals and expatriates in the GCC labour force, 1975–2008

Country	Labour force	1975	1985	1990	1999	2008
Saudi Arabia	Nationals	1027	1440	1934	3173	4170
	Foreigners	773	2662	2878	4003	4280
	Total	1800	4102	4812	7176	8450
	Percentage Foreigners	42.9	64.9	59.8	55.9	50.1
Kuwait	Nationals	92	126	118	221	445
	Foreigners	213	544	731	1005	1780
	Total	305	670	849	1226	2225
	Percentage Foreigners	69.8	81.2	86.1	82	80
Bahrain	Nationals	46	73	127	113	140
	Foreigners	30	101	132	194	438
	Total	76	174	259	307	578
	Percentage Foreigners	39.5	58	51	63.2	84.2
Oman	Nationals	137	167	189	312	374
	Foreigners	71	300	442	503	795
	Total	208	467	631	812	1169
	Percentage Foreigners	34.1	64.2	70	61.7	68
Qatar	Nationals	13	18	21	36	62
	Foreigners	54	156	230	244	766
	Total	67	174	251	280	828
	Percentage Foreigners	80.6	89.7	91.6	87.1	92.5
UAE	Nationals	45	72	96	124	455
	Foreigners	252	612	805	1165	2588
	Total	297	684	901	1289	3043
	Percentage Foreigners	84.8	89.5	89.3	90.4	85
Total in GCC	Nationals	1360	1896	2485	3979	5646
	Foreigners	1393	4375	5218	7114	10647
	Total	2753	6271	7703	11093	16293
	Percentage Foreigners	50.6	69.8	67.7	64.1	65.3

Source: Winckler (2010: 12).

At first, a vast majority of migrants from India were uneducated, low-skilled and semi-skilled labourers. However, by the late 1970s, the demand shifted slightly towards technicians, teachers and paramedics, and India along with Pakistan was the major source for the skilled category of workers. High technological development and changing economies in the 1990s paved the way for the migration of highly skilled professionals or white collar workers – IT professionals, doctors and educated technocrats from India. However, a significant portion of Indian immigrants are engaged in blue collar jobs. For instance, in Qatar, out of 500,000 Indian immigrants, nearly 70 per cent are working in construction, manufacturing and other low-skilled jobs (Kanchana 2012). A recent survey in the UAE shows that 20 per cent of Indian immigrants are engaged in professional and high-tech jobs (Jain 2006).

Presently, a substantial number of migrant workers from South Asia in GCC countries is in the construction sector (Rajan and Narayana 2012). A majority of the South Asian migrants in GCC countries are semi-skilled or unskilled workers, mostly illiterate, single and male (Ozaki 2012). Since the 1990s, the IT boom and technological advancement have altered the skill composition of the migrants as well as the demand of the host countries, particularly in the case of Indian expatriates (Srivastava and Sasikumar 2003). The majority of the Pakistani workers in the GCC region are unskilled, followed by semi-skilled, skilled and highly qualified professionals (Arif 2009). The statistics on Bangladeshi immigrants show that the majority of the migrants are poor and downtrodden. Rita Afsar's study on Bangladeshi migrants points out that hunger and desperation, unemployment and debt traps are the main factors prompting these workers to migrate to oil-rich monarchies.

According to job classifications, skilled categories include nurses, teachers and technicians; semi-skilled categories include masons, drivers, carpenters, and welders; and unskilled categories include construction labourers, cleaners and domestic workers. The average age of migrant workers is nearly 32 years, and the vast majority of migrants are male (Bohra and Massey 2009).

A study conducted by Williams et al. (2010) shows that the vast majority of the Nepali migrants (90 per cent) work as labourers in the GCC region and only 2 per cent are engaged in professional jobs. Moreover, the constitution of the Nepali workforce is as follows: 46 per cent Brahmin/Chhetri, 11 per cent dalit, 21 per cent indigenous hill people, 14 per cent Terai and 7 per cent Newar. A vast majority of the migrant workers from Bangladesh are less educated, unskilled and semi-skilled workers, and work as construction and factory labourers, foremen, carpenters, cleaners, hotel boys, house maids, farm labour, and so on (ibid.). Interestingly, in Sri Lanka, since 2000, the generic profile of migrants has altered in favour of female migration; a majority of the women workers work in the care industry as domestic workers, maids and babysitters. One-third of the Sri Lankan migrants are stationed in Saudi Arabia (Ozaki 2012).

However, the working conditions and protection of labour rights are relatively low in GCC countries. Irregular payment, non-payment of wages, inconsistency between promised and real wages, deduction of salary, non-payment of salary for long durations, denial of medical insurance and long working hours in hostile climatic conditions are quite rampant in the region.

Circular migration to the Gulf, which has crossed over three decades, continues to be characterised by a serious deficit in migrant rights. Some of these so called 'temporary contractual labourers' who have migrated to the Gulf have been there for over 30 years. The large-scale commercialisation of the recruitment industry has made migration in the region not only too costly, but also quite risky. The 2008 ILO Regional Symposium at Dhaka has highlighted the problem experienced by women migrant workers in general, and argued for a gender sensitive management policy. The initiatives with respect to the ASEAN Declaration on the promotion and protection of the rights of migrant workers are presented as an instance. The bilateral agreement between the trade unions of Bahrain, Jordan and Kuwait and Sri Lanka towards protection of the rights of Sri Lankan migrant workers is a good initiative in this context (Kelegama 2011).

Remittances

Remittances from GCC countries play a significant role in foreign exchange reserves, alleviation of poverty and the socio-economic development of South Asia. The flow of remittances to the South Asian region has shown a steady growth from US$16.13 billion in 2000 to US$72.51 billion in 2010 (Ozaki 2012). GCC countries are the main source of remittances to South Asia, as India alone received US$29 billion in 2012 from the GCC region (ibid.). Remittances from GCC countries have been a major source of influence on the annual gross domestic product (GDP) per capita of the South Asian countries, as is evident from the fact that it constituted one-fifth of the total flow to the region in 2008 (Mohapatra, Ratha and Silwal 2012). However, due to the economic crisis, there was a slowdown in the flow of remittances to the South Asian region in 2009, but matters returned to normal by 2011. Remittances contributed significantly in socio-economic development, particularly poverty reduction of the South Asian countries. In his research on the impact of migration in Pakistan, Arif noted, 'The social contribution of migration is even more encouraging in terms of improving children's education, enhancing housing condition, eliminating child labour, empowering women of the migrant household' (2009: 5). In the last decade, there has been a steady growth of remittances to Pakistan, from US$1.1 billion in 2000–01 to US$6.33 billion in 2008–09 to US$9.23 2011–12 (*Pakistan Today* 2013).

Table 1.4 gives a clear picture of the enormous amount of remittances flown to India during the last decade, with a quantum jump from US$14.8 billion in 2002–03 to US$53.9 billion in 2009–10. India continues to be the top recipient of remittances (US$70.0 billion in 2013).

In fact, policymaking centres in South Asia have been more focused on maximising benefits out of the international migration process through the remittances rather than treading any confrontationist path with the generally repressive Gulf regimes (Panicker 2013). But this preoccupation has sometimes come at the cost of ignoring the pitiable conditions under which the labourers work in alien territories, bearing the wrath of a whole host of prejudices and discriminations meted out against them. The remittances to the developing countries have been increasing sharply over the years. In 2008, India, China, Bangladesh, and the Philippines were among the top 10 remittances-recipient countries (Kelegama 2011). Migration and remittances, particularly from the Gulf region, contribute significantly to the overall developmental process of South Asia.

The large flow of remittances have prompted the South Asian countries to formulate policies to attract migrant workers and also to channelise maximum amount of remittances through the formal channels, mainly banks, cheques and telegraphic and post office transfers, rather than informal channels. The informal flow of remittances through *hawala/hundi* is an area of major concern for the recipient counties. To block the inroads of links for informal remittances, South Asian countries have opened branches of major banks in the GCC region, and also provide various schemes to deposit money in these branches of native banks. The South Asian countries have formulated several financial schemes to attract

Table 1.4 Total remittances flow to India (in US$ billion)

Year	Remittances (US$ billion)
1981–82	2.3
1982–83	2.5
1983–84	2.5
1984–85	2.5
1985–86	2.2
1986–87	2.3
1987–88	2.7
1988–89	2.6
1989–90	2.2
1990–91	2.0
1991–92	3.5
1992–93	2.6
1993–94	5.2
1994–95	6.2
1995–96	8.5
1996–97	12.3
1997–98	11.8
1998–99	10.3
1999–2000	12.2
2000–01	12.8
2001–02	12.1
2002–03	14.8
2003–04	18.8
2004–05	21.1
2005–06	25.0
2006–07	30.8
2007–08	43.5
2008–09	46.9
2009–10	53.9
2010–11	55.9
2011–12	70.0
2012–13	70.0

Source: Annual reports of Reserve Bank of India. See also, Ministry of Overseas Affairs, *Annual Reports*, various years (1981–2012), Ministry of Labour, Government of India.

remittances such as the Non-Resident Account (NRI Account) in India, the Non-Resident Foreign Currency Deposit (NFCD) in Bangladesh, the Foreign Employment Bond in Nepal, and the Share Investment External Rupee Account in Sri Lanka (Thimothy and

Sasikumar 2012). The deposit schemes are designed to attract large uninterrupted flow of remittances from migrant workers. Many sending countries have instituted deposit schemes in both local and foreign currencies as well (Gupta and Singh 2012). Nevertheless, a high degree of informal flow of remittances is the key issue of the South Asian migratory system. At the same time, the absence of an effective banking system in South Asia and the social networks among the migrants are the main reasons for the widespread use of informal channels for transfer of remittances. However, money transfer operator (MTO) networks are the most preferred option for receiving remittances in a majority of South Asian countries.

Presently, remittance constitutes one of the major sources of financial flow to Nepal as it reached US$3.5 billion in 2010 (Mohapatra, Ratha and Silwal 2012). Table 1.5 indicates that in 2009 Bangladesh received US$8,392 million and Pakistan received US$4,940.2 million from GCC countries. During 2012, India, Nepal, Pakistan, Bangladesh, and Sri Lanka received nearly US$43,181.79 million from GCC countries (World Bank 2013). The World Bank explains the remittance trends between South Asia and the GCC countries, but the data is largely based on the official flow of remittances. In 2012, India topped the list of remittances-recipient countries from the GCC region with US$29,697 million, followed by Pakistan with US$5,983 million, Bangladesh with US$3,058.76 million, Sri Lanka with US$2,660 million, and Nepal with US$1,783 million (the lowest) (ibid.).

Of the total remittances to each country in 2012, data shows that remittances from GCC countries constituted the major share

Table 1.5 Flow of remittances to Bangladesh and Pakistan from GCC countries, 2008–09 (in US$ million)

	Bangladesh		Pakistan	
	2008	*2009*	*2008*	*2009*
Bahrain	167.4	154.2	147.8	157.0
Kuwait	949.5	993.9	426.9	427.7
Oman	243	337.4	264.4	278.5
Qatar	324.8	366.3	283.6	375.4
Saudi Arabia	2,733.6	3,194.3	1,403.2	1690.6
UAE	1,739.5	1,958.1	1,289.4	2011

Source: Sirkeci, Cohen and Ratha (2012: 93–99).

Table 1.6 Inward remittances to South Asian countries from migrant workers, 2000–09 (US$ millions)

	India	Pakistan	Bangladesh	Nepal	Sri Lanka
	US$ (Millions)				
2000	12,890	1,075	1,968	111	1,166
2001	14,273	1,461	2,105	147	1,185
2002	15,736	3,554	2,858	678	1,309
2003	20,999	3,964	3,192	771	1,438
2004	18,750	3,945	3,584	823	1,590
2005	22,125	4,280	4,314	1,212	1,991
2006	28,334	5,121	5,428	1,453	2,185
2007	37,217	5,998	6,562	1,734	2,527
2008	51,581	7,039	8,995	2,727	2,947
2009 *	47,000	8,619	10,431	3,010	2,892
2009 +	53,227	8,856	10,525	2,812	3,308
	Percentage Change				
2000–01	10.73	35.91	6.96	32.43	1.63
2001–02	10.25	143.26	35.77	361.22	10.46
2002–03	33.45	11.54	11.69	13.72	9.85
2003–04	−10.71	−0.48	12.28	6.74	10.57
2004–05	18.00	8.49	20.37	47.27	25.22
2005–06	28.06	19.65	25.82	19.88	9.74
2006–07	31.35	17.13	20.89	19.34	15.65
2007–08	38.60	17.36	37.08	57.27	16.62
2008–09 *	−8.88	22.45	15.96	10.38	−1.87
2008–09 +	3.19	25.81	17.01	3.12	12.25

Source: Irudaya and Narayana (2012: 98).

Table 1.7 Remittances from GCC countries to India in 2012 (in US$ million)

UAE	14,255
Saudi Arabia	7,620
Kuwait	2,673.42
Oman	2,373.21
Qatar	2,083.99
Bahrain	689.79

Source: Ozaki (2012).

of total remittances received – 49 per cent in Pakistan, 47 per cent in India, 42 per cent in Nepal, 51 per cent in Sri Lanka, and 25 per cent in Bangladesh. In 2012, India's total remittances received from the GCC region included US$14,255 million from the UAE, US$7,620 million from Saudi Arabia, US$2,673.42 million from Kuwait, US$2,373.21 million from Oman, US$2,083.99 million from Qatar, and US$689.79 million form Bahrain (World Bank 2013). Remittances are among the stable forms of external flows as they are less sensitive to interest rates (Gupta and Singh 2012). The trend of remittances in 2012 showed that South Asia received the largest share from UAE and Saudi Arabia, and India alone received US$14,555 million from the UAE in 2012. The World Bank and CDS studies predict that the flow of remittances would continue to grow as global recession has not hindered the volume of remittances to South Asia. In fact, flow of remittances to India increased from US$52 billion in 2008 to US$53 billion in 2009. In India, the southern state of Kerala has been the largest recipient of remittances as the flow of remittances ascended from INR 3025 in 1991 to INR 60,000 in 2012.

GCC economies witnessed a slight drop during the crisis when vast reserves of capital were diverted towards infrastructure projects. The flow of remittances to developing countries has been reduced in 2008 because of the economic crisis and it affected home countries adversely (ibid.). Thus, return migration to South Asia was very low as most migrant workers stayed back unlike earlier. By 2010, the GCC countries had regained some of their economic growth, which had a direct impact on flow of remittances. This economic fluctuation did not affect the flow of migrants, but a shift in domestic economic policies of the Gulf countries are expected to affect the quantum and nature of migration patterns. The recent nationalisation policies and the exodus of a large number of migrant workers from Saudi Arabia and Kuwait would likely to have an impact on the flow of remittances in future (*The Hindu* 2013).

Diaspora formation of South Asian migrants

Though migration to the Gulf is both transitory and circulatory in nature, the ongoing demand for expatriate workers from GCC states has contributed to the existence of both second- and third-generation migrants in the region. The Asia-Gulf transnational movements have a significant impact on the societal and cultural realms of the sending and host countries. By now, the 'Gulf identity' has become part of an accepted lexicon in the region. Social networking between friends and family among Asian migrants supports both the inflow and durability of Asian migrant communities in the Gulf.

The highly professional and well-educated second-generation immigrants are able to integrate quite effectively with the new economic and occupational demands of the region. At the same time, social networking based on family and friends is a major impetus for the long sustenance of the South Asian migrant community in the GCC states, as well as the cause of formation of a strong South Asian community. During field research amongst the Indian community in Kuwait, I found the unbroken existence of three generations, particularly in business families. At the same time, the social-spatial relocation of economically successful immigrants from traditional migrant settlements in the host setting to new areas also shows upward mobility and the creation of a unique identity within the South Asian migrant community. The 'temporary' nature of Gulf migration is quite blurred as both second and third generations of expatriates are now residing in the region without violating existing rules.

The business community has leverage over others as far as staying on in the GCC region and maintaining the family without much complication are concerned. The findings in Kuwait show that the children who left the GCC region to either their home countries or to other countries for higher studies had returned back and joined their parents after completing their education abroad. In fact, it was easier for the highly educated second generation to integrate into IT and high-tech professions rather than their parents. Moreover, the families of the Indian business community and individual immigrants who are engaged in business have been continuously living in the GCC countries uninterruptedly though they lack political rights in the host setting. Unfortunately, not much research has been done on diaspora formation of the South Asian community, particularly migratory strategies, identity, socio-economic mobility, sense of belonging and connection with the home country of second-generation South Asian immigrants.

Conclusion

The strategic and economic implications of Asianisation of migrant workers in GCC countries, particularly its impact in terms of migration and remittances, are undoubtedly an important aspect in the context of the emerging Gulf-South Asia strategic relations. The unprecedented and massive exodus of migrant workers to the oil-rich monarchies is surely a blessing in disguise for many South Asian countries as remittances constitute the largest external financial flow. The recent global economic crisis and nationalisation policies have not reduced the steady flow of migrants from the South Asian region. The education, health care and care industries and construction and manufacturing sectors are highly dependent on workers from South Asia; thus the recent attempts made by the GCC countries to implement the Nitaqat Law may not be successful due to the reluctance of the nationals to participate in blue collar and private sector jobs. The South Asia-Gulf migration corridor will emerge in the foreseeable future as a vital component in South Asia-Gulf strategic relations. At the same time, the rise of unemployment among young nationals and also the inflow of migrant workers from other Asian countries might reduce the monopoly enjoyed by South Asians in the job market.

The apolitical and passive approach of South Asian workers in the political sphere of Gulf society and their hardworking attitude are attributed to the uninterrupted flow of migrant workers to the GCC states. Social networking and informal links provide additional impetus to the South Asia-Gulf migratory process, and flow of workers to the Gulf region will continue to flourish in the future. Though migration to the Gulf region is both transitory and circulatory in nature, the ongoing demand for expatriate workers from the GCC states has contributed to the existence of both second and third generation migrants in the region. However, the flow of migration from South Asia still revolves around certain geographical locations, communities and families, and it is yet to permeate horizontally in the sending societies.

The voluminous remittances from the GCC countries have played a significant role in the socio-economic mobility and reduction of poverty in the South Asian region. The unprecedented socio-economic mobility of migrants in the 'Gulf Pockets' reflects the productive and constructive utilisation of the remittances in the host settings and women contributed significantly in managing the remittances economy. Interestingly, a vast amount of the economic capital earned abroad is used by the migrant families for the education, health and progress of the second generation. Though several studies have examined the economic impact of migration to the Gulf region, limited attempts have been made to understand how migratory process and remittances affected the sociocultural landscape of the sending countries. At the same time, due to manifold factors, the complex nuances and the real lives of South Asian migrants in the Gulf countries is not fully researched or explored, barring few ethnographic studies.

The lack of a unified voice, a visibly weakened South Asian Association for Regional Cooperation (SAARC) and the insensitive attitude of the sending countries have intensified the socio-economic uncertainties of migrant workers. Though remittances from GCC countries constitute a major portion of external financial flows for South Asia, migrant workers are not the focus in strategic planning of the sending governments. The bilateral agreements on labour rights and minimum wages are quite inadequate to safeguard the social insecurity and gross human rights violations in the host setting. Therefore, both sending and receiving countries should approach the multifaceted concerns of South Asian migrants more holistically and sensitively. In addition, issues concerning women migrant workers should be addressed with utmost care and policies should be formulated without curtailing their basic rights.

Note

1 The original version of this chapter was published in Migration and Development, Vol. 4, Issue 1, 2015.

References

Afsar, Rita. 2009. 'Unraveling the Vicious Cycle of Recruitment: Labour Migration from Bangladesh to the Gulf States', Working Paper, International Labour Organization, Geneva

Allen, Jr. Calvin. 1981. 'The Indian Merchant Community of Masqat', *Bulletin of the School of Oriental and African Studies*, 44(1): 39–51.

Arif, G. M. 2009. 'Economic and Social Impacts of Remittances on Households: The Case of Pakistani Migrants Working in Saudi Arabia', International Organization of Migration, Geneva, pp. 3–6

Baldwin-Edwards, Martin. 2011. 'Labour Immigration and Labour Markets in the GCC Countries: National Patterns and Trend', Kuwait Programme on Development, Governance and Globalisation in the Gulf States, Paper no. 15, London School of Economics, London.

Basheer, K. P.M. 2013. 'Saudi Arabia's Nitaqat Blues', *Business Line*, 30 June.

Bindulakshmi, P. 2010. 'Gender Mobility and State Response: Indian Domestic Workers in the United Arab Emirates', in Rajan S. Irudaya (ed.), *Governance and Labour Migration: Indian Migration Report*, pp. 44–63. New Delhi: Routledge.

Bohra, Pratikshya and Douglas S. Massey. 2009. 'Process of Internal and International Migration from Chitwan, Nepal', *International Migration Review*, 43(3): 621–51.

Bureau of Manpower, Employment and Training (BMET). 2010. 'Overseas Statistics'. http://www.bmet.org.bd/BMET/index (last accessed on 7 June 2013).

Chandha, Nayan. 2008. 'The Early Globalizers', *India and Global Affairs Journal*, 11(5): 58–65.

Claude, Markovits. 1999. 'Indian Merchant Networks outside India in the Nineteenth and Twentieth Centuries: A Preliminary Survey', *Modern Asian Studies*, 33(4): 883–911.

Dixit, Kanak Mani. 2013. 'Long Walk to Normalcy', *The Hindu*, November 14, p. 9.

Fargues, Philippe. 2011. 'Immigration without Inclusion: Non-nationals in Gulf State Nation Building'. Paper presented at the 2011 Gulf Research Meeting (Workshop 12, Migration in the Gulf) University of Cambridge, 6–9 July. http://grm.grc.net/index.php?pgid=Njk=&wid=Mjc#sthash.TuH9nDwW.dpuf (last accessed on 9 November 2013).

Fuccaro, Nelida. 2009. *Histories of City and State in the Persian Gulf: Manama Since 1800*. Cambridge, UK: Cambridge University Press.

Gamburd, Michele Ruth. 2010. 'Sri Lankan Migration to the Gulf: Female Bread Winners–Domestic Workers', in Middle East Institute (ed.), *View Points: Migration and the Gulf*, pp. 13–15. Washington DC: Middle East Institute.

Graner, Elvira and Ganesh Gurung. 2003. 'Arabko Lahure: Looking at Nepali Labour Migrants to Arabian Countries', *Contribution to the Nepalese Studies*, 30(2): 295–325.

Gupta, Poonam and Karan Singh. 2012. 'Trends and Correlates of Remittances to India', in Ibrahim Sirkeci, Jeffrey H. Cohen and Dilip Ratha (eds), *Migration and Remittances during the Global Financial Crisis and Beyond*, pp. 93–9. Washington DC: World Bank.

Jain, Prakash C. 2006. 'Indian Labor Migration to the Gulf Countries', *GRC Papers*, Gulf Research Centre, United Arab Emirates, June.

———. 2008. 'Globalization and Indian Diaspora in West Asia and North Africa: Some Policy Implications', in Anwar Alam (ed.), *India and West Asia in the Era of Globalisation*, pp. 161–87. New Delhi: New Century Publications.

Kabeer, Naila. 2007. "Footloose' Female Labour: Transnational Migration, Social Protection and Citizenship in the Asia Region', Working

Paper on Women's Rights and Citizenship, International Development Research Centre (IDRC), Canada.

Kanchana, Radhika. 2012. 'Qatar's 'White-collar' Indians', No. 8, e-migrinter, France. http://www.mshs.univ-poitiers.fr/migrinter/e-migrinter/201208/e-migrinter2012_08_045.pdf (last accessed on 29 January 2014).

Kapiszewski, Andrzej. 2006. 'Arab Versus Asian Migrant Workers in the GCC Countries', United Nations Expert Group Meeting on International Migration and Development in the Arab Region, Population Division, Beirut, United Nations Secretariat, 22 May.

Kelegama, Saman (ed.). 2011. *Migration, Remittances and Development in South Asia*. New Delhi: Sage Publications.

Manoramaonline.com. 2011. ' "Gaddama" Paves Way for the Return of the Melody', 18 February. http://www.manoramaonline.com/cgi-bin/mmonline.dll/portal/ep/contentView.do?programId=1080132927&contentId=8842035&tabId=19&BV_ID=@@@ (last accessed on 17 November 2014).

Migration News. 2012. 'GCC: Migrants', 19(2), April. http://migration.ucdavis.edu/mn/more.php?id=3759_0_3_0 (last accessed on 15 January 2014).

Ministry of Labour. 2003. *Annual Report, 2003*. New Delhi: Government of India.

———. 2004. *Annual Report, 2004*. New Delhi: Government of India.

———. 2005. *Annual Report 2005*. New Delhi: Government of India.

———. 2012. *Annual Report 2012*. New Delhi, Government of India.

———. 2013. *Annual Report 2013*. New Delhi, Government of India.

Mohapatra, Sanket, Dilip Ratha and Anil Silwal. 2012. 'Migrant Remittances in Nepal: Impact of Global Financial Crisis and Policy Options', in Ibrahim Sirkeci, Jeffrey H. Cohen and Dilip Ratha (eds), *Migration and Remittances during the Global Financial Crisis and Beyond*, pp. 129–32. Washington DC: World Bank.

Natrajan, Chitra. 2013. 'Migration to Gulf and its Impact on Tamilnadu, 1991–2010', Unpublished Ph.D. dissertation, Centre for West Asian Studies, Jawaharlal Nehru University, New Delhi.

Nepal Institute of Development Studies (NIDS). 2010. *Nepal Migration Year Book 2009*. Kathmandu: NIDS.

Oishi, Nana. 2005. *Women in Motion: Globalisation, State Policies and Labour Migration in Asia*. Stanford: Stanford University Press.

Ozaki, Mayumi. 2012. 'Worker Migration and Remittances in South Asia', *South Asia Working Paper Series*, Manila, Asian Development Bank.

Pakistan Today. 2013. 'Remittances Rise to $6.33b in 1HFY12', 16 July. http://www.pakistantoday.com.pk/2012/01/11/news/profit/remittances-rise-to-6–33b-in-1hfy12/ (last accessed on 15 January 2014).

Panicker, Krishnakumar Sulochana. 2012. 'Migration, Remittances and Development in South Asia" ' *Diaspora Studies*, 5(2): 219–24.

Percot, Marie. 2006. 'Indian Nurses in the Gulf: Two Generations of Female Migration', *South Asia Research*, 26(1): 41–62.

Rahman, Md Mizanur. 2012. 'Bangladeshi Labour Migration to the Gulf States: Patterns of Recruitment and Processes', *Canadian Journal of Development Studies*, 33(2): 214–18.

Rajan, S. Irudaya and D. Narayana. 2012. 'The Financial Crisis in the Gulf and its Impact on South Asian Migration', in Ibrahim Sirkeci, Jeffrey H. Cohen and Dilip Ratha (eds), *Migration and Remittances during the Global Financial Crisis and Beyond*, pp. 67–81. Washington DC: World Bank.

Rajan, S. Irudaya and Sukendaran S. 2010. 'Understanding Female Migration: Experience of House Maids', in Rajan S. Irudaya (ed.), *Governance and Labour Migration: Indian Migration Report*, pp. 182–96. New Delhi: Routledge.

Rajan, S. Irudaya and K. C. Zacharia (eds). 2012. *Kerala's Demographic Future: Issues and Policy Option*. New Delhi: Academic Foundation.

Ramachandran, Sudha. 2013. 'Saudi's Nitaqat Law: Trouble for Indian Expats', *The Diplomat*, 25 April.

Sananda Kumar, S. 2013. 'After Saudi Arabia's Nitaqat, it is Kuwait's Turn to Crack Down on Illegal Workers', *The Economic Times*, 3 June.

Seccombe, I. J. and R. I. Lawless. 1986. 'Foreign Workers Dependence in the Gulf and the International Oil Companies 1910–50', *International Migration Review*, 20(3): 548–74.

Shah, M. Nasra. 2000. 'Relative Success of Male Workers in the Host Country: Does the Channel of Migration Matter', *International Migration Review*, 34(1): 59–78.

Sharma, Jeevan Raj. 2012. 'Nepal: Migration History and Trends', in Ibrahim Sirkeci, Jeffrey H. Cohen and Dilip Ratha (eds), *Migration and Remittances during the Global Financial Crisis and Beyond*, pp. 133–7. Washington DC: World Bank.

Silva, Cargo Varga and George Naufal. 2012. 'Migrant Transfers in MENA Region: A Two Way Street in which Traffic is Changing', in Sirkeci Ibrahim, Jeffrey H. Cohen and Dilip Ratha (eds), *Migration and Remittances during the Global Financial Crisis and Beyond*, pp. 377–87. Washington DC: World Bank.

Sirkeci, Ibrahim, Jeffrey H. Cohen and Dilip Ratha (eds). 2012. *Migration and Remittances during the Global Financial Crisis and Beyond*. Washington DC: World Bank.

Sri Lankan Bureau of Foreign Employment (SLBFE). 2011. *Annual Statistical Report of Foreign Employment 2011*. Sri Lanka: SLBFE.

Srivastava, Ravi and S. K. Sasikumar. 2003. 'An Overview of Migration in India: Its Impact and Key Issues'. Paper presented at the Regional Conference on Migration, Development and Pro-poor Policy Choices in Asia, jointly organised by DFID, UK and RMMRU, Dhaka, 22–24 June.

The Economic Times. 2013. 'Saudi Arabia's Nitaqat Law may Restrict Remittances to Pakistan: Report', 1 July.

The Himalayan Times. 2013. 'Labour Diplomacy Must in GCC Countries: Envoys', 10 May. http://www.thehimalayantimes.com/fullNews.php?headline=Labour+diplomacy+must+in+GCC+countries%3A+Envoys+&NewsID=375940 (last accessed on 14 January 2014).

The Hindu. 2013. 'Nitaqat Fallout: 18,000 Indians Prepare to Leave Saudi', 8 May.

The Indian Express. 2013. 'Most Indian Workers meet Nitaqat Deadline, Regularize Stay in Delhi', 4 November.

Thieme, Susan. 2006. *Social Networks and Migration: Far West Nepalese Labour Migrants in Delhi*. Berne: NCCR North-South Dialogue.

Thimothy, Rakkee and S. K. Sasikumar. 2012. 'Migration of Women Workers from South Asia to the Gulf', Research Project, V. V. Giri National Labour Institute, NOIDA, pp. 84–8.

Williams, Nathalie, Arland Thornton, Dirgha J. Ghimire, Linda C. Young-DeMarco, and Mansoor Moaddel. 2010. 'Nepali Migrants to the Gulf Cooperation Countries: Values, Behaviors and Plans', in Mahran Kamrava and Zahra Babar (eds), *Migrant Labour in the Persian Gulf*. New York: Colombia University Press.

Winckler, Onn. 2010. 'Labour Migration to the GCC States: Patterns, Scale and Policies', *Migration and the Gulf*. http://www.voltairenet.org/IMG/pdf/Migration_and_the_Gulf.pdf (last accessed on 17 December 2014).

World Bank. 2013. 'Migration and Development Brief 20', Migration and Remittances Unit, Development Prospects Group, 19 April. http://siteresources.worldbank.org/INTPROSPECTS/Resources/334934–1110315015165/MigrationandDevelopmentBrief20.pdf (last accessed on 16 November 2014).

2

Arab versus Asian migrant workers in the GCC countries

Andrzej Kapiszewski[2]

A difficult economic situation in many Arab and South East Asian countries in the last few decades has made labour emigration an attractive option for citizens of these states (Abella 1995; Al-Najjar 2001). Such emigration has generally been supported by the governments of these countries to ease the pressure on labour markets, reduce unemployment and accelerate development. The migration of the workforce has become one of the most dynamic economic factors in the Middle Eastern and North African (MENA) countries; remittances from migrant labour back to these states exceed the value of regional trade in goods as well as official capital flows (Fergany 2001; Nassar and Ghoneim 2002). Similarly, the migrations to the Gulf states speed up the development of certain regions of India, Pakistan, Bangladesh, the Philippines or Indonesia (Amjad 1989; Eelens et al. 1992).

One of the largest markets for Arab and Asian jobseekers has been the Gulf region: Saudi Arabia, Kuwait, Bahrain, Qatar, the United Arab Emirates (UAE), and Oman, all members of the Gulf Cooperation Council (GCC) which was established in 1981. Since the discovery of oil, these countries, lacking a local workforce, have been employing a large expatriate labour force. That process has had a very significant impact on the economy, politics and the social structure of the GCC states. It has allowed for a rapid development of these countries, but at the same time has involved them in various foreign affair developments and brought a number of negative cultural and socio-economic consequences. Although foreigners in the GCC states have not created problems of the magnitude of those found in other immigrant countries of the world, different economic and political interests of governments and individuals have brought numerous tensions and conflicts, which intensified in the post 9/11 era.

This paper analyses the population dilemmas of the GCC states as well as the economic and political determinants of the labour policies. In particular, such issues as the heterogeneity of the local populations, the national composition of the foreign workforce, the segmentation of the labour market, and the localisation of the workforce are discussed.

Divided populations: nationals vs expatriates

Since the discovery of oil, political entities of the Persian Gulf have transformed themselves from desert sheikhdoms into modern states. This process has been accompanied by a rapid population growth. The population in the current GCC states has grown more than eight times in 50 years; to be exact, from 4 million in 1950 to 40 million in 2006, which marks one of the highest rates of population growth in the world. This increase has not been caused primarily by a natural growth of the indigenous population but by the influx of foreign workers. The employment of large numbers of foreigners has been a structural imperative in these countries, as oil-related development depends upon the importation of foreign technologies and requires knowledge and skills alien to the local Arab population. In consequence, unlike in Western Europe, where foreign workers have only complemented the national workforce, usually by filling lower-status jobs, in the GCC states they have become the primary, dominant labour force in most sectors of the economy and the government bureaucracy. The percentage of foreigners in the GCC populations has systematically been growing over the last decades, increasing from 31 per cent in 1975 to over 38 per cent in the mid-1990s, levelling and diminishing slightly at the beginning of the 2000s, to only grew again lately. Towards the end of 2004, the year of the latest relatively reliable statistics, the GCC states were inhabited by 12.5 million foreigners, who constituted 37 per cent of the total population (Table 2.1). In Qatar, the UAE and Kuwait, foreigners constituted a majority; in the UAE they accounted for over 80 per cent of the population. Only Oman and Saudi Arabia managed to maintain a relatively low proportion of foreigners: about 20 per cent and 27 per cent, respectively.

The dominance of foreigners has been more pronounced in the workforce than in the total population. Non-nationals constituted

Table 2.1 Population of the GCC states (2004) and latest (2005–06) estimates

	Nationals 2004	%	Expatriates 2004	%	Total 2004	Current total
Bahrain	438,209	62.0	268,951	38.0	707,160	707,160
Kuwait	943,000	35.6	1,707,000	64.4	2,650,000	2,992,000
Oman	2,325,812	80.1	577,293	19.9	2,903,105	3,102,000
Qatar	223,209	30.0	520,820	70.0	744,029	855,000
Saudi Arabia	16,529,302	72.9	6,144,236	27.1	22,673,538	27,020,000
UAE	722,000	19.0	3,278,000	81.0	4,000,000	4,700,000
GCC	21,181,323	62.9	12,486,349	37.1	33,677,832	39,376,160

Notes: Various government agencies often present different data. The preliminary results of the Saudi Arabia 2004 Census, presented above, contradicts other reports. For example, in May 2004 the Saudi labour minister said that there are about 8.8 million expatriates in the kingdom. Other reports suggested that the total Saudi population in 2005 crossed 27 million, with some 20 million expatriates and 7 million nationals. In turn, in May 2005, the UAE Ministry of Labour announced that at the end of 2004 the population of the Emirates reached 4.33 million and is expected to reach 5 million by the end of 2005. Some reports suggest that the total Omani population exceeded 3.2 million already in 2004.

Source: Publications of the government agencies of the GCC states for mid- or end 2004. See also: Quarterly reports of the *Economist Intelligence Unit* (London). Numbers for nationals and expatriates in Qatar are rough estimates due to lack of official data.

a majority of the labour force in all the GCC countries, with the average for the year 2004 being close to 70 per cent. The lowest rates were recorded in Bahrain and Saudi Arabia, but even there expatriates constituted above 50 per cent and 65 per cent of the workforce, accordingly; in Kuwait 82 per cent of the workforce were foreign, in Qatar almost 90 per cent, and in the UAE, 90 per cent (Fasano and Goyal 2004; Girgis 2002; Gulf Cooperation Council 2002; Human Rights Watch 2004).

This development has posed security, economic, social, and cultural threats to the local population. As a consequence, to maintain a highly privileged position of the nationals, numerous restrictions have been imposed: the sponsorship system, the rotational system of expatriate labour to limit the duration of foreigners' stay, curbs on the naturalisation and citizenship rights of those who have been naturalised, etc. However, many of these measures have not brought the expected results; in particular, the planned rotation of the workforce has proved impossible to achieve. The free market economy has been more powerful than the policies the authorities have been eager to implement. The majority of expatriates have stayed beyond the term of the original contract as employers usually prefer to keep workers who have already gained some local experience rather than bring in the new ones. Moreover, importing a new worker involves additional costs to employers. As a result, the average period of time that foreign workers spend in the GCC countries continues to extend, and the number of 'almost permanent' foreign workers has increased, albeit not formally.

What makes the situation more difficult is the fact that that the exceptionally favourable situation which the nationals have enjoyed for decades has started to change.[3] A growing number of them have experienced difficulties in finding the kind of employment they have been looking for. The public sector, in which most nationals used to find employment, has already become saturated, while the private sector has remained too competitive for a great majority of them.[4] As the unemployment among nationals began to grow, which was a phenomenon unheard of in the past, the GCC governments decided to embark on the formulation of labour market strategies to improve this situation, to create sufficient employment opportunities for the nationals, and to limit dependence on expatriate labour (the so-called localisation, nationalisation or indigenisation of labour, depending on the country, referred to as Saudisation, Omanisation, Emiratisation, etc.).

A number of measures have been proposed to achieve these objectives: some professions have been reserved as 'for nationals only', the employment quotas for nationals and expatriates have been introduced in certain professions, wage subsidies and state retirement plans for nationals in the private sector were established parallel to fees and charges on the foreign labour to make it less competitive (Kapiszewski 2001: 201–50). Private companies meeting quota requirements have been rewarded in public tenders. Moreover, large efforts have been made to improve the education and training of nationals. Nevertheless, all these measures have so far brought only limited results. Only the public sector has been successfully nationalised. In the private sector, the localisation is still very low. In 2004, in Kuwait, out of a total workforce of 850,000 in the private sector, Kuwaitis accounted for only 1.8 per cent, i.e. ca 16,000 (Jassen 2004). In general, in Qatar, Oman and the UAE, there were around 10 per cent of nationals in the workforce; in Bahrain 27 per cent, and only in Saudi Arabia in excess of 30 per cent (Fasano and Goyal 2004). The unsuccessful nationalisation attempts have been caused by the fact that employment in the private sector is usually unattractive for nationals. The salaries it offers are usually low, working hours long, and the work environment, with its competitiveness and the need to recognise an expatriate supervisor – difficult to accept. Moreover, working in the private sector, unlike in the public sector, is sometimes perceived as debasing the nationals' social status. Another problem is that nationals are culturally disinclined to enter low-skilled posts, while, at the same time, the educational systems are not properly prepared to deal with the problem of reorienting traditional work values. Finally, a forceful approach to localisation, like the quota system, has encountered strong opposition from local businessmen, as potentially harmful and adversely affecting productivity and profitability of firms.

Women in the workforce

In the GCC states there has been another very important determinant of the situation in the labour market, namely the participation of women. In general, that participation has been limited due to religious norms and tradition (Kapiszewski 2001: 101–19). In Saudi Arabia, the law even forbids women to work in the presence of men, and in effect women amount to only some 10 per cent of the Saudi labour force (Qusti and Al-Zahrani 2006). Nevertheless, the improving education of women, the existing economic needs and changing attitudes to their work outside homes in the society at large are among the factors that have recently increased national women's participation in the workforce. Their presence in the labour market created a possibility to replace some foreign workers. Just the act of granting Saudi women the right to drive cars alone should result in removing around 100,000 foreign drivers from the labour force.

The issue of female employment poses a dilemma for the authorities: some would like to promote it but are often anxious to do so, as moves in that direction may strengthen radical anti-government Islamic forces that oppose the emancipation of women. These movements are especially strong in Saudi Arabia but their power is also growing in Kuwait and Bahrain. Yet, in recent years, the rulers of many GCC states have made a number of symbolic gestures to support women's position in the society: in Oman, Bahrain, Kuwait, Qatar, and the UAE they have nominated a number of national women to ministerial positions. In Oman, Bahrain and Qatar, they have allowed them to participate in local elections; in Kuwait they will be able to do so in the next election; even in Saudi Arabia they have been allowed to participate in the election to the Chambers of Commerce and Industry.

The majority of women in the GCC workforce are foreign (Kapiszewski 2001: 107–9). Their ratio has varied: in the UAE, over 80 per cent of employed women have been expatriates, while in Bahrain only some 55 per cent. In turn, national women constituted 2–10 per cent of the total national workforce, while expatriate women between 10 per cent and 25 per cent of the expatriate workforce. Most of the expatriate women have been Asian domestic workers.

Arabs vs Asians: de-Arabisation of the labour market

Another problem which has developed in the labour market has been its controversial national make-up.

For historical, political and economic reasons, people of various nationalities have traditionally searched for work in the GCC states. The composition of these foreign populations has been changing with time.

At the beginning of the oil era, the majority of the workforce migrating to the lower Gulf countries came from the poor neighbouring Arab states. The largest groups among them were the Yemenis and the Egyptians looking for better employment opportunities, particularly in Saudi Arabia. There were also traditional local migrant labourers from the peninsula, Omanis in particular, who looked for jobs in the more developed neighbouring states. At various times, other Arabs used to arrive in the Gulf states, compelled to leave their home countries as a result of the domestic political situation. There were Palestinians, who began emigrating to the Gulf very early, after the Arab-Israeli War of 1948 and the occupation of Palestine; some Iraqis, following the 1968 Ba'ath party coup in Baghdad; and Yemenis, after the civil wars in their country. For years, many Indian, Pakistani and Iranian traders and labourers used to go to the Gulf as a result of their long-time ties that their countries had maintained with the region (developed especially during the British presence in the Indian subcontinent). A new phase in the migration started with the post-1973 economic boom. With the upsurge in oil revenues, the Gulf states made development efforts on an unprecedented scale, unmatched in other states of the world. Total investment rose almost 10 times between the first and the second half of the 1970s. In Saudi Arabia alone, the growth of capital formation averaged an incredible 27.8 per cent a year during the whole decade (Abella 1995: 418). A massive labour emigration followed these developments: Yemenis, Egyptians, Sudanese, Jordanians/Palestinians, Syrians, Pakistanis, and Indians began to arrive in the Gulf states in large numbers.

Initially, Arab workers were particularly welcomed. Their linguistic, cultural and religious compatibility with the local populations made them more attractive to nationals than other immigrants. The migrant Arabs set up a familiar Arab-type government administration and educational facilities, helped to develop health services, build the necessary infrastructure for these rapidly developing countries, and run the oil industries. Nevertheless, relatively quickly, the preference of the oil-states' governments changed, and they began to be more open to Asian workers. There were several economic, political, social, historical, and pragmatic reasons for this change.

First, the Gulf authorities became worried about non-local Arabs bringing and spreading radical social and political concepts (in particular, the secularist and frequently pro-Soviet ideologies), and cultivating undesirable loyalties. The leftist, pan-Arab ideas promoted by Arab expatriates called for the abolition of monarchies in the Gulf. Some organisations of the type of the Popular Front for the Liberation of Bahrain, the Popular Front for the Liberation of Oman, and the Popular Front for the Liberation of the Occupied Arab Gulf were established and began anti-government activities in the Gulf states. In the 1970s and 1980s, numerous immigrant Arab workers were prosecuted, jailed and deported because of their participation in the activities of these organisations (Kapiszewski 2001: 133–44). The internal stability of some of the GCC countries, including Saudi Arabia, Kuwait, Bahrain, and Qatar, was also shaken by the Arab expatriate-led labour strikes.

Some other ideas promoted by expatriate Arab workers also worried the GCC authorities. Many young Arabs regarded borders in the Middle East as artificial lines imposed by Western imperialists, and, consequently, expected them to be eliminated. Another popular pan-Arab view, that of a single Arab nation in which labour 'circulates' freely, was also rejected by the Gulf governments for security reasons. Yet another problem was related to the regional distribution of the oil-generated wealth. While the oil-producing countries, which preferred to retain that wealth, began to link the entitlement of oil revenues to state sovereignty, poorer states increasingly stressed their Arab identity as a good reason to demand their share in the revenues: Iraq even used the oil-related arguments as a justification to invade Kuwait in 1990.

Another dimension of the Arab presence in the GCC states which worried many nationals was the supposed 'Egyptianization' of the local dialects and culture that were believed to have resulted from the predominance of Egyptians in the field of education (Graz 1992: 220–1).

Finally, the presence of Palestinians, which pushed the GCC states into an involvement in politics related to the Arab-Israeli conflict, was also considered a problem.

The stereotypical attitudes of the nationals towards the non-GCC Arabs have not helped to promote them in the labour market either. Their attitudes have often not been as positive as the cultural and religious bonds between the nationals and the non-GCC Arabs could suggest. Birks and Sinclair noted: 'Many GCC nationals feel a detachment from Palestinians and Jordanians, a lack of respect for Yemenis, and mistrust and dislike of Egyptians' (1980: 116). Mohammed Al-Fahim, a leading UAE businessman, presents the attitudes of nationals towards non-Gulf Arabs in the following way:

> Because we had a common religion and for the most part, a common language, we felt we were dealing with friends not foes. In the case of our neighbours, we shared the same Arab perspective on life and the world. Or so we believed. Unfortunately, we found to our dismay that it took more than such commonalties to build a solid foundation for trustworthy relationships. (Al-Fahim 1995: 160)

On the other hand, Asians did not represent any threat to the Gulf nationals and were preferred to Arabs for various other reasons.

First, Asians were less expensive to employ, easier to lay-off and believed to be more efficient, obedient and manageable (Ghobash 1986: 138–42; Girgis 2002: 29). Second, they were used to leaving their families at home, whereas Arab immigrants usually brought their families to the Gulf with the hope of settling there permanently. This possibility was not acceptable to the GCC authorities. Third, in the post-1973 oil boom, the demand for foreign workers in the GCC states outstripped the Arab countries' ability to supply them (Chuocri 1983). In contrast, Asian governments often became involved in the recruitment and placement of their workers, facilitating their smooth flow to the Gulf. Efficient recruitment agencies in Asia were able to provide a constant supply of manpower, fully satisfying the needs of the Gulf employers. Moreover, at that stage of the GCC countries' development, the so-called 'turnkey' projects, in which Asian contractors specialised, were implemented with increasing frequency. In many cases, Asians were also logistically easier to bring to the GCC states as this region had closer historical links with some parts of Asia than with many, more geographically distant, parts of the Arab world.

Finally, many Asians were Muslims too, so the religiously-sensitive Gulf Arabs felt more comfortable having such people around.[5]

For all these reasons, the number of Arab workers in the GCC countries reduced considerably over the years, although there were never any official policies announced to sanction such an approach. Arabs were replaced not only by workers from the states already well established among the GCC workforce, for example, India or Pakistan, but also from such countries as the Philippines, Thailand, Sri Lanka, Bangladesh, and Indonesia.

The percentage of expatriate population represented by Arabs in the GCC countries decreased from 72 per cent in 1975 to 56 per cent a decade later (Table 2.2). In turn, in 1970, non-Arabs constituted only 12 per cent of all workers in the Gulf, yet by 1980 their number had grown to 41 per cent, and by 1985 Asian workers formed 63 per cent of the Gulf workforce (Russel and Teitelbaum 1992).

Table 2.2 Arab share in foreign populations, 1975–2002/04* (%)

	1975	1985	1996	2002/04
Bahrain	22	15	12	15
Kuwait	80	69	33**	30**
Oman	16	16	11	6
Qatar	33	33	21	19
Saudi Arabia	91	79	30	33
UAE	26	19	10	13
GCC	72	56	31	32

Source: The ratios for 1975 and 1985, see Birks (1988), Birks, Seccombe and Sinclair (1988) and Winckler (2000); for Kuwait, in 1996, data is from the Public Authority for Civil Information; for Oman, in 1996, the data is from the Ministry of Planning, *Statistical Yearbook 1996* (Muscat); the ratios for the other countries in 1996 and in 2002/04 are the author's estimates based on various sources. See also: the GCC Demographic Report (1998). See Kapiszewski (2005) for: * data for the years 2002, 2003 or 2004; ** including the *bidun*.

There was some concern about the possible social consequences of the de-Arabisation of the population as a result of Asian influence. For example, in 1982, Abd al-Rahman al-Dirham from the Qatari Ministry of Labor, noted that:

> The question of foreign labor is of great concern. Our social customs are threatened by foreigners. The problem is not just in Qatar but also in other Gulf countries. We prefer it if we can get suitable people from Arab countries who can live in the Gulf area without changing it. (*MEED*, August 1982, p. 40)

The labour laws enacted in most GCC countries stressed that employment should be first offered to the national citizens, second to the citizens of other GCC states, then to non-Gulf Arabs, and finally to other foreigners. That approach was in line with the overall Arab position on the issue. In 1968, the Arab Labor Organization (ALO) called all the Arab states to give priority to Arab workers; in 1975, a similar resolution was adopted by the Arab League. The Strategy for Joint Arab Economic Action of the 1980s stated that 'Arab manpower must be resorted to increasingly reduce dependence on foreign labor'. In 1984, the Arab Declaration of Principles on the Movement of Manpower stressed once more the need to give preference to Arab nationals before the nationals of third countries.

In 1980, the UAE formally introduced a policy that Arabs should constitute at least 30 per cent of the foreign workforce, and signed agreements with Tunisia, Morocco and Sudan to recruit more Arab workers (Al-Alkim 1989: 30–2). Similarly, in 1974, Qatar signed an agreement with Egypt to receive 9,000 workers annually from that country; in 1982 it signed one with Tunisia providing for the recruitment of Tunisian military personnel and technicians for the Qatari army as well as blue collar workers (Winckler 2000: 27).

Despite all these declarations and agreements, the pro-Arab labour policies were never really implemented. Nader Fergany wrote that 'attempts to organize the pan-Arab labor market have fizzled out into ineffective declarations of intent that have been impeded in reality by perceived narrow national interests, particularly of countries of employment, acting the mind set of buyers in a buyers-market'. Moreover, 'labor movement in the Arab region has been captive to the ups and downs of Arab politics, sometimes with devastating consequences to the welfare of embroiled migrants' (Fergany 2001: 12).

It is only recently that the GCC authorities have begun to admit publicly the negative consequences of this situation. During the October 2004 meeting of the GCC labour ministers, Majeed Al-Alawi, the Bahraini Minister of Labor and Social Affairs warned that 'non-Arab foreign workers constitute a strategic threat to the region's future'.[6] Similarly, during another ministerial meeting of that kind in November 2005, Abdul Rahman Al Attiya, the GCC Secretary General, warned about the possible consequences of the situation.

> The GCC countries need to look at the massive presence of expatriates basically as a national security issue, and not merely as an economic matter . . . International accords are pressing for the settlement of expatriates and imposing giving them salaries equal to nationals and greater rights in the areas of education and health.

At the same time James Zogby, the president of the Arab American Institute stated that the guest workers were a 'time bomb waiting to explode and unleash riots like those that rocked France'.[7]

The regional politics occasionally also influences the situation on the labour market to a considerable extent. In particular, some significant changes in the composition of the foreign workforce occurred as a result of the events of the second Gulf War. Both the Iraqis and those whose governments were supportive of Iraq (including Palestinians, Jordanians, Yemenis, and Sudanese) were distrusted and forced to leave the GCC states during and in the aftermath of the crisis. Altogether, over 1.5 million people were expelled: up to 1 million Yemenis were expelled from Saudi Arabia along with 200,000 Jordanians and 150,000 Palestinians – mainly from Kuwait and Saudi Arabia. Several hundred thousand foreign workers (including 158,000 Egyptians) left Kuwait voluntarily or were evacuated by their governments (Shaban, Assaad and Al-Qudsi 2002: 41). In addition, many Asian workers were evacuated from Kuwait by their governments, but most of them were able to return to the country after the crisis.

Many Arabs who left the GCC states during the Gulf war and in its aftermath did not return following the conflict. The resultant vacuum in the labour market, despite the GCC governments' intentions, was not filled by the nationals. The free market dynamics led Asians in particular to take the vacant jobs, enlarging their share in the workforce again.

The workforce has witnessed further change in the 1990s, partly because of the end of the Cold War and the processes of globalisation. The jobseekers from China and from the newly-independent states of the former Soviet Union began to arrive in the Gulf looking for employment opportunities. Cheap to employ and often quite well educated, these migrants created additional competition in the labour market.

The policy of nationalisation of the workforce combined with political preferences has also had an impact on the foreign workforce. For example, in the mid-1990s, when trying to reduce expatriate labour in order to find more jobs for young unemployed Saudis, Saudi Arabia reduced the number of work permits issued to Egyptians. As a result, their number decreased from 900,000 in 1995 to 670,000 two years later.

Following all these developments, the percentage of the expatriate population represented by Arabs in the GCC countries continued to decrease further in the following years: by the early 2000s, they accounted only for 32 per cent (see Table 2.2). In Saudi Arabia, the percentage of Arabs went down from 91 per cent in 1975 to 33 per cent by 2004. In Kuwait, the decline was from 80 per cent in 1975 to 30 per cent in 2003. In other countries, where the proportion of non-native Arabs in the population was traditionally lower, their share nevertheless declined even further, to as little as 6 per cent in Oman and 13–15 per cent in Bahrain and the UAE (all these numbers are estimates only, as the precise data are not available).

Altogether, among the 12.5 million foreigners who lived in the GCC countries in 2004, there were about 3.2 million non-Gulf Arabs, half the number of Asians, who were represented by 3.3 million Indians, 1.7 million Pakistanis and about 0.7 million people from Bangladesh, the Philippines and Sri Lanka each (Table 2.3). Thus, the percentage of Asians in the foreign populations varies from almost 70 per cent in Kuwait and Saudi Arabia to over 90 per cent in Oman.

The exact size of foreign communities in the GCC states is, however, difficult to establish, as authorities usually do not reveal any information about them, thinking probably that it is better not to make foreign communities aware of their actual size.

The non-Gulf Arab community has mainly been composed of Egyptians (almost 1.5 million), Yemenis (0.9 million) and Palestinians/Jordanians (0.5 million) (Ambrosetti and Tattolo 2004; CAPMAS 2004). There are also over 300,000 Sudanese living in the GCC states nowadays.

Table 2.3 Major expatriate communities in the GCC countries (2004)

	Bahrain 2004	Kuwait 2003	Oman 2004	Qatar 2002	Saudi Arabia 2004	UAE 2002
Indians	120	320	330	100	1,300	1,200
Pakistanis	50	100	70	100	900	450
Egyptians	30	260	30	35	900	140
Yemenis					800	60
Bangladeshis		170	110		400	100
Filipinos	25	70		50	500	120
Sudanese					250	30
Sri Lankans		170	30	35	350	160
Jordanians/ Palestinians	20	50		50	260	110
Indonesians		9			250	
Syrians		100			100	
Iranians	30	80		60		40
Turks					80	
Nepalese				70		
Bidun		80				

Source: Various sources.

Numerous reports gave much larger numbers for particular Asian communities, especially in Saudi Arabia. Many claim the Kingdom hosted over 1 million Bangladeshis, about 900,000 Sudanese, a similar number of Filipinos, 850,00 Sri Lankans, and over 500,000 Indonesians.[8] If such numbers are correct, it means that the number of foreigners in Saudi Arabia is much higher than officially reported in the last census results (that this can be true, see the note to Table 2.1). In turn, some sources spoke of only 40,000 Sri Lankans in Kuwait and just 100,000 Indonesians in Saudi Arabia.[9]

The consequences of large Asian and non-Gulf Arab populations in the GCC states

The employment of foreign workers is both profitable and costly for the receiving countries. The benefits of importing foreign labour are fairly clear: foreigners provide a basic workforce as well as specialists to compensate for the limited number of nationals with required skills and attitudes, stimulate the domestic consumption of goods supplied by local merchants and boost local property markets. The costs, although much more difficult to estimate, consist of salaries, and the increased spending required to expand the educational and health services, housing, roads, communications, and other elements of infrastructure in order to accommodate the needs of the newcomers. Moreover, the foreign labour force substantially drains the GCC states' hard currency earnings, with remittances to migrants' home countries amounting to US$27 billion each year; US$16 billion coming from the migrant workers in Saudi Arabia alone (Al-Bassam 2004). These remittances constitute a large portion of the GCC countries' GDP; for example, in Saudi Arabia, in 2001, they amounted to about 10 per cent of the total GDP of the kingdom.[10] Nevertheless, the relative costs and benefits of hosting foreign labour have more or less balanced each other out in economic terms. It has been shown that the percentage of the GDP that foreign labour generates is roughly equal to what the state has to spend on them.[11]

On the other hand, foreigners benefit from their employment in the GCC countries. They are usually able to find better-paid jobs than they would have at home, enjoy a high standard of living and often have a chance for quick career advancement. In particular, they are able to save large sums of money and send or take them home, often significantly stimulating the economy in their home countries.[12] The presence of a large number of expatriates constitutes, however, a major threat to the stability of the GCC countries; it endangers the culture, influences the structure of society and, furthermore, has an impact on foreign policy. During the GCC summit in Manama in December 2004, the Bahraini king submitted a report on the danger posed by foreign labour to the social and cultural life as well as economy of the GCC states. Majeed ibn Muhsen Al-Alawi, his Minister of Labour and Social Affairs, said in an interview that 'we should save future generations from having their culture lost' and that although 'we are not against the foreign labor' at the same time 'we do not want these workers to become citizens in the region'. The submitted proposal was aimed at limiting the period a foreigner can work in a Gulf state to six years.[13] The summit left it to further discussions which have continued ever since.

Expatriates have often been perceived by the nationals as disloyal to their hosts, and even as potentially dangerous political agents who spread hostile ideas or work as a 'fifth column' for the benefit of foreign powers (Whitley 1993: 30). Abdul-Reda Assiri has commented that 'certain elements of the expatriate labor force could potentially be quasi militant', function as 'intelligence instruments, to instigate disputes and sabotage', or serve as tools 'for political pressure, and monetary and economic extortion' (Assiri 1996: 19; El Rayyes 1988: 86; Fergany 1984: 160; Khalifa 1979: 113). In 2005, the GCC Secretary General clearly stated that 'expat workers are 'security issue".[14] Thus, quite often, the security situation has an impact on the labour market. For example, in August 2005, the Kuwaiti Ministry of Interior banned workers from Iraq, Iran and Syria from entering Kuwait due to 'security reservations'.[15] It also became compulsory for persons of certain nationalities to get security approval before applying for residency in the country.

In the GCC states, as elsewhere, migration can be an important foreign policy issue, and migrants can influence both their host and sending countries' policies. According to Hassan Hamdan al-Alkim, 'the roles played by the expatriates . . . in the GCC states are of great importance in political articulation on foreign policy-making' (Al-Alkim 1994: 29; Davisha, 1970: 60). Although in the monarchies of the GCC members, expatriate communities do not usually have any formal rights in the political process, they can influence their host countries' foreign policy via the local media. Expatriates also exert influence through the informal access to top-ranking nationals, which some of them enjoy, and through the expatriates' involvement in the overall functioning of the state. According to Al-Alkim, 'the expatriate community, though without citizenship (. . .) exerts more real political influence than most local citizens, and in many ways is considered to be crucial to the relatively smooth functioning of the political process' (Al-Alkim 1994: 49). In a similar way, expatriates can often influence their home countries' foreign policy towards the GCC (Crystal 1997: 208).

The presence of large groups of expatriates sometimes causes problems between their home and host countries. For example, in 1996, the Qatari government accused Egypt of its involvement in the attempted coup, and expelled ca 700 Egyptian workers, particularly those employed in the Ministry of Interior. Several hundred Egyptian workers were also fired by the Qatari authorities in 1997 and 1998, basically due to the tensions between the countries resulting from Cairo's criticism of Doha's developing relations with Israel. In turn, in December 1999, around 3,000 Yemeni workers were deported from Saudi Arabia, apparently due to renewed tensions between the countries related to border issues. In October 1999, a mass riot involving hundreds of Egyptian and

Kuwaiti workers took place in Kuwait. About 120 people were wounded in the event, and 16 Egyptian workers were arrested and accused of arson, damage to private property, participation in an illegal gathering and resisting arrest in the riots. At the root of the incident were the inadequate working and living conditions of Egyptian workers, most of whom were employed illegally and as such were not protected by either Kuwaiti or Egyptian authorities (Kapiszewski 2004: 128). In 2005, the low-paid Asian workers also staged protests, some of them violent, in Kuwait, Bahrain and Qatar, for not receiving salaries on time. In March 2006, hundreds of mostly South Asian construction workers stopped work and went on a rampage in Dubai, UAE, to protest their harsh working conditions, low or delayed pay, and the general lack of rights.

Such incidents demonstrate the tense relations which have developed between the nationals and the expatriates in some cases. Foreigners, non-Gulf Arabs in particular, have often suspected the nationals of desiring to exploit them on unfair economic terms and have feared the possible consequences of a total dependence on their sponsors, given the lack of laws that could protect them adequately. They have felt the nationals have often acted out of prejudice and discriminated against them both in the labour market and in their attempts to establish business enterprises or purchase real estate (Alessa 1981: 44–50). Non-Gulf Arabs have also been frustrated that the nationals' attitudes towards them were not more positive than towards non-Arab or non-Muslim expatriates. They 'naturally expect to be better treated and somehow more naturally welcomed in the Gulf than [let us say] Indians or Koreans', and when their expectations are not met, they sometimes 'repeat tales of 'arrogance,' 'greed,' 'exploitation,' and 'discrimination' encountered in the Gulf' (Salame 1988: 242). Such claims are often justified. According to James Zogby, 'workers are trapped in horrible conditions, denied justice and their basic humanity'.[16] Even Sheikh Sabah al-Ahmed, the Kuwaiti foreign minister, said once that foreign workers were often treated by unscrupulous contractors as 'slaves'.[17] Of course, the non-Gulf Arabs' perception of the treatment they receive in the GCC countries depends, as is the case with all the expatriates, on their personal experiences (failures or successes), as well as their expectations and motivations before immigration.

Non-Arab labourers, Asian women especially, have also often complained about their treatment in the Gulf.

The sexual harassment of Filipino housemaids by local employers, especially in Saudi Arabia, has become a serious matter in recent years (Gamburd 2005). Among other things, it has resulted in a ban on the under 21 years of age for female migration. Also, in Indonesia the maltreatment of women in the GCC states has been widely reported; it has been viewed as a national 'embarrassment', and led to calls to the government to stop sending housemaids altogether (Silvey 2004: 258).

When several Nepalese contract workers were murdered in mid-2004 by their hostage-takers in wartime Iraq, anger over this situation spilled into the streets of Kathmandu, where the incident was indexed as an act of Arab aggression against guest workers in the Gulf, and the Nepal offices of the Qatar Airways were torched (Chaudoir 2005). Earlier, in 2001, female labour migration was banned by the Kathmandu government.

There are also other social and cultural implications of the presence of a large number of foreigners in the GCC states. The negative influence of expatriates on the national cultures, identities and values as well as social structures remains a big concern for the nationals (Kapiszewski 2001: 157–68). In particular, authorities are worried about the influence of Asian nannies or expatriate teachers, who form the majority of school staff, on local children; their concern is over raising of children without proper attention being given to Islamic and Arabic values. They are also unhappy at the growing influence of the foreign media and a large number of foreign women married to the nationals. Strangely enough, the authorities seem to be less worried about the overwhelming presence of Western material civilisation and Western consumption patterns in the GCC states, probably the most threatening factors for local culture and identity.

The future of the GCC foreign labour market

The demand for foreign workers in the GCC countries in the years to come will depend on several factors: the number of young nationals entering the labour market, the effect of the nationalisation of labour markets (mainly due to government regulations), the capacity of the economy to generate new jobs, the employment qualifications of the national labour force in relation to the requirements of the job market, the willingness of the nationals to take low-prestige jobs, as well as political and security considerations (Fasano and

Goyal 2004; Girgis 2002). Probably the most important factor will be the overall state of the economy; the high oil prices at the beginning of the 2000s allowed for further rapid development of several GCC states and, in consequence, a large growth in population, the foreign one in particular. The reality has greatly exceeded earlier predictions.[18]

In terms of the numbers, were the trend of the last decade to continue, the number of the expatriates would grow in the next 10 years by another 10 million or so (between 1995 and 2004 the number of the expatriates went up from 7 million to 12.5 million, that is by 80 per cent). There are also indications that the percentage of foreigners in the population may grow as well, at least in some countries.[19] Most of the newcomers will be Asians, as employers in the GCC states will probably continue to prefer them to Arab workers.[20] It is unlikely that in the near future the wage rate in such Arab countries as Egypt or Jordan will fall low enough to make non-Gulf Arab labour wage-competitive with Asian labour. Moreover, Arab labour will remain less attractive for foreign employers due to the non-Gulf Arabs' inferior level of education and technical training compared to that of many Asians.[21]

What may, to some extent, slow down the growth of the foreign labour? This may occur because of the following reasons:

1 There will be a growing number of nationals looking for jobs each year due to demographic factors: the birth rate of nationals in the GCC states is very high (3.5 on average), and almost half of the local population is under 15 years of age.
2 The nationals will become better educated, which will allow them to compete more effectively against foreign labour in the private sector. Moreover, when facing growing unemployment (especially high in Saudi Arabia),[22] the nationals will gradually change their work ethic and grow more willing to accept the low-prestige jobs currently held by foreigners (Kapiszewski 2001: 210–11).
3 National women will increase their presence in the workforce, in terms of their numbers, especially in Saudi Arabia.
4 The nationalisation policies will create more jobs for nationals each year.[23]

Moreover, decisive action can be expected from some GCC governments in that matter. Saudi Arabia seems to be the adopting most radical measures. According to the 2002 guidelines of the Shura Council, by 2007, 70 per cent of the workforce will have to be Saudi.

On 2 February 2003, Prince Naif bin Abdulaziz, Saudi Arabia's Minister of Internal Affairs and the chairman of the Manpower Council, announced that the Saudi government had decided to lower the number of foreigners in the kingdom to a maximum of 20 per cent of its indigenous population within the next 10 years, and to establish a quota system for foreigners in which no nationality may exceed 10 per cent of the total population.[24] This decision, if implemented fully, will have a dramatic effect on the foreign population in the kingdom, and on Arab immigrants in particular. In terms of the 2004 situation (16.5 million nationals, 6.1 million foreigners), the execution of the new policies would imply the expulsion of over half of the foreign workers currently residing in the kingdom, a decrease in the size of the Indian population from 1.3 million to around 300,000, and a reduction of the number of Egyptian, Yemeni and Pakistani populations from almost a million (each) to a similar number.

In October 2004, Ghazi al-Ghosaibi, the labour minister, announced that the government plans to cut the number of foreign workers by no less than 100,000 every year, and in March 2005 he declared that the number of job visas was reduced from 832,244 to 684,201 during one year (Ghafour 2005).

Naturally, only time will show whether the Saudi authorities will be able to realise these ambitious plans. In the Five-Year Plan adopted in 1985, a 22.6 per cent reduction of foreign labour was planned by the year 1990 (i.e., by some 600,000 people). In reality, the foreign workforce increased during that period by 200,000.

The Kuwaiti government was similarly unsuccessful in trying to implement such policies. In 1997, a decision was issued that ministries must replace 10 per cent of their expatriate staff every year with young Kuwaitis. The decision was implemented only for two years as ministries could not find enough qualified Kuwaitis to substitute the expatriates (Taqi 2005).

In 2005, a proposal was made to limit the stay of expatriates, at least of the unskilled labour, to six years. Labour ministers submitted a recommendation to this effect to the GCC leaders in December 2005 but it evoked varying reactions.[25]

To sum up, in the years to come, in all the GCC states, the employment of nationals and labour migration will remain politically a very sensitive issue as it will cause further tensions between the profit-driven concerns of the private sector, the indigenisation efforts of the states and national security considerations. Moreover, a large number of foreigners residing in these countries will bring new social and cultural challenges of consequences difficult to estimate, especially as the naturalisation of many foreigners will take place. Asians will continue to dominate the foreign workforce at the expense of the non-Gulf Arab labour.

Notes

1 There is a general lack of reliable population data for the GCC states. Author's comments on that written in 2000 are still valid (Kapiszewski, 2001, pp. 26, 27, 45, 46). Therefore, numbers presented in this paper should be treated as estimates only, especially ones for Saudi Arabia and Qatar.

2 This article, written in 2004, could not be updated due to the sudden demise of Professor Andrzej Kapiszewski. However, the general trends observed and the issues raised by him continue to be relevant.

3 For example, in Saudi Arabia, between 1990 and 2000, the gross domestic product (GDP) grew, on average, 1.6 per cent annually, but the country's population grew at an annual rate of 2.7 per cent, thus producing a declining trend in per capita income (Looney 2004). In turn, over the 1997–2004 period, the average nominal salary for Saudi nationals declined by 12 per cent, compared to a 17 per cent fall for foreigners (Fasano and Goyal 2004).

4 Nationals prefer to work in the public sector because of usually high wages, job security, generous social allowances, and retirement benefits, short working hours (allowing workers to be involved in additional private business on the side), lack of work discipline, etc.

5 Nevertheless, many Gulf Arabs have perceived non-Arab Muslims as potential troublemakers, often trying to use their shared Muslim identity to buttress their claims to resources and economic wealth, which the GCC nationals believe are necessarily and naturally only theirs (Ahmad 2005).

6 http://www.middle-east-online.com, 12 October, 2004.

7 *Gulf News*, 24 November 2005.

8 For example, according to the spokesperson for the Philippine Embassy in Riyadh in 2005 there were between 850,000 and 900,000 Filipinos in the Kingdom (*Saudi Gazette*, 17 December 2005).

9 According to the official Indonesian government data for 2003, there were 104,698 Indonesians workers in Saudi Arabia. See http://www.nekatrans.go.id/statistik_naker/pptkln.php.

10 *Al-Madinah*, 16 July 2002.

11 Abdul Rasool Al-Moosa and Keith McLachlan (1985: 85) calculated that foreign workers in Kuwait generate 26 per cent of the GDP, while the state spends 30 per cent of the GDP to sustain this workforce.

12 Workers' remittances constitute a large share of home countries' GDP: in the 1990s this contribution came to 12.4 per cent in Egypt, 15.7 per cent in Jordan and 22.4 per cent in Yemen. Apparently each dollar of remittance increased Egypt's gross national product (GNP) by US$2.2 (Abella 1992: 157; Kandil and Metwally 1990: 159–80; Shaban, Assaad and Al-Qudsi 2002: 27).

13 One of the reasons for such a proposal was the problem caused by international regulations imposing naturalisation of foreign workers who had lived in the country for more than five years.

14 *Gulf News*, 24 November 2005.

15 *Arab Times*, 29 August 2005.

16 *Gulf News*, 24 November 2005.

17 *IPS*, Cairo, 5 December 1999.

18 For example, Girgis (2002), widely quoted in the literature on the subject, predicted in the year 2000 that by the year 2010 the demand for expatriates in the GCC states will increase to 10,799,000. That number was achieved already in 2002.

19 In Kuwait, in 2004, foreign labour grew by 12 per cent while national labour grew by only 6.6 per cent (Jassen 2005).

20 Girgis (2002: 39–40) estimated that in the years 2003–07, 485,000 non-Gulf Arabs will lose their jobs in the GCC states. The lost income that will result from the consequent outmigration will reach US$3.6 billion from Arab workers. While the calculations leading to these precise numbers are debatable, one should agree with Girgis that in the years to come '[non-Gulf] Arab countries are well advised to anticipate less remittance, more workers returning home and perhaps high unemployment rates at home'.

21 Nader Fergany (*Al-Ahram Weekly*, 23–29 December 1999) stressed this problem in relation to Egypt: 'We have a problem of human resource quality. This is a part of our problem with the Gulf. Today, to be competitive in the global market you have to have efficient, cheap and highly trained labour. In this new era of rapidly and continuously changing knowledge and high rates of obsolescence, workers require access to on-going education programs. [But] our education, training and re-training systems are very weak'.

22 There are various estimates of the level of unemployment in Saudi Arabia. In January 2005, Saudi Labour Minister Ghazi al-Ghosaibi said that there were 180,443 unemployed nationals. The minister also said that there are numerous unofficial estimates that are greatly exaggerated and that the only figures which should be accepted are those from the General Statistics Authority. The problem is, however, that according to the Authority, the unemployment figure was twice as high as mentioned by the minister, namely around 300,000 or 9.6 per cent (*Arab News*, 13 January 2005). Undersecretary for Planning and Development for the Ministry of Labour, Abdul Wahid Al-Humayid, revealed on 4 January 2006, that there were only 155,000 Saudi male jobseekers, i.e. 5 per cent. The unemployment of women was unknown. Other sources quoted from 14 per cent to 20 per cent, with 32 per cent among young workers (United Nations ESCWA 2001: 44), see

also Saudi Monetary Agency statistics (*Arab News*, 5 March 2003). In Bahrain, in 2004, there were 16,000–20,000 unemployed workers, i.e. 13–17 per cent of the national workforce (Almazel 2005). In the UAE, the number was put at 32,000 (Karimkhany 2005).

23 Nationalisation policies did not bring much change in the composition of the workforce so far, but eventually they will (Kapiszewski 2001: 212–43). Failures of the nationalisation policies can be easily observed, for example, in Saudi Arabia. The Saudi Manpower Council mandated 5 per cent of Saudization annually, while in reality that number was achieved only between 1998 and 2003 (Pakkiasamy 2004).

24 *Riyadh Daily*, 3 February 2003.

25 *Arab Times*, 14 December 2005.

References

Abella, Manolo I. 1992. 'The Troublesome Gulf: Research on Migration to the Middle East', *Asian and Pacific Migration Journal*, 1(1): 145–67.

——. 1995. 'Asian Migrant and Contract Workers in the Middle East', in Robin Cohen (ed.), *The Cambridge Survey of World Migration*. Cambridge: Cambridge University Press.

Ahmad, Attiya. 2005. 'Pakistanis Citizens' Call to the Ummah in Kuwait: Contradictions and Interconnections'. Paper presented at the 'Transnational Migration: Foreign Labor and its Impact in the Gulf Conference', Bellagio, Italy, 20–25 June.

Al-Alkim, Hassan Hamdan. 1989. *The Foreign Policy of the United Arab Emirates*. London: Saqi Books.

——. 1994. *The GCC States in an Unstable World: Foreign Policy Dilemmas of Small States*. London: Saqi Books.

Al-Bassam, Majed. 2004. '$16b Remittances', *Arab News*, 26 March.

Al-Fahim, Mohammed. 1995. *From Rags to Riches: A Story of Abu Dhabi*. London: Center for Arab Studies.

Al-Moosa, Abdul Rasool and Keith McLachlan. 1985. *Immigrant Labour in Kuwait*. London: Croom Helm.

Al-Najjar, Baqer. 2001. *Dream to Migrate to Wealth: Migrant Labour in the Gulf*. Beirut: Center for Arab Unity Studies.

Alessa, Shamlan Y. 1981. *The Manpower Problem in Kuwait*. London: Kegan Paul International.

Almazel, Muhammad. 2005. 'Bahrain Strained by Expat Rush', *Gulf News*, 8 February.

Ambrosetti, Elena and Giovanna Tattolo. 2004. 'Petrole et migrations de travail vers les Pays du Golfe'. Paper presented at 13e colloque de l'AIDELF, Budapest, 20–24 September.

Amjad, Rashid (ed.). 1989. *To the Gulf and Back: Studies on the Economic Impact of Asian Labour*. New Delhi: UNDP and ILO.

Assiri, Abdul-Reda. 1996. *The Government and Politics of Kuwait: Principles and Practices*. Kuwait.

Birks, J. S. 1988. 'The Demographic Challenge in the Arab Gulf', *Arab Affairs* (London), 1(1): 72–86.

Birks J. S. and C. A. Sinclair. 1980. *Arab Manpower: The Crisis of Development*. London: Croom Helm.

Birks, J. S., I. J. Seccombe and C. A. Sinclair. 1988. 'Labour Migration in the Arab Gulf States: Patterns, Trends and Prospects', *International Migration*, 26(3): 267–86.

Central Agency for Public Mobilisation and Statistics (CAPMAS). 2004. *The Statistical Yearbook 2003*. Cairo: Government of Egypt.

Chaudoir, David C. 2005. 'Mapping Work in the Gulf: Guest Workers in Qatar's Luxury Hotels'. Paper presented at the 'Transnational Migration: Foreign Labor and its Impact in the Gulf Conference', Bellagio, Italy, 20–25 June.

Chuocri, N. 1983. *The Hidden Economy. A New View of Remittances in the Arab World*. Cambridge: MIT. Mimeographed.

Crystal, Jill. 1997. 'Social Transformation, Changing Expectations and Gulf Security', in David E. Long and Christian Koch (eds), *Gulf Security in the Twenty-First Century*, pp. 208–25. Abu Dhabi: The Emirates Center for Strategic Studies and Research.

Dawisha, Adeed. 1977. 'The Middle East', in Christopher Clapham (ed.), *Foreign Policy Making in Developing States*. Farnborough: Saxon House.

Eelens, F., T. Schampers and J. D. Speckmann (eds). 1992. *Labour Migration to the Middle East: From Sri Lanka to the Gulf*. London: Kegan Paul International.

El Rayyes, Riad N. 1988. 'Arab Nationalism and the Gulf', in B. R. Pridham (ed.), *The Arab Gulf and the Arab World*. London: Croom Helm.

Fasano, Ugo and Rishi Goyal. 2004. 'Emerging Strains in GCC Labour Markets', Working Paper, International Monetary Fund, Washington, D.C.

Fergany, Nader. 1984. 'Manpower Problems and Projections in the Gulf', in M. S. El Azhary (ed.), *The Impact of Oil Revenues on Arab Gulf Development*. London: Croom Helm.

———. 2001. *Aspects of Labour Migration and Unemployment in the Arab Region*. Cairo: Almishkat Center for Research. Mimeographed.

Gamburd, Michele Ruth. 2005. '"Lentils there, Lentils here!' Sri Lankan Domestic Labour in the Middle East'. Paper presented at the 'Transnational Migration: Foreign Labor and its Impact in the Gulf Conference', Bellagio, Italy, 20–25 June.

Ghafour, Abdul. 2005. 'No Ban on Foreign Recruitment', *Arab News*, 26 March.

Ghobash, M. 1986. *Immigration and Development in the United Arab Emirates*. Cairo: Al Wafa Press.

Girgis, Maurice. 2002. 'Would Nationals and Asians Replace Arab Workers in the GCC?' Paper presented at Fourth Mediterranean Development Forum, Amman, Jordan, 6–9 October. Mimeographed.

Graz, Liesl. 1992. *The Turbulent Gulf: People, Politics and Power*. London: I. B. Tauris.

Gulf Cooperation Council (GCC). 2002. *GCC Secretariat Report*. Riyadh: GCC Secretariat. http://gcc-sg.org (July 27).

Human Rights Watch. 2004. 'Migrant Communities in Saudi Arabia', in *Bad Dreams: Exploitation and Abuse of Migrant Workers in Saudi Arabia*. www.hrw.org.

Jassen, Nirmala. 2004. 'Plans to Increase Kuwaiti Manpower Quota in Private Sector', *Gulf News*, 5 December.

———. 2005. 'Kuwait Sees Rise in National Workforce', *Gulf News*, 18 February.

Kandil, M. and M. F. Metwally. 1990. 'The Impact of Migrants' Remittances on the Egyptian Economy', *International Migration Review*, 28(2): 159–80.

Kapiszewski, Andrzej. 2001. *National and Expatriates. Population and Labour Dilemmas of the GCC States*. Reading: Ithaca Press.

———. 2004. 'Arab Labour Migration to the GCC States', in *Arab Migration in a Globalized World*, pp. 115–33. Geneva: International Organization for Migration.

———. 2005. 'Non-indigineous Citizens and 'Stateless' Residents in the Gulf Monarchies', *Krakowskie Studia Miedzynarodowe*, 2(VI): 61–78.

Karimkhany, Azita. 2005. 'Viability of 'Emiratization' Stirs Debate', *The Daily Star*, 12 April.

Khalifa, Ali Mohammed. 1979. *The United Arab Emirates: Unity in Fragmentation*. Boulder, Colorado: Westview Press.

Looney, Robert. 2004. 'Saudization and Sound Economic Reforms: Are the Two Compatible?' *Strategic Insights*, III(2).

Nassar, Heba and Ahmed Ghoneim. 2002. Trade and Migration. Are they Complements or Substitutes: A Review of Four MENA Countries. Cairo: Center for Economic and Financial Research and Studies, Cairo University. Mimeographed.

Pakkiasamy, Divya. 2004. 'Saudi Arabia's Plan for Changing its Workforce'. Mimeo, Migration Policy Institute.

Qusti, Raid and Al-Zahrani. 2006. 'Obstacles before Saudi Women's Employment Discussed', *Arab News*, 6 February. http://www.arabnews.com/node/279971 (last accessed on 17 November 2014).

Russel, Sharon Stanton and Michael S. Teitelbaum. 1992. 'International Migration and International Trade', Discussion Paper no. 160, World Bank,Washington, D.C.

Salame, Ghassan. 1988. 'Perceived Threats and Perceived Loyalties', in B. R. Pridham (ed.), *The Arab Gulf and the Arab World*. London: Croom Helm.

Shaban, Radwan A., Ragui Assaad and Sulayman Al-Qudsi. 2002. 'Employment Experience in the Middle East and North Africa', in Djavad Salehi-Ishfahani (ed.), *Labour and Human Capital in the Middle East. Studies of Markets and Household Behavior*, pp. 21–67. Reading and Cairo: Ithaca Press with the Economic Research Forum.

Silvey, Rachel. 2004. 'Transnational Domestication: State Power and Indonesian Migrant Women in Saudi Arabia', *Political Geography*, 23(3): 245–64.

Taqi, Ali. 2005. 'Government Rejects Plea for Job Nationalization', *Gulf News*, 4 July.

United Nations ESCWA. 2001. *Globalization and Labour Movements in the ESCWA Region*. New York: United Nations Economic and Social Commission for Western Asia.

Whitley, Andrew. 1993. 'Minorities and the Stateless in Persian Gulf Politics', *Survival*, 35(4).

Winckler, Onn. 2000. *Population Growth, Migration and Socio-Demographic Policies in Qatar*. Tel Aviv: The Moshe Dayan Center for Middle Eastern and African Studies.

3

Indian labour in the Gulf

Issues of migration and the British Empire

Kundan Kumar

Indians have been migrating to various parts of the world for a long time. The frequency of this emigration, for various purposes or reasons, got strengthened during the modern period, especially after the colonial powers established their control over most of the globe. The advent of industrialisation and the related prospects of growth demanded cheap and politically neutral labour. The case of Indians migrating to the Gulf is a unique example of movement of labour which has fulfilled both these criteria and also, in a way, helped in institutionalising British colonial authority. The Gulf region has always been a place of movement in terms of peoples, goods and ideas, wherein, during the 19th and 20th centuries, streams of colonially regulated Indian labourers and workers were exported. In fact, the existence of the modern Indian diaspora came into being mainly due to the subjugation of India by the British and its incorporation into the empire (Reid 1993).

Indians moved to many parts of the empire including the Gulf in the 18th and 19th centuries, and since then they have been living there as culturally distinct communities. The Gulf arena was connected by specialised flows of intermediary capital and migrant workers in the age of global empire. In addition, there were streams of Indian professional people and service groups seeking opportunities in different fields. These finely tuned networks of inter-regional specialisation drew on earlier ties but were effectively forged during the 19th century. They were utterly indispensable to the working of global colonial capitalism.

West Asia, in general, has always been a major destination in global migration of labour, and the Gulf countries, in particular, are the main receptors of the migration flows, as together they have migrants constituting one-third of their total population

(Kapiszewski 2001: 39, 2006: 4). In all the Gulf countries today, foreign labour comprises a majority of the total workforce, and in some countries like the United Arab Emirates (UAE), Kuwait and Qatar, foreign workers comprise an absolute majority of the population (Abella 1995: 418–23).

Though there is no dearth of studies focusing on this contemporary flow of Indian migration to the Gulf and its socio-economic processes, there are only but a few which have examined the previous historical stages of migration, especially during British times. This chapter argues that basically there are three waves of migration of Indian labour to the Gulf countries – during pre-oil times, during the development of the oil industry and during the contemporary emigration from 1960s onwards – and that they were characterised by colonial imperatives.

Indian labour in the Gulf: the pre-oil period

Although Indian migrant labour flows into the Gulf region were considerably accelerated by the dramatic oil price increases of 1973–74 and 1979, the region's dependence on Indian workers dates back to the oil-induced economic boom which followed the initial discovery of oil in the Gulf in the early part of the 20th century. This, however, does not negate their migration in the pre-oil age. For example, the population of Aden, which became the busiest port after being taken over by the British as a coal depot in 1839 (Ewald 2000: 82), increased from 1,300 to 21,000 between 1839 and 1856 (Gavin 1975: 445). Right from the middle of the 18th century, the expansion of British imperialism necessitated the constant mobility of peoples, goods and services for maintaining the empire without falling short in the vast resources it needed. In this connection, the example of Aden must be discussed, as Indians used to migrate there before the discovery of oil in the Gulf.

The case of Aden: labour migration in the pre-oil era[1]

In the period between 1757 and 1857, Britain assumed a steadily growing imperial role in India, and her imperial interests spread outward from there to the Persian Gulf, to Aden (Gilbert 2002: 7–34). During this period, British officials sponsored the migration of convict labour and free workers from India, as they wanted an 'inexpensive and controllable work force' (Ewald 2000: 82). It was the Indian migrants who helped in transforming Aden into a major steamship port. In the 1840s, with the import of Indian labour for the construction work related to defence, Aden became more an Indian than Arab town (Jain 2003a: 102).

In 1856, there were 8,229 Indians in Aden, and this number remained almost the same till 1931. In 1955, it increased to 15,817 and then subsequently to 20,000 in the 1960s (*ibid.*: 104–6). In 1935, Aden was no longer under the jurisdiction of India's government. At the time there were over 7,000 Indians living there (Bose 2010: 93). In 1955, an Indian, V.K. Joshi, was even elected to the Legislative Council and became a minister. Because of the difficulty of inducing experienced, good domestics to live in Aden, far away from their native country, as well as the expensive nature of settling there, the wages of Indian servants were very high in Aden (as shown in Table 3.1).

Table 3.1 Aden: occupations of Indians and wages in the 1870s

Occupations	Wages (in rupees)
Head servant	20 to 30
Second servant	15 to 20
Washerman (depend on the number in family)	7 to 25
Cook	15 to 25
Coachman or groom	10 to 18
Female servants	10 to 20
Peons or messengers	10 to 15
Boatmen	10 to 15
Tailor	15 to 20
Boiler maker	45 to 60
Hammerman	25 to 30
Blacksmith	50 to 70
Bellows boy	7 to 9
Carpenter	45 to 160
Engineer	90 to 150
Clerks	30 to 300
Fireman, stoker	12 to 20
Labourer	10 to 15
Mason	30 to 45

Note: All the above expect also a daily ration of one gallon condensed and two gallons of brackish water, or a corresponding increase in pay.

Source: Hunter (1877: 31).

Indians were employed as sweepers, jewellers, blacksmiths, carpenters, shipbuilders, bumboatmen, masons, bricklayers, mechanics, shoemakers, tailors, dyers, bakery men, 'accountants and clerks in mercantile firms' (Hunter 1877: 34) and government offices (*ibid*.: 27–36, 79–86; Kour 2005: 52; Playfair 1859: 14–16), shopkeepers, artisans and skilled labourers, fishermen, military men, moneylenders (Kour 2005: 51)[2] etc. A considerable number of Indians worked as sailors and boatmen (Hunter 1877: 36; *ibid*.). As most Indian Muslims came to be in Aden by force of circumstance,[3] some found employment with the police force, and many engaged themselves as masons; the poor worked as tailors or domestic servants (Kour 2005: 50).

Against the backdrop of the strengthening links between India and the Gulf during the 19th century, the British used their Indian subjects as a valuable human resource in the running of the administration. The same links subsequently began to serve the private sector oil businesses when oil was found in the region in the second quarter of the 20th century.

Development of the oil economy: rising need for imported labour

The development of the oil industry during the early 20th century had provided an additional need for workers in clerical as well as skilled and semi-skilled manual occupations, and as the local labour available in the region had limited experience in industrial employment, the oil companies were obliged to import large numbers of foreign workers. The development of the early oil industry in the Gulf provided the stimulus for new patterns of Indian labour movement into and within the region (Seccombe and Lawless 1986a: 549) as the demand for labour was greater than the supply (Seccombe 1983: 5). From the outset, Britain exercised effective use of migrant workers. Seccombe and Lawless (1986a: 554) argue that 'while the concession agreements permitted the oil companies to import whatever foreign labor was necessary, the political agreements ensured that the local British authorities retained their control over the nationality of those imported'. As a result, in Kuwait and Qatar, where British authority was relatively strong, workers from British colonies, particularly those from the Indian subcontinent, dominated the foreign workforce.

Concessional agreements: encouraging emigration from India

The composition of the immigrant workforce was closely controlled by the terms of the oil concessions and subject to certain political controls. Almost all the concessional agreements between the British and the Gulf oil companies made specific reference to the nationality of company employees.[4] In particular, all the operating companies undertook to employ local nationals as far as practicable, while reserving the right to import and employ foreign labour if the local market could not supply the specific skills requested. In spite of the concession agreements which specified the import, primarily of Arab labour, the British, right from the beginning, through their political control, ensured and preferred the recruitment of Indians in oil companies operating in the Gulf region (Seccombe and Lawless 1986a: 557–8).

Indians in the Anglo-Persian Oil Company (APOC)

The number of Indians employed in APOC between 1910 and 1932 is shown in Table 3.2, which is self-explanatory.

Table 3.2 APOC: employment of Indians, 1910–32[5]

Year	Number of Indians	Year	Number of Indians
1910	158	1922[6]	4285
1911	379	1923	4715
1912	553	1924	4731
1913	917	1925	4890
1914	1074	1926	3588
1915	979	1927	3272
1916	1366	1928	3050
1917	n.a.	1929*	2518
1918	n.a.	1930	2411
1919	2641	1931	1675
1920	3616	1932	1420
1921	4709		

Note: Due to the Great Depression of 1929–32, it decreased to 1,420 in 1932 and finally to 800 in 1933. See Seccombe and Lawless (1986a: 559).

Source: Seccombe and Lawless (1986a: p. 557, Table 2).

The Indians migrating to the Gulf during this period were absorbed by the large oil companies as clerical staff, skilled artisans and semi-skilled manual workers, which shows that Indians dominated the clerical, technical and artisan grades. For example, the Bahrain Petroleum Company (BAPCO) during 1939–44 employed more Indians for these services than any other foreign nationality (Seccombe and Lawless 1986a: 559).

Bahrain/Bahrain Petroleum Company (BAPCO)

In Bahrain, the development of oil resources in 1932 stimulated the inflow of Persians from neighbouring Iran. However, the American-owned BAPCO, whose presence in Bahrain was allowed by British authorities, began dismissing Persian workers and formalised the recruitment of Indian workers in the mid-1930s (Nair 1986; Nair 1999). Thus, the employment of Indian workers from the Indian subcontinent by BAPCO increased and accounted for 91.1 per cent of the total artisans employed in 1939. The number of Indian migrants employed in BAPCO in the cadres of artisans, and clerical and technical staff between 1939 and 1944 is illustrated in the Table 3.3.

Besides the recruitment of British and American professionals for managerial and higher technical positions, Indians dominated the monthly paid, largely skilled and semi-skilled, labour force in 1948, as shown in Table 3.4.

Indian labourers were imported through lengthy bureaucratic procedures in accordance with the provisions of Indian emigration

Table 3.3 Indian migrants, by occupational status, in BAPCO, 1939–44

Year	Clerical and technical			Artisans		
	Total employees	Number of Indians	Percentage (%)	Total employees	Number of Indians	Percentage (%)
1939	140	132	94.3	190	173	91.1
1940	143	133	93	168	154	91.7
1941	128	119	93	119	108	90.8
1942	119	109	91.6	95	87	91.6
1943	129	118	91.5	87	81	93.1
1944	191	170	89	201	196	97.5

Source: Seccombe and Lawless (1986a: 566, Table 5).

Table 3.4 BAPCO's monthly paid labour in 1948 (Rs 215–475)

Nationality	Number of employees
Indian	238
Pakistani	35
Portuguese Indian	18
Iraqi	4
Bahraini	51
Iranian	3
Others	5

Source: Seccombe 1983: 10.

Table 3.5 Foreign population, by country of area of origin, Bahrain, 1950, 1959 and 1970

Country or area of origin	1950		1959		1970	
	Number	Percentage	Number	Percentage	Number	Percentage
Arab countries and areas	6,018	33.1	10,547	43.2	17,002	44.9
Oman including Muscat	2,466	13.5	7,314	30.0	10,785	28.5
Yemen (United)	105	0.6	492	2.0	1,538	4.1
Jordan and occupied Palestinian territory	...	...	117	0.5	1,338	3.5
Saudi Arabia	2,526	13.9	1,605	6.6	1,332	3.5
UAE	...	...	...	...	770	2.0
Egypt	...	...	71	0.3	589	1.6
Lebanon	...	...	144	0.6	280	0.7
Qatar	...	...	242	1.0	145	0.4
Iraq	...	...	169	0.7	83	0.2
Other Arab countries	921	5.1	393	1.6	142	0.4
Other Asia	**9,986**	**54.8**	**10,977**	**45.0**	**17,311**	**45.7**
India	...	...	*4,043*	*16.6*	*6,657*	*17.6*
Pakistan	...	...	2,283	9.4	5,377	14.2
Iran	6,943	38.1	4,203	17.2	5,097	13.5
India and Pakistan	3,043	16.7	...	...	...	...

(Continued)

Table 3.5 (Continued)

Country or area of origin	1950		1959		1970	
	Number	Percentage	Number	Percentage	Number	Percentage
Other countries in Asia	...	...	448	...	180	...
Great Britain	1,840	10.1	2,514	10.3	2,901	7.7
United States	...	...	151	0.6	272	0.7
Other countries	363	2.0	212	0.9	400	1.1
Total	**18,207**	**100.0**	**24,401**	**100.0**	**37,886**	**100.0**

Source: State of Bahrain (1967: 5, Table 12) and State of Bahrain (1972: 10, Table 6).

laws. Despite the higher recruitment costs, the Bahraini rulers and their British protectors pressured BAPCO to recruit more Indians.[7] By the 1950s, Europeans and Americans were in management positions, Indians and Pakistanis in intermediate positions and Bahrainis at the bottom in lower clerical and labour jobs (Belling 1960: 159). Table 3.5 shows their configurations in 1950, 1959 and 1970 in comparison to other nationals.

Kuwait

Indian migration to Kuwait predated the creation of the Kuwaiti state and the development of the oil industry, but it was significantly increased by both these factors subsequently. In the period up to the Second World War, it was also significantly influenced by British foreign policy and perceptions of British regional interests, as has been discussed later. Riad argues that before the 1930s Kuwait had two types of migrants: the seasonal migrants who would come to the Gulf shore during pearling season and the long-term non-Arabs who were mainly Persians and Indians (Riad 1983: 244).

The growth of population in Kuwait was closely associated with the growth of migration, which was heralded by the finding of oil in the 1930s and later by its extraction from 1946 onwards. The composition of migrants in Kuwait in terms of their nationalities, as shown in Table 3.6, indicates that migrants from the Indian subcontinent constituted 10 per cent of the total foreign population, which was 1,098 in numbers (see Table 3.6).

Table 3.6 The composition of migrants in Kuwait up to 1947 (%)

Nationality of immigrants	Before 1917	1917–27	1927–37	1937–42	1942–47
Iraqi	17	10	17	22	29
Irani	48	48	42	37	22
Omani	2	10	13	16	17
Saudi	21	20	18	12	17
Indian	1	1	1	3	5
Pakistani	1	1	2	3	5
Others	10	10	9	8	14

Source: Ffrench and Hill (1971); Hill (1969: 88; 1972, 1973, 1982); Hill (1980, 1983: 117–48).

Table 3.7 Foreigners in Kuwait before 1947

Country of origin	Numbers
Iran	1,611
Iraq	2,476
Jordan	665
Lebanon	299
Oman	917
India	744
Pakistan	354
Syria	239
UK	99
Egypt	333
Others	1,038
Total	8,775

Source: Hill (1969: 83).

With the development of oil, the nature of migration began to change, primarily as a result of the KOC's demand for skilled labour. This demand for labour went beyond what could be imported from the surrounding areas and as shown in Table 3.7, labour was recruited from two principal sources: from those countries of the Arab world with more skilled labour than could be provided by the existing indigenous labour force of Kuwait, and from India and Pakistan. This South Asian labour greatly differed from the already settled Indian population in the Gulf, they being especially imported as skilled workers for the oil industry (Ashtiany 1982: 11–12).

Kuwait Oil Company (KOC)

Apart from the above categories of occupation, Indians were employed in semi-skilled and even unskilled categories of the workforce. The number of Indian workers in KOC increased from four in 1935 to 4,908 in 1949, which accounted for 85.6 per cent of the total clerical, foreman and technical staff of the company. In fact, Indians accounted for nearly 23 per cent of the total unskilled labour employed by KOC in the late 1940s (Nair 1986: 92). Large-scale immigration to the oilfields increased from the 1940s onwards. The number of foreign workers engaged by the KOC increased from 70 in 1936 to 8,734 in 1949. Table 3.8 depicts the variations in the total number of foreign workforce in KOC between 1936 and 1950.

In spite of strong views on the part of the British as well as the local ruler, 'the Kuwait Oil Company (KOC) increased its employment from 1,900 in January 1947 to 18,000 by January 1949, of whom 4,053 were Indians' (Seccombe 1983: 14). The predominance of Indian and Pakistani labour in 1948 as the major chunk of junior staff, i.e. semi-skilled and skilled manual and clerical employees, can easily be ascertained by the Table 3.9. Furthermore, it highlights their pre-eminent position as the major expatriate element

Table 3.8 Total foreign workers brought in by KOC and their numbers, 1936–50

Foreign workers in KOC	Numbers
1936	70
1937	55
1938	56
1939	72
1940	65
1941	63
1942	67
1943	16
1944	8
1945	13
1946	142
1947	417
1948	2,782
1949	8,734
1950	5,528

Source: Seccombe and Lawless (1986b).

Table 3.9 KOC: comparison of labourers and junior staff between March 1948 and September 1948

Countries	March 1948		September 1948	
	Labourers	Junior staff	Labourers	Junior staff
India (including Pakistan)	**2,004**	**515**	**2,574**	**637**
Kuwait (including other Gulf nationals)	5,656	62	6,136	78
Bahrain	4	3	6	3
Oman/Muscat	2	—	52	2
Saudi Arabia	3	1	7	1
Iran	15	—	102	—

Source: Seccombe (1983: 15, Table 8).

Table 3.10 Kuwait: foreign population, by country or area of origin, 1965 and 1970

Country or area of origin	1965		1970	
	Number	Percentage	Number	Percentage
Arab countries and areas	**187,923**	**76.0**	**312,849**	**80.0**
Jordan and occupied Palestinian territory	77,712	31.4	147,696	37.8
Iraq	25,897	10.5	39,066	10.0
Egypt	11,021	4.5	30,421	7.8
Syrian Arab Republic	16,849	6.8	27,217	7.0
Lebanon	20,877	8.4	25,387	6.5
Oman	19,584	7.9	14,670	3.8
Yemen (United)	2,779	1.1	10,967	2.8
UAE	1,105	0.4	4,436	1.1
Other Arab countries	7,467	3.0	2,092	0.5
Non-Arab countries	**59,357**	**24.0**	**78,341**	**20.0**
Iran	30,790	12.5	39,129	10.0
India	*11,699*	*4.7*	*17,336*	*4.4*
Pakistan	11,735	4.7	14,712	3.8
Other non-Arab countries	5,133	2.1	7,164	1.8
Total	**247,280**	**100.0**	**391,190**	**100.0**

Source: State of Kuwait (1974: 23, Table 10).

in the unskilled labour force. It is also interesting to note that the Indian/Pakistani[8] 'labourers' grew in both absolute (570) and relative (28 per cent) terms more rapidly than the indigenous labour supply (480 and 8.5 per cent) over the six-month period.

Like in Bahrain, the number of Indians also continued to rise in Kuwait after the 1950s. Table 3.10 shows their figures in comparison to other foreign populations in 1965 and 1970. Though less in numbers vis-à-vis other foreigners, Indians were still employed in Kuwait.

Qatar/Petroleum Development Qatar (PDQ)

In PDQ, the number increased to 841 in 1950 from a meagre five workers in 1937. In Arabian American Oil Company (ARAMCO), this number increased from 37 in 1940 to 1,122 in 1950. In fact, in nearly all oil companies, Indians comprised 94.3 per cent of the total clerical and technical employees among foreign workers. It is estimated that by 1950, the large oil companies in the Gulf employed nearly 8,000 immigrants from the Indian subcontinent (Seccombe and Lawless 1986a: 568). The overall numbers of Indians between 1948 and the early 1970s gradually increased from about 1,400 to 40,000.[9] In comparison with Kuwait and Saudi Arabia, Qatar's oil

Table 3.11 Qatar: foreign population, by country or area of origin, 1970

Country or area of origin	Number	Percentage
Arab countries and areas	**21,080**	**31.8**
Jordan and occupied Palestinian territory	9,780	14.8
Oman	3,270	4.9
Yemen (United)	2,280	3.4
UAE	2,240	3.4
Saudi Arabia	2,040	3.1
Egypt	1,370	2.1
Iraq	100	0.2
Non-Arab countries	**41,570**	**62.7**
Iran	20,840	31.4
Pakistan	17,080	25.8
India	*3,650*	*5.5*
Not specified	3,630	5.5
Total	**66,280**	**100.0**

Source: Birks and Sinclair (1980: 152, Table 39).

resources were relatively small. However, because of its small population, it had the highest level of oil production per capita among the oil-producing countries during the 1950s and 1960s (Fukuda 1996). In 1970, foreigners represented 83 per cent of its total labour force (United Nations Population Division 2003: 12). Indians constituted one of the largest segments of this migrant population. Separating Indians from Pakistanis, Birks and Sinclair (1980) have analysed the foreign population in terms of origin in Qatar in 1970, as shown in Table 3.11.

Saudi Arabia/Arabian American Oil Company (ARAMCO)

In Saudi Arabia, which was not a British protectorate, the American-owned ARAMCO held an exclusive oil concession. As a result, different patterns of migration and recruitment of workers emerged in that country. Table 3.12 shows that very few Indian

Table 3.12 Indians employed by the oil companies in the Gulf, 1933–53

Year	BAPCO	KOC	PDQ	ARAMCO	APOC
1933	24	n.a.	n.a.	n.a.	795
1934	45	n.a.	n.a.	n.a.	925
1935	61	4	n.a.	n.a.	955
1936	328	40	n.a.	n.a.	780
1937	472	40	5	n.a.	785
1938	422	41	n.a.	n.a.	1,340
1939	375	54	5	n.a.	1,155
1940	349	54	28	37	1,160
1941	272	47	46	40	1,005
1942	248	52	n.a.	n.a.	1,720
1943	297	11	n.a.	50	2,100
1944	444	8	n.a.	n.a.	2,500
1945	681	28	n.a.	599	2,785
1946	635	177	n.a.	323	2,560
1947	553	723	194	602	2,470
1948	658	3,211	552	914	n.a.
1949	659	4,908	690	1,063	2,125
1950	622	3,203	841	1,122	1,980
1951	n.a.	3,044	901	1,813	
1952	n.a.	n.a.	n.a.	2,430	
1953	n.a.	1,125	n.a.	2,406	

Source: Seccombe and Lawless (1986a: 563, Table 3).

workers were recruited by ARAMCO until the mid-1940s. The urgency to supply oil to allied forces in East Asia during the Second World War demanded an increase in oil production and expansion of its refinery which led to increased recruitment of workers from colonial India. After the war, the demand for oil kept only increasing. Thus, from only 200 Indian employees that ARAMCO had in 1945, the number of Indian workers increased to 1,122 in 1950 and reached 2,430 in 1952. A growing number of skilled Palestinians, especially in the aftermath of the establishment of the State of Israel in 1948, were also recruited during this period for whom ARAMCO opened a recruitment office in Beirut in 1949. There is no reliable data regarding foreign migrant workers before 1970. Even the first census conducted in 1962–63 does not provide any surveys or tables. However, the number of foreign workers in 1963 is believed to have been about 150,000.

Indian labour: nature and extent of migration

The number of Indians employed and engaged in various capacities by the major oil companies in the Gulf region is shown in Table 3.12.

These data corroborate that both in Kuwait and in Qatar, prior to the Second World War, the scale of operations of oil companies was still small, so that there were few Indians employed. Oil production was suspended during the war, but its resumption in the post-war period led to increased employment of Indian workers in the late 1940s.

Channels of migration and methods involved

For the sustenance of the oil economy of the Gulf, a continuous supply of migrant workers was indispensable. The labour from India was recruited through various methods. The oil companies, with the help of British assistance, had their own agents placed in Bombay and Surat. Besides, other private firms were also employed to maintain the labour supply. The independent agents who facilitated this used to get commissions. Some of the firms had even hired private agents to visit the interiors and persuade the labour to understand the benefits of working in the Gulf. Apart from the formal recruitment channels, a large number of Indian workers migrated to the Gulf through informal channels. For example, thousands of

Indians who migrated to Bahrain on their own were absorbed by BAPCO during the 1930s and 1940s.[10] Indian labour reaching the Gulf through formal or informal methods and not employed by the big oil companies worked in unskilled sectors like gardening and domestic services. In addition to these formal and informal migrations, Indians also migrated illegally to the Gulf countries on their own bearing a high degree of risk such as travelling in country-made launches without any valid documents.[11]

The primary motive behind Indian migration to the Gulf was the substantial wage differential which existed between the labour markets in the Gulf and India for the same occupational groups. For example, during 1941, in BAPCO, persons in the occupational groups of clerical and technical, artisans and domestics were paid Rs 275, Rs 159 and Rs 71 per month, while in CALTEX, one of the highest paid oil companies in India, they got Rs 140, Rs 78 and Rs 45 respectively (Seccombe and Lawless 1986a: 568).[12]

After the First World War, Indians migrated to various parts of the Gulf to work in government departments (e.g., customs, postal and passport departments), and also as doctors, nurses, midwives, clerks, and agricultural advisors. In Kuwait, Indians were employed in a number of sectors such as education, postal services, communication, and other government departments (Jain 2004: 441); in Oman, Indian were employed as army and police personnel, carpenters, etc.; in Muscat, they were employed as Indian soldiers from 1913 to 1921 (Peterson 1978: 79) and as carpenters in shipbuilding (Jain 2003b: 8); in Aden (from two Indian workers in 1839 to 160 Indian workers in 1855), and in most of the Gulf region, they were employed as subordinate administrative officials, policemen, blacksmiths, carpenters, mechanics, sweepers, shopkeepers, bricklayers, domestics, clerks, accountants, schoolteachers, postmen, street vendors, caretakers, guards, petty entrepreneurs, salesmen, etc.

1950–70 and beyond: contemporary scene

Due to their small populations the Gulf countries attracted a large number of migrants and India was one of the primary countries which filled the gap this labour gap. The contemporary wave in the history of Indian labour migration to the Gulf countries started in the 1960s, accelerating in the 1970s, and continues to today. The tremendous global demand for oil and the resulting growth

Table 3.13 Foreign workforce in the Gulf countries, 1957–71

Countries	Number of migrant workers					
	1957	*1959*	*1963*	*1968*	*1970*	*1971*
Saudi Arabia	...	...	150,000	...	...	...
Qatar	...	...	...	...	66,000 (83% of the total workforce)	...
Bahrain	...	15,800	...	...	...	22,400 (37% of the total workforce)
UAE	...	...	...	66,000 (one third of the total population)	...	...
Kuwait	55,700 (69% of the total workforce)	...	...	...	176,800 (73% of the total workforce)	...

Source: United Nations Population Division (2003: 11–16).

of the oil industry throughout this region lead the Gulf economies to establish a variety of modernisation plans. The oil embargo of the 1970s, and the already improved wealth of the Gulf countries, stimulated a dramatic rise in the number and scope of these projects. At this juncture, Indian migration to the Gulf grew rapidly with a major shift in its nature and composition. While in the past Indian labour migrants to the Gulf were typically skilled workers or entrepreneurs, the new arrivals were predominantly unskilled labourers.[13] Table 3.13 shows the number of foreign nationals in the Gulf countries during 1957–71.

British interests in the Gulf: preferring Indian labour migrants

Signing exclusive treaties with the Gulf states in the latter half of the 19th century, Britain had taken over their foreign policy, controlling their diplomatic access to the outside world. During the 1920s, and more so in the 1930s, a number of political and economic changes occurred, affecting the regional and international situation, which in turn influenced British foreign policy in the area. The most fundamental of these changes was the discovery of oil which attracted the eager interest of global capital. This period was one of intense imperialist rivalry, between essentially American and British companies, over the granting of oil concessions.

This major economic change influenced British policy in two related ways. First, Britain viewed the granting of concessions by Gulf rulers to non-British companies as an invitation to foreign interests to move into the area, something it saw as a violation of its exclusivist treaties signed with the Gulf rulers. Second, British officials were concerned that the concessions meant that companies needed labour for oil prospecting and extraction. This labour needed to come from outside, because the existing local labour force was small, unskilled and mostly composed of mariners. The British objected to this import of labour, because they saw that the governments of the migrants' countries would eventually demand diplomatic representation in the Gulf states and in the event of disturbances or unfortunate incidents, this foreign labour could be used as a lever to gain political representation for foreign interests in the Gulf' (Seccombe and Lawless 1986b). It was not the entry of foreigners into the labour market of the Persian Gulf per se that the British saw as a potential threat, but rather the consequences of their entry because they regarded the Gulf region as a vitally strategic area (Shwadran 1973: 407–10). Equally, the clauses that were inserted in the oil concessions[14] also obstructed the entry of other foreign nationals, mostly Arabs from the countries of the Fertile Crescent. The political agreements and their provision of subsequent control by British authorities ensured that the oil companies' labour imports were mostly from India (Seccombe and Lawless 1986b). Labourers from India were naturally not perceived by Britain as contravening imperial control. As a result, the number of Indians increased in the 1940s, when the KOC set up two recruiting offices in Bombay and Karachi to contract labour for its oilfields.

It is clear thus Britain's preference for Indian labour stemmed from the need to pursue a number of foreign policy objectives centring on the desire to maintain British hegemony in the Gulf, but also involving the changing political climate of the 1920s, and particularly the 1930s. A number of regional factors like that of the Palestinian General Strike of 1936 also influenced the British attitude to the entry of foreign labour.

Conclusion

Against this backdrop, it can be argued that the recent growth of immigration from the Indian subcontinent is not a new phenomenon but the recrudescence of a tradition of migration dating back to the 1930s, encouraged by the rapid exhaustion of Arab labour supplies. The above discussion establishes the fact that the Persian Gulf has had a long tradition of migration and that from the earliest part of this century, the nature of this migration, especially during the British period, was neither 'natural' nor 'accidental', but was in fact shaped and transformed by conscious decisions and active agencies – by British foreign policy and by oil companies needing a stable workforce. This intervention continued a process that had existed for long, but also deeply altered it. Oil provided the region with new wealth and power but also with the need for a new workforce at every level of the economy. The potential problems constituted by such a new social force ensured that the state would act to govern and regulate the migrant population – just as different interests had previously given the British an interest in regulating entry into the area.

Notes

1 The example of Aden is given only to underscore the general trends, nature and extent of mobility of Indians and does not, in any way, imply that Indians did not migrate to other countries of the region before the discovery of oil. For example, Indian labour was engaged in pearling in Bahrain and Kuwait; in Oman Indians engaged themselves in various other professions – moneylending, petty jobs and shipbuilding being the major ones.
2 Mainly Hindu Banias and Indian Muslims like the Memons from the Kutch region of western India.
3 This was due to the lack of transportation back to India after Hajj. The Hajj pilgrims, especially those who were poor and destitute, used to stay back and move around the surrounding areas of the Gulf to make their living.
4 The British entered into concessional agreements with Anglo-Persian Oil Company (APOC) in 1935, Iraq Petroleum Company (IPC) in 1925, Petroleum Concessions Ltd. (PCL) in 1935, Petroleum Development Qatar (PDQ) in 1936, Kuwait Oil Company (KOC) in 1934, and Bahrain Petroleum Company (BAPCO) in 1933.
5 The pattern was repeated in other oil companies in the 1930s and 1940s.
6 The Indian Immigration Act, passed in 1922, effectively ended the indentured labor system and introduced stricter controls on Indian emigration for employment, APOC were obliged to open a formal recruiting office in Bombay. Thus, the number of Indians in APOC increased from 4,285 in 1922 to 4,890 in 1925.

7 They feared that an increased Iranian presence might foster the Shah's claim over Bahrain. It may be mentioned here that before their conquest by the Al-Khalifa family in 1783, the islands of Bahrain were under the sovereignty of Iran.

8 India and Pakistan gained independence in 1947.

9 The figures are for India and Pakistan taken together. The figures can roughly be estimated based on a number of studies. See, Khadria (2006: 14); Kondapi (1951: 528); Tinker (1977: 12). Also see Seccombe and Lawless (1986a: 548–74).

10 The modus operandi of this migration was that in return for a 'commission fee', Indian merchants and businessmen in Bahrain used to obtain a No Objection Certificate (NOC) from the state to import one or more immigrants for expansion of their own business. Once the immigrant had arrived and paid his sponsor an agreed sum, he would subsequently apply for employment with any company.

11 Such a stream of illegal migration took place mainly from India's West coast – Mumbai being the most important centre of origin. Economic pressures at home and the massive demonstration effect of the amount of wealth acquired by the Gulf migrants were the reasons for this illegal migration.

12 This is not to say that the living conditions of the Indian workers were satisfactory as most of them faced severe housing problems and were put up in tents in the deserts. However, the situation improved in the 1960s as the large oil companies started giving more and more importance to the provisions of basic needs like housing, drinking water, etc., to their workers. Table 3.12 shows the number of Indians in various Arab countries.

13 These historical factors explicate the increasing flow of Indian migrants to the Gulf. However, a number of other explanations can also be provided as to why India in particular came to play a predominant role in providing labour to the Gulf countries. India contained a comparatively inexpensive supply of educated and trained clerks, supervisors and assistants (Weiner 1986: 47–74). Besides, in comparison with the established flows of Arab migrants to the Gulf, Indian labourers usually arrived without their families, and hence had no intentions to reside there permanently. It is also important to point out that many Indian migrants were neither Arab nor Muslim and this also made for a more pliable and docile workforce (*ibid.*: 53–4).

14 Like in the case of the Kuwaiti Oil Concession of 1934, whereby the entry of a restrictive clause created obstructions on American personnel in the 1930s and 1940s despite the fact that American companies operated in the Gulf, and that the Americans were partners in the concession agreement with the British.

References

Abella, Manolo I. 1995. 'Asian Migrant and Contract Workers in the Middle East', in R. Cohen (ed.), *The Cambridge Survey of World Migration*, pp. 418–23. Cambridge: Cambridge University Press.

Al-Baharna, Husain M. 1968. *The Legal Status of the Arabian Gulf States: A Study of their Treaty Relations and their International Problems*. Manchester: Manchester University Press.

Ashtiany, Julia. 1982. *The Arabic Documents in the Archives of the British Political Agency, Kuwait, 1904–1949, IOR:R/15/5*. London: Indian Office Library and Records.

Belling, W. 1960. *Pan-Arabism and Labour*. Cambridge, Massachusetts: Harvard University Press.

Birks, J.S. and C.A. Sinclair. 1980. *International Migration and Development in the Arab Region*. Geneva: International Labour Office.

Bose, Sugata. 2010. *A Hundred Horizons: The Indian Ocean in the Age of Global Empire*. New Delhi: Permanent Black.

Ewald, Janet J. 2000. 'Crossers of the Sea: Slaves, Freedmen, and other Migrants in the Northwestern Indian Ocean, c. 1750–1914', *American Historical Review*, 105(1): 69–91.

Ffrench, G. E and A. Hill. 1971. *Kuwait: Urban and Medical Ecology*. New York: Springer-Verlag.

Fukuda, Sadashi. 1996. 'The Changing Nature of Economic Development and Industrialization', in *Oil Economic Development and Industrialization with Arabian Gulf States*, pp. 3–50. Tokyo: Institute of Development Economics.

Gavin, R.J. 1975. *Aden under British Rule, 1839–1967*. London: C. Hurst & Co.; New York: Barnes and Noble.

Gilbert, Erik. 2002. 'Coastal East Africa and the Western Indian Ocean: Long-Distance Trade, Empire, Migration, and Regional Unity, 1750–1970', *The History Teacher*, 36(1): 7–34.

Hill, A. 1973. 'Segregation in Kuwait', in *Social Patterns in Cities*, Institute of British Geographers. Special Publications, No. 5.

———. 1982. 'Population, Migration and Development in the Gulf States', in Shahram Chubin (ed.), *Security in the Gulf*, Vol. 1, Domestic and Political Factors. The International Institute of Strategic Studies.

Hill, A.G. 1969. 'Aspects of the Urban Development of Kuwait', Unpublished PhD Thesis, Durham University.

———. 1972. 'The Gulf States: Petroleum and Population Growth', in J.I. Clarke and W.B. Fisher, *Populations of the Middle East and North Africa*. London: University of London Press.

Hill, Enid. 1980. *Modernization of Labour and Labour Law in Arab Gulf States*, Cairo Papers in Social Science, Monograph 3, Cairo: American University in Cairo.

———. 1983. 'The International Division of Labour: Saudi Arabia and the Gulf, Kuwait', *Journal of the Social Sciences*, pp. 117–48.

Hunter, Captain Frederick Mercer. 1877. *An Account of the British Settlement of Aden in Arabia*. London: Trübner & Co.

Jain, Prakash C. 2003a. 'Indian Diaspora in Yemen', *Journal of Indian Ocean Studies*, 11(1): 99–111.

———. 2003b. 'Indians in Oman', Working Paper, Gulf Studies Programme, Centre for West Asian and African Studies, School of International Studies, Jawaharlal Nehru University, New Delhi.

———. 2004. 'Indians in Kuwait', *Journal of Indian Ocean Studies*, 12(3): 440–50.

Kapiszewski, Andrej. 2001. *Nationals and Expatriates: Population and Labour Dilemmas of the Gulf Cooperation Council States*. Ithaca, New York: Ithaca Press.

Kapiszewski, Andrej. 2006. 'Arab versus Asian Migrant Workers in the GCC Countries', *United Nations Expert Group Meeting on International Migration and Development in the Arab Region*, Population Division, Department of Economic and Social Affairs, Beirut.

Khadria, Binod. 2006. 'India: Skilled Migration to Developed Countries, Labour Migration to the Gulf', Jawaharlal Nehru University, New Delhi, and Asia Research Institute and the Department of Economics National University of Singapore.

Kondapi, C. 1951. *Indians Overseas, 1838–1949*. Madras: Oxford University Press.

Kour, Z. H. 2005. *The History of Aden, 1839–1872*. London: Frank Cass.

Nair, P. R. Gopinathan. 1986. 'India', in Godfrey Gunatilebe (ed.), *Migration of Asian Workers to the Arab World*, pp. 66–106. Tokyo: The United Nations University; London: Minority Rights Group.

Nair, P. R. Gopinathan. 1999. 'Return of Overseas Contract Workers and their Rehabilitation in Kerala (India),' *International Migration: A Quarterly Review*, 37(1): 209–42.

Peterson, J. E. 1978. *Oman in the 20th Century*. London: Croom Helm.

Peterson, J. E. 2007. *Historical Muscat: An Illustrated Guide and Gazetteer*. Leiden and Boston: Brill.

Playfair, Captain Robert Lambert. 1859. *Selections from the Records of the Bombay Government*, New Series xlix, History of Arabia Felix or Yemen from the Commencement of the Christian era to the Present Time; including an Account of the British Settlement of Aden, issued by the Bombay Political Department. Bombay: Bombay Education Society Press.

Reid, Anthony. 1993. *Southeast Asia in the Age of Commerce 1450–1680: Volume 2, Expansion and Crisis*. New Haven: Yale University Press.

Riad, M. 1983. 'The Gulf and its People Before 1930: A Study in Geography, Economy and Population', *Journal of the Gulf and Arabian Peninsula Studies*, No. 36.

Seccombe, I. 1983. 'Labour Migration to the Persian Gulf: Evolution and Characteristics', *Bulletin of the British Society for Middle Eastern Studies*, 10(1): 3–20.

Seccombe, I. and R. Lawless (1986a). 'Foreign Worker Dependence in the Gulf and the International Oil Companies 1910–1950', *International Migration Review*, 20(3): 549–74.

————. 1986b. 'Duty Sheikhs, Sub-Contractors and Recruiting Agents: the Impact of the International Oil Industry on Recruitment and Employment in the Persian Gulf 1900–1950', *Orient*, 27(2): 252–70.

Shwadran, Benjamin. 1973. *The Middle East, Oil and the Great Powers*, third edition, New York: John Wiley.

State of Bahrain, *Statistical Abstract, 1967*. Manama: Statistical Bureau.

State of Bahrain, *Statistical Abstract, 1972*. Manama: Statistical Bureau.

State of Kuwait. 1974. *Statistical Yearbook of Kuwait, 1974*. Kuwait City: Central Statistical Office.

Tinker, Hugh. 1977. *The Banyan Tree: Overseas Emigrants from India, Pakistan and Bangladesh*. London: Oxford University Press.

United Nations Population Division. 2003. 'Levels and Trends of International Migration to Selected Countries in Asia', Department of Economic and Social Affairs Population Division, New York.

Weiner, Myron. 1982. 'International Migration and Development: Indians in the Persian Gulf Region', *Population and Development Review*, 8(1): 1–36.

————. 1986. 'Labour Migrations as Incipient Diasporas', in Gabriel Sheffer (ed.), *Modern Diasporas in International Politics*, pp. 47–74. New York: St. Martin's Press.

Winckler, Onn. 2009. *Arab Political Demography*, second edition. Brighton: Sussex Academic Press.

4

GCC's immigration policy in the post-1990s

Contextualising South Asian migration

Zakir Hussain

Introduction

The Gulf Cooperation Council (GCC) is one of the hotspots of con-tractual workers in the world. The migration influx into the Gulf commenced after the mid-1970s when the region witnessed the first oil boom, leading to a massive augmentation of oil wealth. Conse-quent to the economic surge, the resource-rich monarchical states embarked upon large-scale construction and developmental activi-ties. Such activities necessitated a huge workforce, especially of 'blue collar' workers, which the native GCC labour markets could not fulfil. Consequently, the bloc pursued an 'open door' demo-graphic policy, inviting a large workforce from outside the region.

The inflow of expatriates to the Gulf, however, continued even after the oil wealth began to decline. Gradually, the migrant popu-lation in the GCC swelled from 5 million to the current 17 million and is expected to grow to 20.5 million by 2020, according to the World Bank estimates. At the same time, the oil wealth has wit-nessed a drastic decline, due to a decrease in crude prices, which shrunk to US$15 a barrel in the late 1990s. Figure 4.1 indicates the growing percentage of expatriate workers in a decade. In 2001, the expatriates' share in the GCC population was 36 per cent, which increased to 48 per cent in 2011, while the native population declined from 64 per cent to 52 per cent during the same period.

During the 1980s and the 1990s, the declining oil prices even forced some GCC countries to borrow as well as depend upon defi-cit financing. While at one end, the declining oil wealth constrained the state's capacity to provide employment in the public sector, at the other end, population explosion, including a youth bulge, forced the 'rentier' economies to reconsider their open door demo-graphic policy. Consequently, the GCC states launched a massive

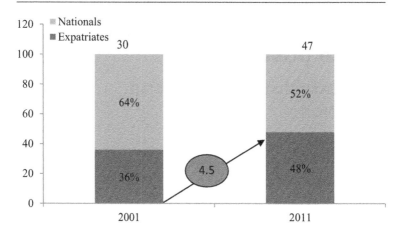

Figure 4.1 GCC population, 2001–11

Source: QNB 2013.

drive towards localisation of jobs and introduced waves of restrictive immigration policies.

Against this backdrop, this chapter examines different dimensions, such as causes, magnitude, performance and implications of restrictive immigration policies in the GCC, which have intensified in the post-1990 era. While Part I traces the historical trend of migration in the GCC bloc, Part II analyses the prevailing conditions leading to a revision of immigration policies in the region. Part III explains the factors responsible for influencing GCC authorities to introduce restrictive immigration policies and Part IV addresses the policy options to manage migration. This chapter also attempts to evaluate the performance of the localisation of job policies and its impact on South Asia.

Historical trend of migration

Initially, we find that these oil-rich states preferred a large number of workers from the neighbouring labour abundant but oil-deprived Arab states.[1] Oman, Bahrain, Yemen, Syria, Lebanon, Egypt, Sudan, Iran, Iraq, Jordan, and other Arab states were the primary labour suppliers to the GCC.[2] It is pertinent to underline that labourers from Oman and Bahrain migrated to higher-income group countries in the GCC bloc, such as Saudi Arabia, the United Arab Emirates (UAE), Kuwait, and Qatar, while in their own countries, expatriate workers, primarily from Asia, were invited to work mostly in 3D (dingy, dangerous and demanding) jobs.[3] Oman and Bahrain hold a unique position: they were simultaneously labour-importing as well as labour-exporting countries.

The dominance of Arab workers in the GCC countries continued till 1975 and thereafter started declining. They were eventually replaced by workers from Asia. In 1975, the percentage of Arab expatriates in GCC, on an average, was around 75 per cent; within two decades, it declined to 36 per cent in 1996. Country-wise, Saudi Arabia hosted the highest percentage. From the entire foreign labour force present in the kingdom, 90 per cent were Arabs, and by 1996, this figure declined to 30 per cent. Kuwait was the second country to host a large percentage of Arab labourers: around 80 per cent, which declined to 33 per cent during the same period. According to a 2006 migration report of the League of Arab States (LAS):

> A recent development over the past years in labour migration streams, as an overall orientation especially towards Arab Gulf states, has been the decrease of opportunities for Arab labour migration. Arab immigrants in Gulf Cooperation Council states have dropped from 72 per cent of the total immigrants in 1975 to 31 per cent in 1990, down to barely 25–29 per cent in 2002. At the same time, Asian labour has risen up to two-thirds of the incoming labour to the Gulf. Estimates indicate that Indians alone in the Gulf make up almost the total number of all Egyptian, Yemeni, Syrian and Jordanian immigrants.[4]

The detailed share of Arab workers in GCC countries is shown in Table 4.1, which shows a declining share of the Arab workforce.

Table 4.1 Share of Arabs in expatriate population of GCC countries, 1975–96 (%)

	1975	1985	1996	2000
Bahrain	22	1	12	15
Kuwait	80	69	33	30
Oman	16	16	11	6
Qatar	33	33	21	19
Saudi Arabia	91	79	30	33
UAE	26	19	10	13
GCC	72	56	31	32

Source: Kapiszewski (2006).

Arabs versus Asians

The declining ratio of Arab workers in the GCC bloc was replenished by the growing share of Asian workers. Several economic, socio-political and security factors led to the decline of Arab workers in the GCC. Economically, two main reasons forced GCC countries to substitute Arabs with Asians. First, the changing nature of the GCC economy demanded a new kind of workforce, especially semi-skilled and skilled, which the Arab states could not provide. As the GCC countries were being transformed from 'desert to cosmopolitan economies', their workforce demand also underwent changes. Now, these economies required relatively skilled and semi-skilled workers. Consequently, neither the labour-exporting Arab countries nor the labour-importing GCC countries were technically equipped to sustain the migration flow.

A second factor was the profit motivation of the private sector. Being of Arab origin as well as proximate to the host region, workers from Arab countries used to migrate with their families; hence, they would demand and avail full benefits equivalent to the native Arabs of the GCC. They resisted any sub-standard treatment and demanded equal treatment in all respects. The private sectors in the GCC experienced labour-related problems with Arab workers on all these issues. At the other end of the spectrum, Asian workers did not possess any 'unwanted baggage'. Majority of Asian workers were not accompanied by their families and did not demand high salaries either. Furthermore, they were relatively better skilled and suited to the new labour-intensive economy. Hence, the private sector preferred Asian workers.

Consequently, a segmented labour market developed in the GCC countries at two broad levels: public versus private and Arab versus Asians. Within the Arab versus Asian segmentation, different sets of wage structures and benefits were developed. In the first segmentation, the native GCC workforce was paid the highest salaries and benefits; the second segment consisted of the neighbouring Arab workforce and they were treated with a relatively lower wage policy; and the third segment comprised Asian workers. Asian workers were given the lowest wage packages, including housing, perks, allowances and medical facilities. On an average, Asian workers are paid two and half time less than the Saudi workers (House 2013).

Besides payment differences, Asian workers were also convenient for the employers to handle. The *kafeels* (employers/masters) found it easy to make them work for longer hours without much problems vis-à-vis their overtime allowances. They are easy to hire and fire without much concern about their health insurance, living conditions and other amenities. In contrast, employers have to meet all the mandatory labour standards while hiring native Arab workers. In addition, some professions, such as household work, and women employed in certain professions don't come under the purview of the labour laws of the GCC countries. Consequently, workers engaged in these professions do not have any legal status.

The Asian workers migrate to the Gulf purely for economic reasons. The Asian labour-exporting countries have also considered 'overseas employment' generation as one of the objectives of the emigration policies. For instance, the Emigration Act of 1983 of India is focused on the management, promotion and welfare of expatriate workers, particularly the large contractual workforce going to the Gulf (Sasikumar and Hussain 2008).

For Asian countries, overseas migration offered twin benefits. It worked as a safety valve as well as provided economic gain. According to World Bank estimates, in 2012, approximately more than 60 per cent of the total remittances, US$401 billion, went to Asian countries, as out of a total 300 million international economic migrants, more than half are from developing countries and the bulk are from Asian countries (World Bank 2013).

Table 4.2 shows the objectives of the emigration policies of Asian countries in general and the South Asia in particular. It is evident that, except India, the emigration policies of almost all major South Asian labour-exporting countries (such as Pakistan, Bangladesh and Sri Lanka) are poised to promote migration. Nepal has also shown a tendency of exporting labour to the GCC countries.

Table 4.2 Emigration policies of South Asian labour-sending countries, 2007

Country	View	Policy
India	Satisfactory	Maintain
Pakistan	Satisfactory	Raise
Bangladesh	Too low	Raise
Sri Lanka	Too low	Raise

Source: UN (2010).

Overall, employing Asian workers proved economically profitable to the private sector, and we find that the percentage of Asian workers increased consistently. Over a period, we notice that despite GCC authorities' repeated insistence on the 'localisation of jobs', the private sector neither followed the policy mandates nor did they stop issuing visas to foreign workers in general and Asian workers in particular. For instance, we notice that in Saudi Arabia, 90 per cent of the total 8 million expatriates are employed in the private sector. Similar is the case in other GCC states.

Security is another important factor which has forced the GCC authorities to revise their Arab versus Asian immigration policy. Workers from neighbouring Arab countries have been found indulging in local politics. During the Gulf War in 1990, for instance, workers from Yemen, Palestine and other neighbouring Arab countries actively supported Saddam Hussein despite the anguish of the host GCC countries. After the war, around 2 million Arab workers from different countries were, consequently, expelled by Saudi Arabia and Kuwait alone, which Nader Fargany, author of the first Arab Human Development Report (AHDR), termed a 'human tragedy.' Even third-generation Palestinians living in Kuwait, who supported Saddam Hussein, were expelled. The workforce deficiency was immediately neutralised by the GCC countries, which began inviting more workers from Asia in general, and South Asia in particular. The history of South Asian workers, especially those from India, going to the GCC region has been a history of non-interference, dedication as well as loyalty. Asian workers rarely interfere in either the local or the administrative affairs of these monarchical states and are not a security hazard.[5]

The convenience associated with Asian workers encouraged the authorities and the private sector in GCC countries to prefer the Asian workforce over the neighbouring Arabs. Thus, we find that the share of Asian workers grew rapidly in all GCC member countries during the 1970s and the 1980s. Figure 4.2 shows the growing percentage of expatriates in GCC countries. The rise in expatriate workforce in GCC countries has been largely contributed by the Asians. Table 4.3 indicates that from 1975 onwards, the share of Arab workers declined from 72 per cent in 1975 to less than 30 per cent in 2000. This gap was filled by the Asian workforce.

Besides increasing the share of the labour force in the GCC region, the percentage share of the expatriate population also swelled.

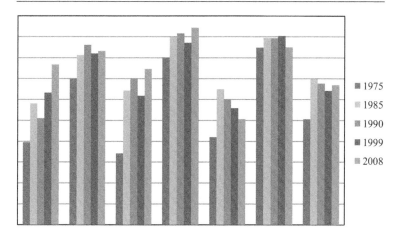

Figure 4.2 The growing percentage of expatriates in GCC countries

Source: Figure made by the author based on Hertog (2013).

Table 4.4 shows the percentage share of the expatriate population in total population of the GCC bloc.

Dominance of South Asia in GCC migration

Over the period, South Asia has become the dominant part of the Asian workforce. The Asianisation of GCC migration was substituted by South Asianisation. From South Asia, India, Pakistan, Bangladesh, and Sri Lanka have contributed the bulk of the labour force to the GCC bloc. The presence of South Asian workers has increased substantially after the Gulf War in 1990. The GCC countries expelled around 2 million workers from neighbouring Arab countries and that was compensated by the readily available and better quality South Asian workers. Tables 4.5 and 4.6 show the growing numbers of Asians in the GCC region during 1990–2009.

In 2009, 97.3 per cent of the total Indian migrants went to the GCC region, followed by Pakistan (97.2 per cent), Sri Lanka (86.9 per cent), Bangladesh (79 per cent), and Nepal (55 per cent).[6] In recent times, migration from Afghanistan to the GCC countries has also increased. Tables 4.6 and 4.7 show the share of migrants to the GCC region from the Asian countries.

Table 4.3 Native and foreign components of GCC labour forces, 1990–2010

Country	1990		1995		2000		2005		2010	
	Total migrants	Percent female migrants	Total migrants	Percent female migrants	Total migrants	Percent female migrants	Total migrants	Percent female migrants	Total migrants	Percent female migrants
Bahrain	173,200	28	205,977	30	239,366	31	278,166	32	315,403	33
Kuwait	1,585,280	39	1,089,545	31	1,500,442	32	1,869,665	30	2,097,527	30
Oman	423,572	21	582,463	21	623,608	21	666,263	21	826,074	21
Qatar	369,816	26	405,915	26	623,608	21	666,263	21	826,074	21
Saudi Arabia	4,742,997	30	461,694	26	470,731	26	712,861	26	1,305,428	26
UAE	1,330,324	33	1,715,980	30	2,286,174	28	2,863,027	28	3,293,264	27
GCC	8,625,189	31.5	4,461,574	28	5,743,929	27	7,056,245	27	8,663,770	27

Source: UN (2009).

Table 4.4 Share of nationals and expatriates in the population and labour force of GCC countries, 2005–08

Country	Year	Total population in GCC		Total labour force in GCC	
		Total (thousands)	Percentage of expatriates	Total (thousands)	Percentage of expatriates
Bahrain	2006	742.6	30	360	58.3
Kuwait	2007	3,328	68.8	0	—
Kuwait	2008	3,441	68.4	2,088	83.9
Oman	2007	2,743	29.9	—	—
Qatar	2007	1,167	85	828	92.5
KSA	2005	24,573	25.9	6,242	49.6
KSA	2007	23,981	27.1	7,766	53.8
UAE	2007	4,488	80.7	2,840	85.5
All GCC countries					
GCC	2005	35,862	35.7	11,103	About 70.0
	2007	36,200	—	—	—

Source: Shah (2009).

Table 4.5 Flow of migrant workers from South Asia to the Gulf, 2005–09

Year	Bangladesh	India	Nepal	Pakistan	Sri Lanka
1990	97,965	137,265	—	113,103	—
1991	143,152	184,381	—	146,819	—
1992	175,364	402,813	—	195,472	112,455
1993	172,307	418,364	—	156,101	115,994
2005	207,089	454,628	88,230	127,810	192,004
2006	304,620	618,286	128,306	172,837	170,049
2007	483,757	770,510	182,870	278,631	188,365
2008	643,424	818,315	169,510	419,842	215,793
2009	—	538,090	152,272	407,077	226,299

Source: Data between 1990 and 1993 collected from the respective countries' emigration departments; data from 2005 onwards taken from Rajan and Narayana (2010).

Asian versus GCC Arab

The image that the Asian workers created in the GCC countries during the 1970s and the 1980s underwent a makeover from the 1990s onwards. The presence of a large number of the Asian workers in the

Table 4.6 South Asian migrants in GCC countries (in thousands)

Serial no.	Country of origin	Bahrain	Kuwait	Oman	Qatar	KSA	UAE	Total	Percentage of nationalities in total
1	Egyptians	—	271	35	29	1,200	100	1,635	17.5
2	Yemenis	—	—	—	—	500	—	500	5.3
3	Jordanians/ Palestinians	—	—	—	40	270	100	410	4.4
4	Syrians	—	95	—	—	170	—	265	2.8
5	Sudanese	—	—	—	—	250	—	250	1.3
6	Kuwaitis	—	—	—	—	120	—	120	1.3
7	**Total Arabs**	—	**366**	**35**	**239**	**2,340**	**200**	**3,180**	**34.0 (%)**
8	Indian	110	262	300	90	1,250	1,000	3,012	32.2
9	Pakistanis	70	100	70	60	800	400	1,500	16.0
10	Bangladeshi	—	142	120	—	450	100	812	8.7
11	Filipinos	25	60	—	40	500	100	725	7.8
12	Sri Lankan	—	167	25	30	150	125	497	5.3
13	Indonesians	—	—	—	—	250	—	250	2.7
14	Iranians	—	69	—	20	—	—	89	1.0
15	**Total Asians**	**205**	**658**	**395**	**240**	**2,950**	**1,625**	**6,073**	**65.0**
16	Others	—	—	—	—	**95**	—	**95**	1.0
	Total Expatriate Population	**242**	**1,409**	**614**	**365**	**6,000**	**2,038**	**9,348**[a]	

Source: Kapiszewski (2006).

Table 4.7 Estimated sizes of the principal migrant communities in the GCC Region (in thousands)

Nationality	Bahrain (2004)	Kuwait (2003)	Oman (2004)	Qatar (2002)	Saudi Arabia (2004)	UAE (2002)	Total
Indians	120	320	330	100	1,300	1,200	3,370
Pakistanis	50	100	70	100	900	450	1,670
Egyptians	30	260	30	35	900	140	1,395
Yemeni	—	—	—	—	800	60	860
Bangladeshi	—	170	110	—	400	100	780
Filipinos	25	70		50	500	120	765
Sri Lankan	—	170	30	35	350	160	745
Jordanians/ Palestinians	20	50		50	260	110	490
Sudanese	—	—	—	—	250	30	280
Indonesians	—	9	—	—	250	—	259
Iranians	30	80	—	60	—	40	210
Syrians	—	100	—	—	100	—	200
Turks	—	—	—	—	80	—	80
Bidoun	—	80	—	—			80
Nepalese	—	—	—	—	70	—	70

Source: Kapiszewski (2006).

Table 4.8 Immigration levels and the policies of the GCC countries

Country	1975		1980		2007	
	View	Policy	View	Policy	View	Policy
UAE	Satisfactory	Maintain	High	Lower	Too high	Lower
Saudi Arabia	Too low	Raise	High	Lower	Too high	Lower
Qatar	Satisfactory	Maintain	Satisfactory	Maintain	Too high	Lower
Oman	Satisfactory	Maintain	Too high	Lower	Too high	Lower
Kuwait	Satisfactory	Maintain	High	Lower	Too high	Lower
Bahrain	Satisfactory	Maintain	Satisfactory	No Intervention	Satisfactory	Maintain

Source: UN (2010).

bloc is now being seen as a more difficult choice than once a better substitution of the Arab workers. Invariably, all the bloc members found it difficult to justify the import of a large number of Asian expatriates, particularly when they themselves were facing a high rate of unemployment among their native workforce (Hussain 2008). One after the other, the GCC countries began considering the reduction of expatriate workers. There are several reasons that forced the GCC authorities to revise their open door demographic policy. Table 4.8 shows the changing perception and policy choices of the GCC countries. Except Bahrain, the rest of the five GCC members view their current immigration as very high and their policy choice is to reduce the expatriates in their respective countries.

Reasons for restrictive immigration policies

Political factors

During the 1990s, the region underwent a severe political crisis. The Iraqi president, Saddam Hussein, occupied Kuwait in July 1990 and, consequently, the entire region suffered. A large number of foreign forces, including 150,000 from the United States (US), landed in the region. This created a political crisis in Saudi Arabia and its neighbouring countries. The average Arab was apprehensive of the presence of external forces. The hard-line section of Arab society vehemently opposed the presence of non-Arab forces, including the US and the Europeans. The GCC authorities faced an uphill task of maintaining law and order in their respective societies. Although the GCC authorities tried to manage the hardliners, the latter went underground only to emerge later in the form of Islamic terrorism, including the 9/11 attacks, followed by a series of terrorist attacks in Saudi Arabia between 2003 and 2007.

Economic factors

Economically, too, the Iraq war proved to be a heavy burden, especially for Saudi Arabia and Kuwait. Almost 40 per cent of the total war expenditure was borne by these two countries. While on the other hand, we notice that during the entire 1990s and more specifically in the second half, the oil prices, which have been the main source of revenue of GCC countries, continuously declined. Due to the East Asian economic crisis in the late 1990s, crude prices plummeted to the lowest in history, touching less than US$14 a barrel. As a result, the GCC countries, along with other oil-exporting countries, suffered a massive income loss. The Iraq war and the subsequent historical lowering of oil prices proved to be a double whammy for the GCC states.

The main brunt of low oil prices was borne by Saudi Arabia. Its economy, suffering from a low level of development since the mid-1980s, was left with very limited options. The country was forced with the option of deficit financing or borrowing money from both domestic and outside sources. Economically, the kingdom's gross domestic product (GDP) failed to increase for more than a decade; per capita income declined to almost half, from US$19,000 to US$9,000, and due to low prices, revenue from oil exports also declined (Figure 4.3).

Figure 4.4 shows the GDP growth of the GCC. It is noted that, on average, during 1980–2010, the GDP growth rate of the GCC

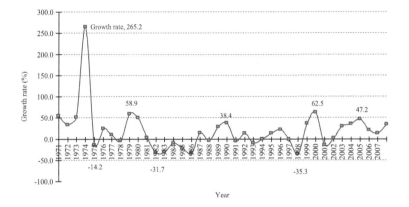

Figure 4.3 Annual growth rate of oil revenue of the four GCC countries, 1970–2008

Source: *OPEC Bulletin* (relevant issues).

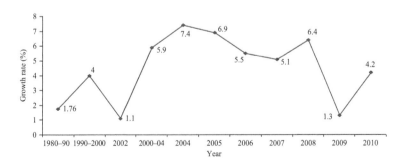

Figure 4.4 GDP growth rate of the GCC region, 1980–2010

Note: 1980–90 and 2000–04 figures are averages.

Source: Collected and compiled from country reports of the International Monetary Fund (IMF) and the Middle East Central Asia annual reports (relevant issues).

was only 1.76 per cent. It only started rising after 2002, when the third spike in oil prices occurred, which continued till 2008.

More or less, the remaining GCC countries were also passing through a similar situation. Being 'rentier' economies, these countries enormously depend upon oil income; still, 80–90 per cent of export earnings, 60–70 per cent of government revenue and more than 35–50 per cent of the GDP is composed of revenue from oil. Although the GCC countries recognised the pitfalls of overdependence on oil and emphasised 'diversification', they have not implemented those policies. In the name of industrialisation, except for the hydrocarbon industry and its horizontal and vertical integrations (such as petrochemicals, fertilisers, preparing chemicals for plastics, etc.), the GCC countries could hardly move forward. At the policy level, the GCC countries have never seriously considered developing the other sectors of their economies. Consequently, these economies could not expand and absorb the increasingly growing number of the native labour force.

Population explosion

The high oil income, during the 1970s and the 1980s, allowed the GCC authorities to spend a high percentage of their budgets on health, water, sanitation, and housing facilities. Estimates show that they spent around 30 per cent of their annual budget on human resource development (HRD). Accordingly, in the post-oil boom phase (post-1973–74), the GCC region witnessed a high rate of population growth, similar to what Western society experienced in the 'baby-boom' period after the Second World War. Table 4.9 provides Saudi Arabia's expenditure on HRD during successive five-year plans. The percentage share of expenditure on HRD progressively increased from 20 per cent in the 1st Five-Year Plan to 56 per cent in the 8th Five-Year Plan.

As a result, in all the GCC countries, post-1973 witnessed a high birth rate, high fertility rate and long life expectancy. Improved health, sanitation and water supply further reduced the mortality rates in the desert countries. This led to a population explosion in the GCC bloc and approximately two-thirds of the total population is within the 10–45 age group, which experts have termed the 'ticking time bomb'. Table 4.10 shows the share of the GCC population in the 15–64 age group.

Table 4.9 Saudi Arabia's government expenditure by development agencies in different Five-Year Plans, 1970–2009 (in SR billion)

Plan	1st plan	2nd plan	3rd plan	4th plan	5th plan	6th plan	7th plan	8th plan
Heads of expenditure	Total expenditure	Total expenditure	Total expenditure	Total expenditure	Total expenditure	Total expenditure	Total expenditure	Total expenditure
Economic resources development	9.5 (27.70%)	97.3 (28.0%)	192.2 (30.7%)	71.2 (20.4%)	34.1 (10.0%)	41.6 (10.0%)	41.7 (8.5%)	71.0 (11.5%)
Human resource development	7 (51.0%)	51 (14.7%)	115.0 (18.4%)	115.1 (33.0%)	164.6 (48.0%)	222.3 (53.8%)	276.9 (56.7%)	347.6 (56.6%)
Social & health development	3.5 (27.60%)	27.6 (8.0%)	61.2 (9.8%)	61.9 (17.7%)	68 (20%)	74.2 (18.0%)	95.8 ((19.6%)	116.5 (19.0%)
Infrastructure development	14.1 (41.40%)	171.3 (49.3%)	256.8 (41.1%)	100.7 (28.9%)	74.2 (22.0%)	75.0 (18.2%)	73.8 (15.2%)	79.5 (12.9%)
Total	34.1	347.2	625.2	348.9	340.9	413	488.2	614.6

Note: In brackets is given the percentage of the total expenditure.

Source: 7th Development Plan, 2009; 8th Development Plan, Ministry of Planning, Saudi Arabia.

Table 4.10 GCC: percentage of population in the age group 15–64

	2007	2008	2009	2010	2011	2012	2013
Bahrain	74.6	76.3	77.5	78.1	78.1	77.7	77
Kuwait	71.8	72.1	72.4	72.6	72.8	72.9	73
Oman	64.9	66.5	68.3	70.1	71.7	73.1	74
Qatar	80.5	82.7	84.3	85.2	85.6	85.7	85
Saudi Arabia	64.2	65.0	65.7	66.3	66.9	67.4	68
UAE	83.3	84.7	85.5	85.8	85.7	85.2	84

Source: World Bank, http://data.worldbank.org/indicator/SP.POP.1564.TO.ZS/countries.

Growth in population resulted in greater workforce participation in the GCC countries. In fact, the GCC labour market faced twin pressures. First, young educated natives started entering the labour market for jobs, and second, due to increase in female education, their participation rate in the labour market also increased considerably after 1990. According to the Booze report, in the 1970s, the female participation rate in the labour market was almost less than 10 per cent, but in the post-2000 era it increased up to 30 per cent. Professor Willoughby termed the growing participation of female labour force in the GCC labour market a 'quiet revolution in the making' (Willoughby 2004), which could potentially be the answer to expatriate workers in the bloc. Table 4.11 shows the total labour force participation (LFP), both male and female, in GCC countries.

High population growth leading to 'youth explosion' and an increasingly growing rate of female labour force led to an overall growth in the aggregate workforce in GCC countries. Qatar Bank estimated that in 2012 the total labour force in the GCC region increased to 18.8 million, approximately 40 per cent of the total population. The largest share of the labour force is located in Saudi Arabia, with 8.4 million workers, or 45 per cent of the total GCC countries.

The report further underlines that the growth rate of the labour force during 2007–11 has been higher than the population growth itself. For instance, during the same period, labour force increased at a rate of 7.9 per cent, compared with growth of 4.3 per cent for the total population. Figure 4.5 shows the stocks of labour force in the GCC countries during 2007–11.

Table 4.11 Total labour force participation in the GCC states (%)

Year	Sex	Total GCC[a]	Bahrain	Kuwait	Oman	Qatar	KSA	UAE
1980	M	86.90	87.40	86.80	87.80	56.10	86.40	94.80
	F	11.30	18.10	21.20	7.50	14.50	9.70	16.50
	T	56.40	61.40	61.90	51.30	43.10	53.60	76.30
1990	M	81.20	89.70	85.70	85.40	45.80	86.00	56.40
	F	20.10	29.80	38.60	13.50	34.00	16.40	30.70
	T	57.70	66.70	67.10	56.50	42.70	58.00	49.40
2000	M	84.90	88.70	87.50	83.80	91.30	83.10	90.80
	F	27.10	36.60	48.30	20.50	43.40	23.90	36.80
	T	61.40	68.30	73.40	60.20	76.50	57.10	75.20
2010	M	82.40	86.70	86.20	82.20	88.30	80.40	88.40
	F	35.40	41.60	52.70	31.90	48.30	33.00	39.90
	T	62.30	68.40	73.70	61.80	74.40	58.90	72.70
2020	M	81.20	86.20	83.00	79.60	86.00	80.10	87.20
	F	41.10	44.80	52.20	39.40	55.20	39.70	42.30
	T	63.30	68.70	70.90	62.20	74.10	61.30	70.80

Notes: [a] = includes non-nationals.

Averages are weighted.

M, Male labour force; F, Female labour force; T, Total labour force (M+F).

Source: Compiled by the author from World Bank (2004); Table A.1, A.2; A.3 on pp. 222–4.

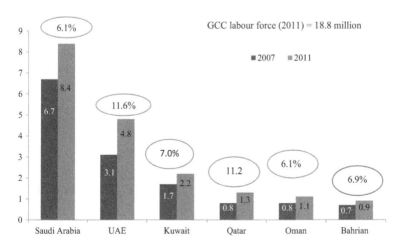

Figure 4.5 Labour force in GCC countries, 2007–11 (with CAGRs shown)
Source: QNB (2013).

Growing non-productive leakages: subsidy, perks, defence, and remittances[7]

Growing expenditure, particularly on subsidy termed a 'cradle to grave' phenomenon, defence, social security, increasing outflow of remittances (see Figure 4.6) on the one hand, and the declining oil revenue (in the 1980s and 1990s) on the other significantly constrained the GCC governments' financial capabilities to expand as well as establish new public sector units which were exclusively reserved for the native Arabs. Consequently, the governments failed to generate enough employment opportunities in the public sector. The segmentation of the labour market in the GCC region further accentuated the problem. The post-oil boom generation of the GCC countries grew in an expatriate-driven environment and had developed a unique mind-set. For them, working below *Mudir* rank (managerial post) was psychologically below their status. Any job below managerial rank neither suited their social status nor was economically worthwhile. These psychological idiosyncrasies among the native labour force generated altogether different kinds of consequences in the GCC economies. People did not like to work below the Mudir rank; their first and last preference was the public sector; the private sector became the hallmark of expatriates. Consequently, in the post-1990s, inter alia, 'voluntary' unemployment, particularly among the native youth, became the common trait of the GCC labour market.

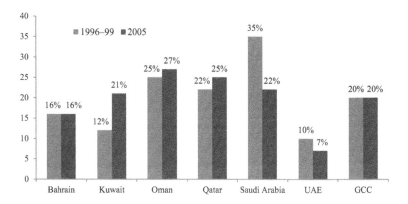

Figure 4.6 Leakage of money through remittances in the GCC region (% of total imports)

Source: Shediac, Haddad and Klouche (2010a).

Unemployment in GCC countries

Although it is tough to get an exact figure of unemployment in these countries, official estimates show that it varies between 12 per cent and 3.5 per cent in different countries. The International Monetary Fund (IMF) expects the GCC to add 6 million new jobs in 2011–15, which would equate to an annual growth in the labour

Table 4.12 Unemployment in GCC countries (%)

	Bahrain	Kuwait	Oman	Qatar	KSA	UAE	GCC
2005	8.82	1.89	8.81	3.24	5.03	3.12	4.68
2006	8.75	2	8.71	0.76	6.25	3.18	5.27
2007	8.33	2.02	8.53	0.48	5.63	3.2	4.82
2008	8.1	2.04	7.99	0.49	4.99	3.99	4.56
2009	8.31	2.2	8.97	0.76	5.38	4.25	4.9
2010	7.88	2.06	8.47	0.68	5.28	4.04	4.72

Source: Gulf Investment Corporation Estimates based on ILO, KILM data.

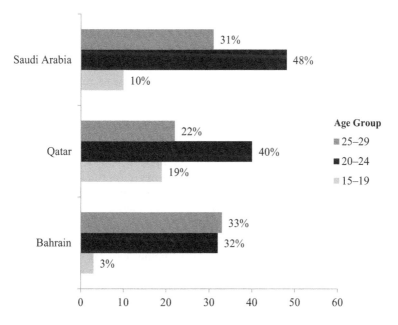

Figure 4.7 Youth unemployment in GCC countries, 2006–07

Source: Shediac and Samman (2010).

force of about 6.1 per cent. Official data indicates that 10 per cent of Saudi nationals are unemployed, followed by the UAE (6.3 per cent), Qatar (4.1 per cent), Kuwait (3 per cent), and Bahrain (less than 4 per cent). However, unofficial sources indicate that a relatively higher rate of unemployment is the order of the day in the GCC bloc (Table 4.12).

Causes of unemployment in the GCC region

Delving into the causes of unemployment in the GCC countries, we find that although it varies from country to country, there are some common features present in all the member countries. This is due to the similar socio-economic and political structures in the GCC countries: (*i*) unemployment in the GCC region is structural by nature; (*ii*) all the economies are termed as rentier, drawing the bulk of their revenue from the hydrocarbon sector; (*iii*) all the economies suffer from the classic Dutch Disease, where other sectors of the economy are underdeveloped; (*iv*) all, except Saudi Arabia, have a low population with a relatively younger base with a low workforce participation rate; (*v*) the labour market is highly segmented in terms of gender, national workers versus expatriate workers, educated workers versus non-educated workers, skilled workers versus non-skilled workers, including vocational, and each segment is characterised by different payment, perk and benefit policies; (*vi*) politically, all are monarchical states cloaked into a religio-welfare mantle.

On the quality of the labour force, it is noticed that the native workforce suffers from a high skill mismatch. It is deficient in skills imperative for a labour market. In fact, the GCC labour force has failed, over the years, to generate the kind of workforce required by its economy. This is inherent in the region's employment and education policy. For instance, the market needs professionals, technicians, medics, management experts, engineers, etc., but the universities in the region are producing non-professionals. Majority of the students are found enrolled in humanities and there is a dearth of student enrolment in medicine, natural sciences, science and technology, and management (Table 4.13). For instance, in Saudi Arabia in 2003, 60 per cent of the total students were enrolled in education and humanities, while only 4.6 per cent were in medicine, 15 per cent in social sciences and 13.1 per cent in science and technology. Considering the massive investment in

Table 4.13 Distribution of university students by field of study in the GCC region (%)

	Education & humanities	Social science	Medicine	Science & technology & engineering	Others
Bahrain (2003)	10	50	7	21	12
Kuwait	—	—	—	—	—
Oman (2003)	54.2	21.1	2.8	14	7.9
Qatar (2003)	19.1	48.3	3.9	19.1	9.5
Saudi Arabia (2003)	60.7	15.1	4.6	13.1	6.1
UAE	57.8	13.6	1.7	24.1	2.8
China (1994)	22.8	9.4	8.9	46.8	12.1

Source: World Bank (2009).

Table 4.14 Percentage share of national workforce in the private sector in the GCC region, 2003

	Bahrain	Kuwait	Oman	Qatar	Saudi Arabia	UAE
Per cent of nationals in private sector	30	3	48	3	46	1
Total workforce (thousands)	254	1,071	158	252	4,315	99

Source: Al-Kibsi, Benkert and Schubert (2007), exhibit 1.

promoting a knowledge-based economy, the kingdom is bound to rely on expatriate workers for the coming decade to meet its requirements.

In the GCC, the private sector has relied upon, as also preferred, the cheap and relatively better skilled expatriate workers. Table 4.14 shows percentage share of national workers in the private sector. Only in Bahrain, Saudi Arabia and Oman has the 'localisation of jobs' been relatively successful.

The segmentation of the labour market is another glaring reality, which has promoted a unique mind-set among the national labour force. Psychologically, they are torn between two mind-sets – public sector versus private sector employment and expatriate versus national nature of employment. Such segmentation has not only promoted wage differentials but privileges and social status as well. Most of the nationals still strictly regard some of the jobs as expatriate jobs and they hardly even think of doing those.

Localisation of employment

Since the 1990s, almost *all the GCC countries* have earnestly begun experimenting with the 'localisation of jobs' policy. They have devised a varied mechanism and policy tools to achieve this objective. The underlying rationale behind 'localisation of jobs' is to reduce unemployment among the national workforce and raise their productivity level, besides solving their growing socio-economic and political problems. The situation has further been aggravated by the Arab Spring. As a result, several GCC members have renewed their efforts towards the nationalisation of their labour policies. For instance, Saudi Arabia, which is facing the highest rate of unemployment, has introduced a new labour policy called *Nitaqat*, which targets the private sector to reduce the expatriate workforce, which constitutes more than 90 per cent of the total 8 million foreign workers present in the kingdom. Under Nitaqat, the Saudi government has categorised the entire private sector companies into four groups and fixed their visa issuing authority on the basis of their performance with regard to the Nitaqat mandates. Table 4.15 schematises the rules of Nitaqat related to four categories of companies.

Table 4.15 Schematising the provisions of Nitaqat

Silver	Incentives	• Complete freedom in hiring employees • Easier visa processing • Freedom to issue new visas • Freedom to change profession of employees Condition-free visa transfer: Freedom to hire • employees from Red and Yellow zones and transfer their visas **Grace period**: One year to improve Nitaqat record
Green	Incentives	• Freedom to apply for new visas • Freedom to change foreign workers' profession • Freedom to renew work permits • Freedom to recruit employees from Red and Yellow zones and transfer their visas **Grace period**: Nine months to improve Nitaqat record
Yellow	Incentives Punitive measures	• None • Not free to issue new visas • Free to issue one visa after the departure of two expatriates • Not free to transfer visas and change professions • Employees barred from renewing their work permit after completing six years **Grace period**: Six months to improve Nitaqat record
Red	Punitive measures	• Banned from: changing profession, transferring visas, issuing new visas, and opening files for new branches. **Grace period**: Six months to improve Nitaqat record

Source: Compiled and processed by the author from various sources.

Evaluation of the policy

Overall, we notice that due to the saturation in the public sector, almost all GCC countries have targeted the private sector to increase the share of the national labour force. The irony is that their own labour force is passing through high rates of unemployment, while more than 17 million foreign workers are employed in gainful professions. This has evoked a nationalistic favour in the bloc and has raised objections to the free flow of migrant workers in the region. Besides, critics have also pointed out the issue of productivity of the labour force, which has considerably declined since the flow of foreign workers in the GCC region.

In the entire bloc, Qatar is the only country to have successfully reduced, unemployment significantly, from 11.3 per cent in 2003 to 3.2 per cent in 2011. Meanwhile, other countries like Kuwait, UAE, Bahrain, Oman, and Saudi Arabia are still struggling to achieve their stated objectives. Figure 4.8 shows the trend of Saudisation in private sector.

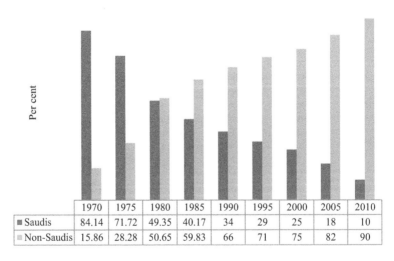

	1970	1975	1980	1985	1990	1995	2000	2005	2010
■ Saudis	84.14	71.72	49.35	40.17	34	29	25	18	10
▨ Non-Saudis	15.86	28.28	50.65	59.83	66	71	75	82	90

Figure 4.8 History of Saudisation in the private sector, 1970–2010

Source: Central Department of Statistics (CDS), Labour Force Statistics in Saudi Arabia, 1977, 1990, 2001 (Jeddah). Figures for 1995, 2000, 2005, and 2010 are author's estimates.

Impact of immigration policy on South Asian migration

Restrictive immigration is bound to have a negative impact on South Asian migration. Under Nitaqat in Saudi Arabia, the share of India, Sri Lanka, Pakistan, and Bangladesh will be considerably reduced. According to one estimate, Saudi Arabia will reduce approximately 2 million foreign workers within a couple of years. Similarly, Kuwait has also announced that it aims to reduce 700,000 foreign workers, with a plan to reduce 100,000 annually. Except Dubai, other emirates of the UAE also plan to decrease the number of foreign workers.

Countries like Sri Lanka and Bangladesh, which supply female migrants, may gain from this opportunity. Prospects of the migration of care workers, particularly nurses, and female paramedics from India and Nepal is also bright (Simel and Smith 2004).

Figure 4.9 shows that out of total migrants in West Asia, 88 per cent are from South Asia. Therefore, if any restrictive policy is adopted by the GCC countries, it is but natural that South Asian workers would suffer the most. According to Indian sources, around 500,000 Indian workers are likely to be deported from

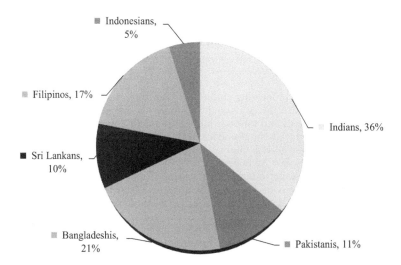

Figure 4.9 Estimated stock of Asian-origin temporary contractual workers in West Asia

Source: IOM (2008: 443).

Saudi Arabia alone; 75,000 have already applied for return. Similarly, in Kuwait too, Indians would suffer the most. The likely policy these labour-exporting countries could adopt is better training and preparation of their workforce to meet the requirements of the GCC economies. For instance, the GCC countries are strongly emphasising a diversification policy. Under this, they have planned to promote five major sectors, namely energy, talent (knowledge economy), finance, knowledge, service (catering and aviation), and the utility-based sector. In order to exploit the GCC labour market, the South Asian labour-exporting countries need better planning and training of their workforce, otherwise workers from the Central Asian republics, China, and perhaps from European countries, due to the protracted economic crisis, will mount stiff competition.

In conclusion, it is obvious that the GCC now is no more a region that absorbs an unlimited foreign workforce. Looking at their internal socio-economic and political dynamics, these countries have adopted a restrictive immigration policy. Nevertheless, it is also a fact that because of a short population base and growing economic profile (approximately more than a trillion plus economy), the GCC economies cannot function properly without support from expatriate workers. The nature of labour demand in the GCC region is drifting towards a more specialised workforce. As a result, the labour-sending South Asian countries need to adjust and revamp their workforce and emigration policies accordingly.

Notes

1   In one of their pioneering studies on Gulf migration, Birks and Sinclair have divided the Arab countries into two categories: labour-poor oil-rich countries and oil-poor labour-abundant countries. During the initial phase, the labour abundant Arab countries catered to the need of the labour-poor oil-rich Gulf countries.
2   Even before the first oil boom in the 1950s and the 1960s, a majority of the workforce was from the neighbouring Arab countries.
3   3D terminology is derived from a Japanese word, which means dirty, demeaning and dangerous. Generally, we find that the blue collar workers are primarily employed in those professions, which are mostly avoided by the native population. For instance, despite a high rate of unemployment, around 10–12 million Bangladeshi workers are present in different parts of India. This is because of the fact that these Bangladeshi workers are mostly employed in those professions where Indians, though unemployed, don't want to work. Bangladeshi male workers are usually present in urban areas as ragpickers and watchmen, or doing household jobs, while Bangladeshi female workers are primarily employed as domestic help for working women.

4 LAS (2006: 4). The report further estimates that the number of emigrants from countries of origin lies between 15 and 20 million, out
   of which 5 million are Palestinians, 2.7 million are Egyptians, 3 million are Moroccans, 1 million are Algerians, 800,000 are Tunisians,
   more than 600,000 are Lebanese, nearly 1 million are Yemenis and
   600,000 are Sudanese. These are just estimated figures. For instance,
   other sources estimate the number of Syrians and Lebanese residing or
   naturalised in South America to be in several millions. Some authorities estimate Sudanese immigrants to also be in several millions. Estimates vary altogether from one source to another, especially between
   labour-sending and labour-receiving countries (*ibid.*: 5).
5 There have been some occasions when Indians and Pakistanis were
   found hassling each other. But these events were not directly related to
   the GCC authorities. Their issues were personal in nature. However,
   there have been some demonstrations, particularly related to discrimination and *payment* issues and excesses of the kafeel.
6 For Detailed discussion see Gurung, Ganesh. 2004. 'An Overview Paper
   on Overseas Employment in Nepal', International Labour Office, Nepal.
7 See Hussain, Zakir. 2011. 'Immigration Policies of the GCC Countries: Implications and Responses', in, Irudaya Rajan and Marie Percot
   (2011) (eds.) *Dynamics of Indian Migration: Historical and Current
   Perspective*, New Delhi: Routledge.

References

Al-Kibsi, Gassan, Claus Benkert and Jörg Schubert. 2007. 'Getting Labor
  Policy to Work in the Gulf', *The McKinsey Quarterly*, February, accessed
  2 June 2013.
Birks, J. S., and S. A. Sinclair. 1980. 'International Migration and Develop-
  ment in the Arab Region', Geneva: International Labour Organization.
Dito, Mohammed Ibrahim. 2007. *Migration Policies and Challenges in the
  Kingdom of Bahrain*. The American University in Cairo.
Hertog, Steffen. 2013. *The Private Sector and Reform in the Gulf Coop-
  eration Council*, Kuwait Programme on Development, Governance and
  Globalisation in the Gulf States, LSE, London.
House, Karen Elliot. 2013. *On Saudi Arabia: Its People, Past, Religious
  Faultline and Future*. New York: Vintage.
Hussain, Zakir. 2008. 'India's Economic Relations with Gulf Cooperation
  Council States: a Study of Labour Migration and Energy Dimension dur-
  ing the Post–1990 Period'. Unpublished Ph.D. dissertation, Department
  of Economics, Jamia Millia Islamia, New Delhi.
International Monetary Fund (IMF). 2011. *Gulf Cooperation Coun-
  cil Countries Enhancing Economic Outcomes in an Uncertain Global
  Economy*. Washington, DC: International Monetary Fund.
International Organisation for Migration (IOM). 2008. *Managing Labour
  Mobility in the Evolving Global Economy*, World Migration Report,
  2008. Geneva: International Organisation for Migration.

Kapiszewski, Andrzej. 2006. 'Arab versus Asian Migrant Workers in the GCC Countries', Department of Economic and Social Affairs, United Nations, Beirut. Available online: http://www.un.org/esa/population/meetings/EGM_Ittmig_Arab/P02_Kapiszewski.pdf.

League of Arab States (LAS). 2006. *Regional Report on Arab Labour Migration 2006*, Population Policies and Migration Department, Cairo and Egypt.

QNB. 2013. *GCC Economic Insight, 2012*, Qatar National Bank, Doha, Qatar.

Rajan, S. Irudaya and D. Narayana. 2010. 'The Financial Crisis in the Gulf And its Impact on South Asian Migrant Workers', Working Paper 436, CDS, Trivandrum.

Sasikumar, S. K. and Zakir Hussain. 2008. 'Managing Internaitonal Labour Migration from India: Policies and Perspectives', ILO-Asia-Pacific Working paper Series, Subregional Office for South Asia, International Labour Organization, New Delhi.

Shah, Nasra. 2009. 'The Management of Irregular Migration and its Consequences for Development', Gulf Cooperation Council, Regional Office for Asia and Pacific, International Labour Organization.

Shediac, Richard and Hatem Samman. 2010. *Meeting the Employment Challenge in the GCC: The Need for a Holistic Strategy*. Abu Dhabi: Booze & Company.

Simel, Esim and Monica Smith (eds). 2004. 'Gender Migration in Arab States: The Case of Domestic Workers', Regional Office of the Arab States, International Labour Organization, Beirut.

United Nations (UN). 2009. *The Demographic Profile of the Arab Countries*, Technical paper 9, Economic and Social Commission for Western Asia (ESCWA), New York.

———. 2010. *World Population Policies 2010*. New York: Department of Economic and Social Affairs, Population Division.

Willoughby, John. 2004. *A Quiet Revolution in the Making? The Replacement of Expatriate Labor through the Feminization of the Labor Force in GCC Countries*, Working paper Series, 2004–18, Department of Economics, American University, http://w.american.edu/cas/economics/repec/amu/workingpapers/2004–18.pdf (accessed on 12 July 2013).

World Bank. 2004. Unlocking the Employment Potential in the Middle East and North Africa toward a New Social Contract, Washington, http://www-wds.worldbank.org/external/default/WDSContentServer/WDSP/IB/2004/06/03/000012009_20040603143832/Rendered/PDF/288150PAPER0Unlocking0employment.pdf.

———. 2009. *Shaping the Future: A Long-Term Perspective of People and Job Mobility for MENA*. Washington, DC: World Bank.

———. 2013. *Migration and Development Brief, 20 April*, http://siteresources.worldbank.org/INTPROSPECTS/Resources/334934–1110315015165/MigrationandDevelopmentBrief20.pdf (accessed on 12 July 2013).

Part II

Dynamics of migration

5

In search of El Dorado
Indian labour migration to Gulf countries

Prakash C. Jain

Contemporary Indian labour migration to the Gulf countries is a phenomenon which is about four decades old. It began after the escalation in oil prices in 1973–74 and subsequent years (Jain 2005). Unlike their predecessors who migrated to the various British colonies before India's independence and the 'brain drain' type émigrés who went to live and work in metropolitan countries of Europe and North America after independence, the Gulf migrants are the transitory migrants as stringent residency and citizenship laws as well as the contractual nature of their work bar them from permanent settlement in these predominantly Muslim countries (see Jain 2003a).

Migration process

The process of migration at the individual level can be said to begin with the decision of the person to seek employment abroad. Potential migrants usually seek employment contracts through their network of relatives or friends or through recruiting agents. This is followed by the registration of the contract with the Protector of Emigrants whose offices are located in a number of major cities in India and which is coordinated by the Office of the Protector-General of Emigrants in the Ministry of Labour and Employment.

Emigration is a costly venture. It usually involves such expenditures as travel costs, visa charges and costs of procuring a No Objection Certificate (NOC). 'An average emigrant from Kerala spent between INR 40,000 to 50,000 for going abroad. Those who have been defrauded by the cheats, the average loss came to INR 22 thousand" (Zachariah, Kannan and Rajan 2002: 18; Breedings 2012). A number of unauthorised agents operate in this market who not only charge an exorbitant fee for it but at times also issue fake certificates. The Gulf workers, particularly semi-skilled and unskilled workers, are the most vulnerable to exploitation and harassment by the recruiting agents as well as government officials during their departure from and arrival to India (Oishi 2005; Shah 2009). Problems in getting a visa, passport and emigration clearance are all too well known. In this connection, the Government of India's resolve to amend the Emigration Act of 1983 in order to have an effective instrument to monitor the flow of Indian labour abroad and protect their interest still remains to be implemented.

Volume and destination

Subsequent to the oil-price boom in the Gulf countries in 1973–74, large-scale infrastructural and economic development projects were planned and initiated which included setting up amenities like schools, hospitals, houses, improvement of transport and communications, etc. These programmes created a spurt in demand for not only highly skilled technical experts but also for semi-skilled and unskilled workers. Therefore, the major outflow of Indian migrant workers and other personnel during the past four decades or so has been to the Gulf countries where about 5.5 million of them are estimated to have been employed. The maximum number of Indian workers is in Saudi Arabia. Other major employers of Indian workers are the United Arab Emirates (UAE), Oman, Kuwait, Qatar, and Bahrain. The number of Indian workers who were given emigration clearance for contractual employment abroad in the past few years and the data on distribution of labour outflow is presented in Tables 5.1 through 5.4.

Indians were the first among the groups of immigrants to flock to the Gulf countries. Moreover, as already pointed out, there has been a tradition of 'outmigration' from India to the various countries, including the Gulf region, at least since the beginning of the 19th century

Table 5.1 presents data regarding migration of Indian contract workers to West Asia. Each year, an overwhelming majority of workers have gone to West Asia, and particularly to the six Gulf Cooperation Council (GCC) countries. Besides the contract workers, several thousand other Indians go to the Gulf countries from the following categories: (*i*) professionals from information technology (IT) and other sectors and skilled and semi-skilled workers

Table 5.1 Annual labour outflows from India to West Asia, 1976–2012

Year	Number of workers	Year	Number of workers
1977	22,900	1995	413,334
1978	69,000	1996	414,214
1979	171,800	1997	416,424
1980	268,200	1998	355,164
1981	272,000	1999	199,552
1982	224,257	2000	243,182
1983	217,971	2001	278,664
1984	198,520	2002	367,663
1985	160,396	2003	466,456
1986	109,234	2004	474,960
1987	121,812	2005	456,479
1988	165,924	2006	619,771
1989	125,786	2007	774,987
1990	143,565	2008	825,373
1991	197,889	2009	598,198
1992	416,784	2010	619,557
1993	438,338	2011	606,929
1994	425,385	2012	725,173

Note: The figures given in Tables 5.1–5.4 do not include the persons who are running the business in partnership with Gulf nationals, those who emigrated on visit visa and stayed on to get a job, and those skilled workers and professionals (like doctors, engineers, chartered accountants, computer specialist etc.) in whose case emigration clearance in India is not necessary.

Source: Ministry of Labour (2002, 2003 and 2005) and Ministry of Overseas Affairs (2009, 2011 and 2012–13).

such as doctors, engineers, managers, supervisors, drivers, cooks, and clerical workers, etc; (*ii*) businessmen, entrepreneurs, etc., who don't require emigration clearance; and (*iii*) illegal migrants (those who overstay their visit visa and get employment).

Data in Table 5.1 further suggests four distinct phases of Indian contract workers' migration abroad: 1976–81 (the period of steady growth), 1982–91 (the period of declining migration); 1992–2001 and from 2002 onwards (a peak period). Fluctuation in migration figures can be explained in terms of a number of political economy factors: oil prices, labour demand and supply factors, geopolitical instability, Arabisation of labour policy, and the recent implementation of Nitaqat law in Saudi Arabia. Data in Table 5.2 shows that though there was slight decline in migration in 2009 (598,198), it reversed by 2011. Thus, in 1999,

Table 5.2 The distribution of annual labour outflows from India to West Asia by country of destination, 1982–90

Country	1982	1983	1984	1985	1986	1987	1988	1989	1990
Bahrain	17,069	18,894	15,514	11,246	5,784	6,578	8,219	8,520	6,782
Iraq	35,268	13,001	11,398	5,855	5,040	2,330	4,284	5,085	1,650
Kuwait	9,764	11,490	5,466	5,512	4,235	7,354	9,653	5,679	1,077
Libya	10,433	5,900	5,179	2,449	2,552	2,272	593	632	305
Oman	39,792	49,120	43,228	37,806	22,417	16,362	18,696	16,574	34,267
Qatar	14,357	7,772	4,362	5,214	4,029	4,751	4,654	7,991	3,704
Saudi Arabia	78,297	83,235	88,079	68,938	41,854	57,234	85,289	49,710	79,473
UAE	19,277	25,559	24,286	21,286	23,323	24931	34,029	26,189	11,962
Others	15,288	7,024	8,410	4,729	4,415	3,544	4,471	5,406	4,345
Total	239,545	219,995	205,922	163,035	113,649	125,356	169,888	125,786	143,565

Source: Ministry of Labour and Employment, *Annual Reports* (different years), Government of India.

Table 5.3 The distribution of annual labour outflows from India by destination, 1991–96

Country	1991	1992	1993	1994	1995	1996
Bahrain	8,630	16,458	15,622	13,806	11,235	16,647
Kuwait	7,044	19,782	26,981	24,324	14,439	14,580
Oman	22,333	40,900	29,056	25,142	22,338	30,113
Saudi Arabia	130,928	265,180	269,639	265,875	256,782	214,068
UAE	15,446	60,490	77,066	75,762	79,674	112644
Others	7,121	13,974	19,974	20,476	28,866	26,162
Total	**191,502**	**416,784**	**438,338**	**425,385**	**413,334**	**414,214**

Source: Ministry of Labour (2002).

Table 5.4 Indian migration to GCC countries, 1997–2012

Country	Bahrain	Kuwait	Oman	Qatar	Saudi Arabia	UAE	Total
1997	17,944	13,170	29,994	–	214,420	110,945	386,473
1998	16,997	22,462	20,774	–	105,239	134,740	300212
1999	14,905	19,149	16,101	–	27,160	79,269	156,584
2000	15,909	31,082	15,155	–	58,722	55,099	175,967
2001	16,382	39,751	30,985	13,829	78,048	53,673	232,668
2002	20,807	48,549	41,209	12,596	99,453	95,034	317,648
2003	24,778	54,434	36,816	14,251	121,431	143,804	395,514
2004	22,980	52,064	33,275	16,325	123,522	175,262	423,428
2005	30,060	39,124	40,931	50,222	99,879	194,412	454,628
2006	37,688	47,449	67,992	76,324	134,059	254,774	618,286
2007	29,966	48,467	95462	88,483	195,437	312,695	770,510
2008	31,924	35,562	89,659	82,937	228,406	349,827	818,315
2009	17,541	42,091	74,963	46,292	281,110	130,302	592,299
2010	15,101	37,667	105,807	**45,752**	**275,172**	**130,910**	**610,409**
2011	14,323	45,149	73,819	**41,710**	**289,297**	**138,861**	**603,159**
2012	20,150	55,868	84,384	**63,096**	**375,503**	**141,138**	**722,139**

Source: Ministry of Labour (2003, 2004–2005) and Ministry of Overseas Indian Affairs, Government of India, Annual Reports (2010, 2011, and 2012).

there was a sharp decline in the number of persons migrating for employment to Saudi Arabia. This was primarily due to the determined efforts to indigenise the labour force. The situation has improved since then and reached an unprecedented peak during

2006–08. In 2008, the annual labor flow of migration workers to West Asia reached a record level of 825,373, and in the later period the flow was slightly reduced, which could be due to the economic crisis.

Table 5.4 provides a detailed account of the India-GCC migratory trends since 1997, based on government sources. As mentioned above, since 2002, the flow of migrants to the GCC region has increased substantially, peaking between 2007 and 2008. The annual labour flow to the GCC countries was 232,668 in 2001 and it had a substantial growth of 818,315 in 2008. Interestingly, data in Table 5.4 indicates that during the years 2002–08 there was upward flow of migrants towards the UAE, but in the later period Saudi Arabia became the favourite destination of migrant workers. In 2012, out of the total 722,139 Indian émigrés to the GCC region, 375,503 migrated to Saudi Arabia. In 2006, the total migrant flow to the GCC countries was 618,286; it was 770,510 in 2007, 818,315 in 2008, 592,299 in 2009, 610,409 in 2010, 603,159 in 2011, and 722,139 in 2012. In the last two decades, from 1998 to 2008, Saudi Arabia remains the favourite destination for Indian migrants (Zacharia and Rajan 2012).

As already pointed out, besides labour, other segments of the Indian expatriate community include traders, entrepreneurs, professional, IT professionals, highly educated technocrats, paramedics and other middle-class personnel. In labour-surplus Yemen, there are very few Indian migrant workers. Yemen has about 150,000 permanently settled Indians, the largest in West Asia (Jain 2003b).

Socio-economic characteristics of migrants

Region/state of origin

During the 1970s and 1980s, an overwhelming majority of Indian migrants to the Gulf countries originated from the south Indian states of Kerala, Tamil Nadu, Andhra Pradesh, Karnataka (generally, in that order), but in recent years a number of other states, such as Rajasthan, Maharashtra, Uttar Pradesh, Punjab, Gujarat, and Bihar, have also started making inroads into this process in significant ways (See Table 5.5). Among other socio-economic characteristics mention must be made of the fact that a majority of migrants tend to be male, young and Muslim (Nair 1986; Jain

Table 5.5 State-wise origin of migrant workers in India, 2000–12

States	2000	2002	2004	2006	2008	2010	2012
Andhra Pradesh	29,999	38,417	72,580	97,680	97,530	72,220	92,803
Bihar	6,726	19,222	21,812	39,493	60,642	60,531	84,078
Delhi	3,165	4,018	6,052	9,098	4,512	2,583	2,842
Gujarat	5,722	11,925	22,218	13,274	15,716	8,245	6,999
Goa	1,331	3,545	7,053	4,063	2,210	1,380	1,338
Karnataka	10,927	14,061	19,237	24,362	22,413	17,295	17,960
Kerala	69,630	81,950	63,512	120,083	180,703	104,101	98,178
Madhya Pradesh	1,706	7,411	8,888	7,047	1,897	1,564	1,815
Maharashtra	13,346	25,477	28,670	21,496	19,128	18,123	19,259
Orissa	576	1,742	6,999	6,696	6,515	7,344	7,478
Punjab	10,025	19,638	25,302	53,942	27,291	30,974	37,472
Rajasthan	10,170	23,254	35,108	70,896	44,744	47,803	42,239
Tamil Nadu	63,878	79,165	108,964	150,842	78,841	84,510	68,732
Uttar Pradesh	9,157	19,288	27,428	91,613	125,783	140,826	155,301
West Bengal	1,940	8,338	8,986	24,817	21,187	28,900	29,795
Others	4,884	10,212	12,150	924	0	0	0
Total	243,182	367,663	474,960	809,453	610,272	641,356	747,041

Source: Ministry of Labour (2003, 2004–2005); and Ministry of Overseas Indian Affairs, Government of India, Annual Reports (2010, 2011 and 2012).

2003a; Rajan and Zachariah 2012). Their average length of stay in the Gulf countries is about four to seven years (Nayyar 1994; Zachariah and Rajan 2004).

As such the phenomenon is slowly acquiring an India-wide character; only the north-eastern states appear to be immune to it. Even in south India, Kerala no longer sends the largest number of contract workers to the Gulf. Interestingly, in recent years, the labour outflow from Uttar Pradesh has increased substantially from 91,613 in 2002 to 125,783 in 2008, 140,826 in 2010, and 155,301 in 2012. At the same time, the migration of workers from Kerala showed a decline as the state sent only 104,101 workers in 2008 and 98,178 workers in 2008, much lesser than Uttar Pradesh. Bihar, too, has emerged in the list of top-sending states, the outflow of migrants being 97,680 in 2006, 97,530 in 2008, 72,220 in 2010, and 92,803 in 2012. Moreover, Kerala, Andhra Pradesh and Maharashtra are the major states from where the maximum numbers of women workers migrate to the GCC region (Rajan and Sukendran 2010). Based on the existing patterns of migration, it can be said that other states from where an extensive outmigration could occur in future are, among others, Tamil Nadu, Punjab, Rajasthan, West Bengal, and Karnataka.

Religion

We do not have an India-wide religious distribution of emigrant workers going to the Gulf, but a study done in Kerala suggests that in 2008 the majority of emigrants were Muslims, around 41.1 per cent; 37.7 per cent are Hindus and the remaining 21.2 per cent are Christians (Zachariah and Rajan 2012: 46–7).

Gender

An overwhelming majority of Indian migrants to the Gulf countries are male. The paternalistic policies of both the sending and the receiving countries and fewer job opportunities for women in the Gulf countries have reduced the flow of female migrants to the GCC countries. Paramedics, nursing, manufacturing, teaching, entertainment and domestic service are some of the few vocations that are open to women.

The patriarchal attitude of Indian society still does not favour independent female migration abroad. Thus, studies conducted in Kerala villages in the 1970s found that not more than 2 per cent of the total number of migrants to the Gulf countries were women (see Commerce Research Bureau 1978; Mathew and Nair 1978; Prakash 1978). The 1987 state survey of Kerala, however, found this figure to be 7.5 per cent (DES 1987). In recent years, the situation in this regard appears to have changed significantly. According to estimates made by the UAE interior ministry, of the 585,000 Indian workers in the UAE in 1995, about 122,000 (17.2 per cent) were female workers (Zachariah, Prakash and Rajan 2004: 2229).

The proportion of women in the Indian population in the Gulf countries is also very low as the majority of Indian migrant workers do not take their families with them. It was estimated that not more than 10 per cent of the total Indian migrant workers in 1983, for example, lived with their families (Gulati 1986: 197). In recent years, the proportion of women migrant workers has gone up. Economic prosperity in the GCC region has simultaneously produced a 'royal-comfort culture' and also led to the restriction of women in the workforce which has increased the huge demand for domestic workers, maids, and female workers in the care industry and manufacturing sector.

Amongst the migrant sending states, Kerala, Andhra Pradesh and Maharashtra are the major states from where maximum women workers migrate to the GCC region (Rajan and Sukendran 2010). The state of Kerala has a high level of female migration and the majority of the Indian nurses working in the GCC region are from here (Percot 2006). The socio-economic mobility of certain communities in Kerala is greatly attributed to the nursing community working abroad. India prohibits women below the age of 30 to migrate. The working conditions of women workers in the GCC region are quite dismal: abuse, harassment by male employers and non-payment of salaries are widely prevalent in the GCC region.

Age, educational and skill levels

A majority of migrants to the Gulf countries happen to be young. According to a study conducted by the Commerce Research Bureau (1978), in Kerala it was found that 79 per cent of migrant workers were 35 years of age or younger. This was further confirmed in a survey conducted in the state by CDS in 2008. The survey found that the majority of migrants (90 per cent of males and 66 per cent females) belonged to the 15–39 age group (Zachariah and Rajan 2012: 23).

Educational and skill levels of Indian migrants to the Gulf countries appear to have been rather low. Data from Kerala state suggests that over two-thirds of the migrants to the West Asian countries in the late 1970s had completed less than 10 years of schooling. The same study also found that about 62 per cent of emigrants were unskilled workers (Gulati 1986: 199). If a sample survey of Indian migrant workers in the UAE in 2001 is to be believed, then these figures have come down to 29 per cent and 36 per cent respectively (Zachariah, Prakash and Rajan 2004: 2230). A recent study conducted by Centre for Development Studies (CDS) suggests that nearly 58.5 per cent of emigrants have a minimum of secondary school level education and the outmigrants are better educated than the return migrants from the GCC region. This study further reveals that a significant number of migrants from Kerala were illiterate and the percentage of illiterates was higher among female migrants than male migrants (Zachariah and Rajan, 2012)

Traditionally, the majority of Indian migrants to the GCC are semi-skilled or unskilled workers, mostly illiterate, single and male. However, the IT boom and the technological advancements of the 1990s altered the skill composition of migrants (Kumar and Srivastava 2003). In the 1970s, along with labourers the demand shifted towards technicians, teachers and paramedics, and India became the major source for the skilled category of workers. The high technological developments and the changing economies in 1990s paved the way for the migration of high-tech white collar IT professionals, doctors and educated technocrats from India. Presently, a significant portion of Indian immigrants are engaged in blue collar jobs. The survey in the UAE shows that only 20 per cent of Indian immigrants were engaged in professional and high-tech jobs. For instance, in Qatar, out of the total 500,000 Indian immigrants, nearly 70 per cent are working in construction, manufacturing/low-skilled jobs (Kanchana 2012).

Legal framework and emigration management

Following the ban on indentured labour in India in 1913, efforts were made by the British government to regulate the migration of Indian workers. This was done by enacting the Emigration Act of 1922. This Act was replaced by the Emigration Act of 1983 which deals with the migration of Indian workers for overseas employment on contractual basis and seeks to safeguard their interests and ensure their welfare. The Emigration Act is administered by the Ministry of Labour through the eight offices of the Protector of Emigrants located at Delhi, Mumbai, Kolkata, Chennai, Chandigarh, Cochin, Hyderabad, Jaipur, and Thiruvananthapuram.

According to the Emigration Act of 1983, only registered recruiting agents can conduct business of recruitment for overseas employment after obtaining a Registration Certificate from the Protector-General of Emigrants. The recruiting agents are allowed to levy service charges from each worker of not more than Rs 10,000. From 1984 to 2001 the Protector-General of Emigrants had issued registration certificates to 3,487 recruiting agents. However, in 2002, only 1,250 recruiting agents were found to be engaged in this business with valid registration certificates.

Presently, there are 1,835 recruiting agencies registered with the Protector-General of Emigrants (Breedings 2012). Besides legal migration, illegal migration of labour has also been taking place from India and other South Asian countries. In her study on Indian recruiting agencies, Breedings has pointed out that private recruiting agencies often violate the rules and the cost of migration is four to five times higher than the amount stipulated by the Ministry of Overseas Indian Affairs (MOIA). The spurious informal networks often jeopardise the free and smooth flow of labour and also their future well-being.

In the meantime, in 2004, the Government of India formed the MOIA to safeguard the rights of the Indian diaspora and expatriate workers, to formulate policies and welfare schemes for migrants, disseminate adequate and authentic information on the emigration process, and promote skilled migration from time to time. With the formation of the MOIA, the Emigration Division of the Ministry of Labour and Employment and the Protector-General of Emigrants were attached to the new ministry from 2004.

The foremost task of MOIA is dissemination of authentic, accurate and timely information to prospective migrants. In order to realise these objectives, Migration Resource Centres (MRCs) have been established in Kerala, Andhra Pradesh, Haryana, and Punjab, and the ministry is likely to open MRCs in more states in the future. Additionally, in 2008, the Overseas Workers Resource Centre (OWRC) was opened in New Delhi with a 24/7 helpline service to provide information to emigrants and their families. In addition, the ministry is also implementing an e-Migrate system to make the migratory process more efficient, transparent and free from irregularities.

There is an element of uncertainty of work and life in the Gulf countries and as such every migrant is potentially a 'stranded' returnee. Migrants may be stranded for several reasons such as premature termination of contract, retrenchment, victimization, accident, illness, etc. The solution of the problem obviously lies in rehabilitation as well as repatriation of such workers. The MOIA has also introduced the Mahatma Gandhi Pravasi Suraksha Yojana (MGPSY), a pension-cum-life insurance scheme for Indian expatriate workers. It was introduced on a pilot basis from May 2012. The main objectives of MGPSY are to save for the future, to encourage the resettlement plans of emigrant workers, and to get a life insurance cover during natural death. In addition, the MOIA has also established the Indian Community Welfare Fund (ICWF) to provide assistance to overseas workers in times of difficulty and distress. The ministry data shows that over 28,421 workers have benefited from ICWF and that nearly Rs 373,829.447 had been spent till 2012.

For the protection and welfare of emigrants, the ministry had signed Memorandum of Understandings on labour with Qatar (2007), UAE (2006), Oman (2008), Kuwait (2007), Malaysia (2009), and Bahrain (2009); the MOIA is also negotiating with Yemen, Saudi Arabia and Jordan to sign agreements on labour welfare. Finally, it needs to be pointed out that the Emigration Act of 1983 is quite outdated and not equipped to handle the challenges of emigration as per current requirements. Thus the ministry has proposed the introduction of an Emigration Management Bill (EMB) in the Indian Parliament and this is likely to prove an innovative step in the protection and welfare of migrant workers.

Return migration

There are no adequate records of return migrant workers. The estimates for the late 1980s in the case of Kerala return migrant workers varied from about 20 per cent to 30 per cent (see Nayyar 1994: 35). The 1990–91 Gulf crisis, involving the annexation of Kuwait and the subsequent war in 1991, had greatly accelerated the return migration process. At least 150,000 Indians living in Kuwait and Iraq had been forced to return home (Jain 1991). Even during normal times, Gulf migrants continue to return home. In recent years, this figure has been running into tens of thousands. The data on return migration is confined to Kerala and in a survey report of Kerala, it was found that during 1999, about 740,000 Keralites had returned home. This figure increased to about 900,000 in 2003 and to 1,160,000 in 2008 (CDS 2011).

Whatever the reasons for return migration, a majority of the returnees faced numerous economic and social problems such as unemployment or underemployment, family disorganisation, marital discord, neglect of children's education, and psychological stress and strains on the remaining family members. The phenomenon of return migration thus throws up a number of problems which require careful attention of social scientists, social workers, social planners, and administrators.

There are several factors associated with return migration of Indian workers from the Gulf region. To begin with, in the late 1980s, there was a situation of economic recession in the oil-producing and exporting countries of West Asia. Consequently, these countries experienced structural changes in their economies which had a noticeable impact on their demographic structures. During the past two decades a similar situation had arisen in most Gulf countries which were already implementing measures to reduce dependence on foreign labour. The fear of 'cultural pollution', unemployment and demographic imbalance were cited as other reasons for reducing the dependence on foreign labour. Though the indigenisation policy has not been successful, it did create uncertainties in the labour market. Saudi Arabia's recent decision to implement Nitaqat law and the Kuwaiti government's crackdown on violating visa norms have further aggravated the situation for thousands of South Asian workers.

Impact of remittances

The economic and sociocultural impact of such contractual migration on both sending and receiving countries has not escaped the attention of social scientists. It has been found that the host countries benefit from such migration in terms of ready availability of skilled manpower which is cheap, unorganised and politically docile, incapable of creating any law and order problem. On the other hand, the impact of international migration in the sending countries can be seen in terms of reduction in unemployment and underemployment, occupational mobility, a construction boom, and the generation of new enterprises. Foreign employment can also lead to a drain of skilled workers, increased concentration of landholdings, higher land prices and social problems among family members left behind. Remittances from the GCC countries play a significant role in foreign exchange reserves, alleviation of poverty and the socio-economic development of India. Available data on the social and psychological impact of international migration in Asia suggests that such migration has both a positive and a negative impact on the family and community life of the migrants. Thus, in a study of the socio-economic conditions and problems of the Korean return migrants from the Middle East, it was found that the father's absence had a negative impact on children's education because of a decrease in discipline and motivation. Contrary to this, studies in the Philippines and Thailand suggested that education was one of the major objectives of expenditure, and remittances obviously helped in this regard (ESCAP 1986).

The remittances have helped the Gulf migrants from Kerala to improve their per capita income, acquire land and fixed and non-fixed assets, enhance the educational attainments of the younger generation, relatively improve the standard of living and access to health-care facilities, and also help in the overall reduction of poverty. Gulf migration has made a commendable contribution in the overall development of the Muslim-dominated Malappuram, Kannur and Kozhikode districts of Kerala. But, at the same time, the flow of remittances has resulted in an unprecedented hike in land prices and basic commodities, and has also lead to the commodification of health and educational services.

Another significant impact has been the commodification of religion and the large investment in religious activities by the newly-moneyed emigrants (Oscella and Oscella 2003). These changing patterns of religiosity and religious practices were obviously influenced by the migrant experiences based on the religious beliefs in their host countries. The proliferation of radical religious movements and sectarian political bargaining based on narrow religious identities in Kerala, which are being observed in the past 20 years, has a connection with the social transformation of Kerala society, influenced by migration.

Significantly, the non-migrant women or 'Gulf wives', as they are called, acquire a more independent outlook by having to manage the household, including financial transactions. In 2008, there were nearly 1.06 million Gulf wives in Kerala (Zachariah and Rajan 2012). It has been found that although such women start with a number of handicaps, they tend to become self-reliant over a period of time. They take on increased responsibilities for running the household on their own, and even for the management of money and property. Furthermore, the 'migration of men breaks down women's isolation, increases mobility and brings them into contact with wider network of institutions than were not in their purview before' (Gulati 1993: 144). On the whole, Gulf migration appears to have a positive impact on the women in India, as Rajan pointed out, as the 'the separation of the Gulf Wife from her emigrant husband made her more independent and self-autonomous' (Zacharia and Rajan 2012).

India remained the largest remittances-recipient country and received US$70 billion as remittances from overseas Indians in 2012. In 2012, India topped among the remittances recipient countries from GCC as it received US$29.7 billion followed by Pakistan (US$5.9 billion), Bangladesh US$3.78 billion), Sri

Lanka (US$2.7 billion), and Nepal (the lowest at US$ 1.8 billion). At the macro-economic level, remittances and investments made by non-resident Indians (NRIs) have played an important role in India's economic development. India's foreign exchange receipts from remittances have increased several times since 1990–91 when foreign exchange reserves had dipped to less than US$1 billion. NRI deposits have helped India immensely in averting its balance of payment crisis. There has been a steady increase in the remittances, except for a couple of years due to the decline in migration of Indian labour. The total remittances to India during 2005–06 were US$25 billion, tripling almost to US$70 billion in 2012. The break-up of the total remittances received by India from the GCC region is as follows: UAE US$14.2 billion, Saudi Arabia US$7.6 billion, Kuwait US$2.6 billion, Oman US$2.4 billion, Qatar US$2.1 billion, and Bahrain US$689.79 million.

The Gulf countries have emerged as the launching pad for Indians for immigrating to more liberal destinations like Britain, Canada, Australia, New Zealand, and the United States (US). A considerable number of NRI children in the Gulf take preliminary undergraduate courses in institutions run by Western countries that offer transfer facilities to the US, Australia, United Kingdom (UK), or Canada. Some of them eventually settle down in these countries.

Conclusion

Indian labour migration to the Gulf countries is about a century-old phenomenon. Initially, Indians went to Iran, Iraq and the Gulf to work for international oil companies in various capacities (Seccombe and Lawless 1986). Their number remained small until the Second World War, perhaps not more than 15,000. During the 1950s and 1960s, the number of Indian workers in the Gulf countries increased to about 50,000. Since then, as a result of the booming oil economies and the shortage of indigenous manpower in the Gulf countries, there has been a phenomenal increase in the number of Indians working there. Presently, there are about 5 million Indian workers in the Gulf region, employed in a wide variety of jobs.

In spite of drastic reduction in the pay and perks, harsh and sometimes humiliating work conditions, changing requirements of manpower and the increasing indigenisation of the workforce, an ever-increasing number of Indians have been making a beeline to the Gulf destinations. The phenomenon, however, appears to be understandable given the fact that besides unemployment and underemployment there are significant wage differentials between India and the Gulf countries. In other states of India the situation is more or less the same. Be that as it may, migration to the Gulf is still an attractive proposition for the country as well as individual migrants and their families. As such the Gulf countries continue to remain the El Dorado for an overwhelming number of Indian migrants. Minor fluctuations apart, the upward trend in Indian labour outflow to the Gulf countries is likely to continue. The following categories of workers will be in demand in the Gulf countries: professional, technical and related workers; administrative, executive and managerial workers; clerical and related workers; service workers; production and related workers; and transport equipment operators and labourers. The GCC countries serve as second home to about 6 million Indian expatriates. Indians make up about 31 per cent of the total expatriate population in the region and about 10 per cent of the total GCC population. The GCC countries as a block are also the biggest sources of NRI remittances into India.

References

Breedings, Mary. 2012. 'India-Persian Gulf Migration: Corruption and Capacity in Recruitment Agencies', in Mehran Kamrana and Zohra Babar (eds) *Migrant Labor in the Persian Gulf*, pp. 137–54. New York: Columbia University Press.

Centre for Development Studies. 2011. Kerala Migrant Survey, 2011. Trivandrum: Centre for Development Studies.

Commerce Research Bureau. 1978. *Emigration, Inward Remittances and Economic Growth of Kerala*. Bombay: Commerce Research Bureau.

Department of Economics and Statistics (DES). 1987. *The Report of the Survey on the Utilization of Gulf Remittances in Kerala*. Trivandrum: Department of Economics and Statistics, Government of Kerala.

Economic and Social Commission for Asia and the Pacific (ESCAP). 1986. *Returning Migrant Workers: Exploratory Study*. Bangkok: ESCAP.

Gulati, Leela. 1986. "The Impact on the Family of Male Migration to the Middle East: Some Evidences from Kerala, India", in Fred Arnold and Nasra M. Shah (eds.), *Asian Labour Migration: Pipeline to the Middle East*, pp. 194–212. Boulder and London: Westview Press.

———. 1993. *In the Absence of their Men: The Impact of Male Migration on the Women*. Delhi: Sage Publications.

Jain, Prakash C. 1991. 'The Social Implications of the Kuwaiti Crisis: Refugees, Returnees and Peripheral Changes', in A. H. H. Abidi and K. R. Singh (eds), *The Gulf Crisis*, pp. 156–76. Delhi: Lancers Books.

————. 2003a. 'An Incipient Diaspora: Indians in the Persian Gulf Region', in Bhikhu Parekh et al. (eds), *Culture and Economy in the Indian Diaspora*, pp. 102–24. London: Routledge.

Jain, Prakash C. 2003b. "Indian Diaspora in Yemen", *Journal of Indian Ocean Studies*, 11(1): 99–111.

————. 2005. 'Indian Labour Migration to the Gulf Countries: Past and Present', *India Quarterly*, 61(2): 50–81.

Kanchana, Radhika. 2012. 'Qatar's 'White Collar' Indians', in Prakash C. Jain and Kundan Kumar (eds) *Indian Trade Diaspora in the Arabian Peninsula*, pp. 303–24. New Delhi: New Academic Publishers.

Mathew, E. T. and P. R. G. Nair. 1978. 'Socio-Economic Characteristics of Emigrants and Emigrant Households: A Case Study of Two villages in Kerala', *Economic and Political Weekly*, 13(28): 1141–53.

Ministry of External Affairs, High Level Committee, Government of India, *High Level Committee Report on the Indian Diaspora*, Indian Council of World Affairs, Delhi, 2001.

Ministry of Labour and Employment. 2002. *Annual Report, 2002*. New Delhi: Government of India.

————. 2003. *Annual Report, 2003*. New Delhi: Government of India.

————. 2005. *Annual Report, 2004–2005*. New Delhi: Government of India.

Ministry of Overseas Indian Affairs. (2009, 2010, 2011, 2012–13). Annual Reports. New Delhi: Government of India.

Nair, P. R. Gopinathan. 1986. 'India', in Godfrey Gunatilleke (ed.), *Migration of Asian Workers to the Arab World*, pp. 66–109. Tokyo: The U. N. University.

Nayyar, Deepak. 1994. *Migration, Remittances and Capital Flows: The Indian Experience*. Delhi: Oxford University Press.

Oishi, Nana. 2005. *Women in Motion: Globalisation, State Policies and Labour Migration in Asia*. Stanford: Stanford University Press.

Oscella, Filippo and Caroline Oscella. 2003. 'Migration and Commoditisation of Ritual: Sacrifice, Spectacle and Contestations in Kerala', *Contributions to Indian Sociology*, 37 (1–2): 109–39.

Percot, Marie. 2006. 'Indian Nurses in the Gulf: Two Generations of Female Migration', *South Asia Research*, 26(1): 41–62.

Prakash, B. A. 1978. 'Impact of Foreign Remittances: A Case Study of Chavakkad Village in Kerala', *Economic and Political Weekly*, 13(27): 1107–11.

Rahman, Anisur 2001. *Indian Labour Migration to West Asia*. Delhi: Rajat Publications.

Rajan, S. Irudaya and S. Sukendran. 2010. 'Understanding Female Migration: Experience of House Maids', in S. Irudaya Rajan (ed.), *Governance and Labour Migration: Indian Migration Report*. New Delhi: Routledge.

Rajan, S. Irudaya and K. C. Zachariah (eds). 2012. *Kerala's Demographic Future: Issues and Policy Option*. New Delhi: Academic Foundation.

Srivastava, Ravi and S. K. Sasikumar. 2003. 'An Overview of Migration in India: Its Impact and Key Issues', Paper presented at the Regional

Conference on Migration, Development and Pro-poor Policy Choices in Asia, Jointly organised by Department for International Development (DFID) and the Refugee and Migratory Movements Research Unit (RMMRU), University of Dhaka, 22–24 June, Dhaka

Seccombe, I. J. and R. I. Lawless. 1986. 'Foreign Workers Dependence in the Gulf and the International Oil Companies 1910–50', *International Migration Review*, 20(3): 548–74.

Shah, Nashra. 2009a. The Management of Irregular Migration and its Consequence for Development, Gulf Cooperation Council. Working Paper No. 19, March. International Labour Organization.

Shah, Nasra M. 2009b. 'Relative Success of Male Workers in the Host Country, Kuwait: Does the Channel of Migration Matter?', *International Migration Review*, 34(1): 59–78.

Zachariah, K. C. and S. Irudaya Rajan. 2004. 'Gulf Revisited: Economic Consequences of Emigration from Kerala' (Emigration and Unemployment), Working Paper Series 363, Centre for Development Studies, Thiruvanthapuram.

Zachariah, K.C. and S. Irudaya Rajan. 2012. *Kerala's Gulf Connection, 1998–2011: Economic and Social Impact of Migration*. New Delhi: Orient BlackSwan.

Zachariah, K. C., K. P. Kannan and S. Irudaya Rajan. 2002. *Kerala's Gulf Connection: CDS Studies on International Labour Migration from Kerala State in India*. Thiruvananthapuram: Centre for Development Studies.

Zachariah, K. C, B. A. Prakash and S. Irudaya Rajan. 2004. 'Indian Workers in UAE: Employment, Wages and Working Conditions', *Economic and Political Weekly*, Vol XXXIX (22): 2227–34.

6

Spatial mobility and migratory strategies of Kerala's immigrants in the United Arab Emirates (UAE)

Philippe Venier

Introduction

A large majority of the population living in the cities of the United Arab Emirates (UAE) is of foreign origin. These immigrants constitute about 85 per cent of the total population of the country and even a higher proportion of the manpower. Since the mid-1980s, migration flows from Asia have been predominant and account for more than half of the total population. This unique demographic situation of the country, that of a large number of migrants, is reinforced by another specificity related to international labour migration – that these migrants are exclusively under contract and therefore temporary. In other words, the foreign manpower is continually renewed on the basis of a limited working permit.

However, with this principle of a temporary expatriation still in force, new strategies have appeared among some socio-professional categories of immigrants. Taking advantage of the evolution of the immigration policy and using opportunities of emerging global economy and metropolisation, the migratory projects have been redefined towards longer stays, an increase in the number of families and in a more stable socio-economic position. This chapter discusses the case of these settlements among Indian immigrants and, more precisely, among those coming from the state of Kerala. In fact, for several decades, the Malayalee community has been representing more or less half of the Indians living in the UAE. The same can be observed regarding the proportion of families. It is for these reasons that this group is largely influenced by the economic dynamics and the urban development of the emirate cities.

Indian immigrants: majority of Keralites

With about 1.3 million immigrants out of a total population estimated at around 4.8 million[1], Indians are one of the most important
expatriate groups living in the UAE. If we look at the state of origin,
Kerala emerges as the main sending place from India. A rough figure of 0.8 million has been given by Zachariah and Rajan (2012),
making this community account for a little less than two-thirds of
the Indian immigrants, and about one inhabitant out of six living
in the country. The specificity of the migratory dynamics between
Kerala and the UAE is not only related to the quantitative aspect,
because, unlike other states of India, international emigration in
Kerala is almost exclusively oriented towards the Gulf countries.
In fact, the region accounts for more than 90 per cent of the total
Keralite international emigration and the UAE itself accounts for
40 per cent to 45 per cent of these flows.

The migratory relations between the Gulf and Kerala have
existed for several centuries through commercial and cultural
exchanges. However, the massive migration to the Gulf started only
in the beginning of the 1970s. Since then, three major emigration
waves have been identified: the first one related to the oil boom of
1973–74, when the UAE, newly independent, launched an ambitious economic programme based on the development of industrialisation and the construction sector, and on the improvement of
infrastructure and the services sector. The lack of local manpower
induced an active immigration policy (Beaugé 1991; Alkobaisi and
Khalaf 1999). Three main reasons were behind the choice of orient-
ing the demand for Asian labourers. First, the traditional source of
immigrants coming from the Middle East and the Near East regions
was not large enough to supply the demand. Second, South Asian
workers were considered more docile, ready to work for lower
wages and without demanding any rights. Third, it was easier to
control migration flows through an exclusive temporary and contractual expatriation. In the beginning of the 1980s, consequently,
the number of Keralites living in the UAE was around 100,000
(Department of Economics and Statistics 1987).

The second massive flow began after 1991, closely related with
the invasion of Kuwait by Iraq, when hundreds of thousands of
Arab immigrants were expelled from the Gulf countries due to
the position of their country in favour of the invasion. Also, the
decrease of South East Asian immigrants gave a new opportunity

to South Asians. In 1998, about 400,000 Keralites were living in the UAE (Zachariah, Mathew and Rajan 2003). The last wave of the immigration flux from South Asia appeared in the beginning of the 21st century. The events of 2001 and 2003 (Twin Towers in New York and the invasion of Iraq by the United States) created a general geopolitical instability in the Persian Gulf. However, the small petro-monarchies, such as the UAE, were seen as politically and economically stable at the regional scale. During the same decade, the oil price hike, the acceleration of globalisation and the metropolisation processes of the state-cities of Dubai and Abu Dhabi produced important economic growth, particularly noticeable in sectors such as industry, international commerce, services and the real estate businesses. Regarding the Keralite immigration, this third massive flow has modified the general position of the migrants in the labour market. Until the 1990s, within the Indian expatriates, the Malayalees were largely employed in unskilled or semi-skilled jobs, mainly in industries, construction or services sectors.

However, for a decade now, an increase in the proportion of qualified migrants working as administrative heads, accountants, technical professionals, engineers, and others has been noticed. In spite of the lack of statistics on the issue in the host country, a study by Zachariah and Rajan in 2007 shows this evolution: in 1998, 10.5 per cent of Keralite immigrants in the Gulf held a degree or more. In 2007, this percentage reached 19.4 per cent. Simultaneously, the number of those without any qualification was decreasing (Zachariah and Rajan 2007: 32). Many reasons explain this general improvement of the migrants' profiles: the higher education level in Kerala for the last 30 years; more accurate selection of job offers by candidates for emigration; increase in the cost of migration which reduces the chance to reimburse it and which, therefore, reduces the number of unskilled migrants; as well as development of entrepreneurial initiatives among Keralite expatriates in the UAE. But some other important sociological reasons are also operating: the increase in emigration from other states such as Tamil Nadu, Andhra Pradesh and now the northern states of India provides crucial unskilled or semi-skilled manpower that is ready to work for lower wages and which is more docile than the Keralite worker!

The second reason is illustrated best by this example: during fieldwork in Dubai in 2010, we met a human resources manager from Kerala. He was in charge of recruiting 700 unskilled Indian workers in the building sector. He told us that he was unwilling to send the contracts to his village in Kerala. According to him, no one would accept such contracts and, moreover, he would be discredited by doing so. Consequently, he looked for Tamils or Telugus. Ten or 15 years earlier, this choice would never have occurred to him. His social prestige and financial benefits would have been sufficient enough. One major consequence of this recent evolution in the proportion of qualified Keralite migrants is the redefinition of migratory strategies. Indeed, the duration of expatriation has expanded, the desire for a good life 'here and now', instead of building a better future after the migration period, has become more common among highly skilled professionals and entrepreneurs. This form of longer-term settlements is particularly visible through family reunification.

Evolution of migratory strategies: longer settlements and family reunifications

The evolution of migratory strategies can be excellently perceived through family reunification, and it is thanks to information regarding women's migration that family reunification dynamics can be better grasped. Generally speaking, gender differentiation is one of the characteristics of Asian migration to the Gulf countries. Migration flows from Sri Lanka or the Philippines are mainly constituted of female migrants, whereas those from Pakistan or India constitute mainly male migrants. In the case of Kerala, until the end of the 20th century, men represented between 91 per cent and 95 per cent of the expatriates (Venier 2003). However, this over-represented male migration has tended to diminish during the last decade. In 2003, compared to 1998, the proportion of women had almost doubled, from 9 per cent to 17 per cent of the total Keralite migrants living in the UAE (Zachariah and Rajan 2007: 64). The 2011 figure gives a slight decline in the percentage of female migrants: around 15 per cent (Zachariah and Rajan 2012: 48). It is also to be noted that the proportion of married women changed from about 75 per cent to around 52 per cent (ibid.: 50). Considering these figures, we can reasonably estimate that more than 100,000 Keralite couples lived in the UAE at the beginning of the century and around 60,000 were still expatriates in the country in 2011. Concurring with this data, personal interviews carried out in 2004, 2007 and 2010 showed the same trend: an increase of families until 2008 and a slight decline or a stabilisation thereafter.

What then are the factors that have contributed to this increase in family reunifications?

The impact of legislation

One of the first legislations regarding family reunification has been linked to migrants' income. As a matter of fact, a migrant has to prove that his monthly income is above 4,000 emirate Dirhams (2010 value) or above 3,000 Dirhams if he/she gets free accommodation. The migrant's family can then get a resident permit for three years, which is renewable. Moreover, since 2001, a migrant himself can be the sponsor of his wife and his kids (only those under 18). If the children are above 18 years of age, they must be registered at university in order to be sponsored a migrant. This right, defined according to the monthly income, de facto excludes most migrants. For the UAE, it is a way of selecting the most qualified migrants while offering only a minority a decent life with their family. In fact, a kind of deal – a declaration of a false salary – is done between the employer and the employee when the salary of the latest does not reach the authorised limit. It is often the case in the poorest states of the UAE (Ras al-Khaimah, Umm al-Quwain, Fujairah) where the cost of living is less than in Dubai or Abu Dhabi. On the contrary, it is not enough to earn more than 4,000 Dirhams to be eligible. The administration investigates the migrant's job and the status of the company before accepting the demand of family reunification. It is obvious that some professions are excluded from the procedure, for example, some small traders. Thus, there is a double selective legislation: monthly income and type of employment.

This legislation of family reunification is inserted into the immigration policy which is itself inserted in a global economic development policy (Cadene and Dumortier 2009; Janardhan 2011). Two aspects are particularly highlighted: the employment of the most qualified and the foreign entrepreneurial initiatives. Regarding the first category, two governmental measures have been taken: in 2001, it became possible for professionals of some sectors to change their sponsor. It means that they were de facto allowed to change jobs. The second measure, from 2003 onwards, related to the education level of the migrants who should be at least above the Secondary School Leaving Certificate (SSLC) level. The objective was clearly to uplift the 'quality' of the new migrants.

Such measures have undoubtedly given an advantage to migrants from Kerala. The aspect on entrepreneurship has progressively been set up since the end of the 1990s (Venier 2011). In other words, a foreign entrepreneur can be the sponsor of his employees. He can also be free of sponsorship in the free zones and enjoys different advantages for investments and partnerships with locals.

Through this presentation of the main legislative aspects related to family reunification and qualified migrants, we notice that the unique objective of the immigration policy of the UAE is to fulfil their economic development through a softening of the highly skilled labour market and structured support to foreign entrepreneurial initiatives (Rycx 2005: 262). This policy has facilitated the redefining of migratory strategies among the most qualified expatriates (Percot and Nair 2011). However, other factors, such as the numerical importance of the Keralite community and its long-term presence, have also undoubtedly played a role in the evolution of migratory strategies.

The wish of a 'real life'

With the third migratory wave came a fundamental change in the idea of 'life as an expatriate,' at least among a part of the Keralite community. This change can be illustrated by the typical sentences collected from many interviews: 'I want a life here' or 'Savings are secondary, you know, we have only one life'. Such expressions reveal the will to be a part of the global society and its consumption attitude. In other words, a kind of 'consumer citizenship' is appearing. This new generation of migrants no longer has the unique obsession of sparing and saving money during the time of migration so as to build a better future in Kerala. Now, it is through going to malls or shopping complexes in different cities or driving fast on highways that migrants derive pleasure and satisfaction and their ostentatious presence can be highlighted. This attitude, which was of a tiny minority of bachelor male migrants 15 or 20 years ago, has become the general attitude among professionals, bachelors or married migrants. In other words, the Indian (Keralite) migrant has become *visible* in public consumption spaces.

This new conception of the migration experience has less to do with the socio-economic transformation of the Emirati society than with the evolution of the Keralite society, deeply modified by

40 years of intense emigration to the Gulf countries (Venier 2009). In fact, it was in the 1990s that the perception of migration to the Gulf began to change. It was the time of the second migration wave and the first massive return of emigrants. Keralites living in the *Gulf pockets* are aware of the reality of expatriation, even for the skilled migrants: frustration, deprivation, obsession with savings, and an absence of a social life. Those who left for the Gulf by the end of the 1990s were aware of the socio-psychological situation. It is in this context that migratory projects started to be modified among the new generation of qualified migrants: why should they experience a hard time in the Gulf for a hypothetical better socio-economic position on their return home?

The changes in the migration experience were also influenced by the evolution of gender relations. Indeed, the improvement in the educational level among women and the development of the nuclear family has led to an increase in married women being able to join their husbands in migration. The wish to have a 'good life' in the Gulf encourages family reunification. Changes have also been facilitated by the development of job opportunities for women, for example, in the health sector and in services (as secretaries, office employees, etc.). Keralite wives, with their educational qualifications, undoubtedly have some advantages in the women's labour market in the UAE. Moreover, having a second source of income is often a necessity for living a 'decent life.' Another important factor which has helped to redefine migratory strategies is related to the development of airways between Kerala and the Gulf countries. With now three international airports in northern (Kozhikode), central (Kochi) and southern Kerala (Thiruvananthapuram), there are numerous daily flights. Fares are also relatively cheaper compared to the 1980s or 1990s. The frequency of short returns is thus facilitated. New technologies, like mobile phones or the Internet, are also factors which help in keeping relations 'tight' with Kerala. In other words, the space-time conundrum between the two parts of the Arabian Sea has been greatly reduced. Migration is progressively perceived less as a spatial distance and a 'physical break' with the country of origin. In fact, it has become quite common to hear people in Kerala saying that UAE cities are 'less abroad' than north Indian states, or that 'Dubai is the capital of Kerala'! The size of the Keralite community and its increasing visibility in the urban space play a major role in this perception.

'Little Kerala' in the UAE

When staying in the UAE, one of the first things to be noticed is the visibility of South Indians, and particularly Keralites, in public spaces such as streets, shops, malls, offices, industrial areas and recreational spaces. This specific visibility of an immigrant group is also expressed by an important social and cultural environment. Keralite associations exist in every UAE city. Simply named as *Indian associations*, most of them (if not all) are controlled by Keralites and people who go to these places are in a large majority Keralite migrants. One of the main activities of these associations is to offer cultural activities such as dancing and music performances, songs, sport events or conferences. National day celebrations are also an occasion to gather and have lunch or dinner together. Moreover, it is a place where Indian citizens can come and meet officers of the Indian embassy, who are present there some days in a week. Indians schools are another sign of the changes in migratory strategies towards a longer settlement for the more qualified migrants. Since the 1990s, the number of educational institutions has doubled in Dubai and Sharjah. In the northern and eastern city-states like Umm-al-Quwain, Ras-al-Khaimah and Fujairah, the number of Indian pupils has doubled. All these Indian schools offer an Indian syllabus but also a 'Kerala syllabus' due to the fact that a majority of the people are from Kerala. It is therefore possible for a Keralite family to provide an education to their children which is recognised by India (at least up to high school), when it comes to the access to universities. In other words, there is no break in education or any disadvantage for the young ones. Finally, the numerous Malayalam radios, TV channels and newspapers that exist in the UAE cities have helped maintain and develop Keralite culture and identity. Music, films, food items and other various cultural items are also available everywhere.

Spatially, the visibility of the Keralite community is defined by some urban quarters named 'Little Kerala'. In Dubai, it is in the commercial and residential neighbourhood of Al Karama where the concentration of Keralites is the most important, while, in Sharjah, it is located around Rollah square. However, in other small city-states in the north and east coast, little Kerala does not exist. The foreign population and ethnic activities are more widespread in the urban space. This spatial distinction between the UAE cities can also be apprehended through family reunification dynamics.

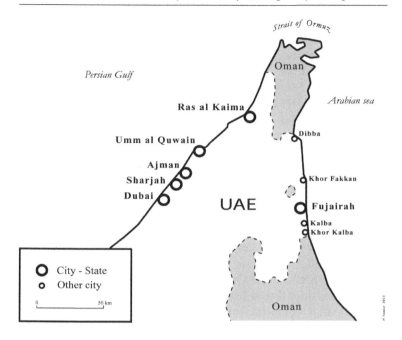

Figure 6.1 City-states and cities of the UAE

Source: Prepared by Philippe Venier.

Family reunification dynamics: spatial differences

For the state as a whole, family reunification among Keralites has clearly increased since the beginning of the 21st century. Nevertheless, a slowdown of the dynamics has been noticeable over the past five or six years. Two different migratory tendencies can be highlighted.

The Dubai–Sharjah–Ajman conurbation: stabilisation of family settlements

'More families live in Dubai or Sharjah? Of course not! It is the opposite! Women and children are being sent back to Kerala. Only those who can afford it stay here. And their move from Dubai to Sharjah or from Sharjah to Ajman [is] in order to reduce the rent and the cost of living.' In few sentences, the president of the Indian Association Sharjah has summed up the situation![2]

It was in the beginning of 2000 that the move from Dubai to Sharjah started for middle-class migrants. The increase of rents and of daily life expenses pushed families to live farther away from their working places. The increase in car traffic jams on larger and larger highways (up to 10 ways nowadays) between the two emirates reveals this situation. The urbanisation boom in Sharjah also gives a significant demonstration of this spatial mobility. About 10 years ago, a vast desert space existed between the two cities. Then, a few blocks of small skyscrapers started to emerge from the sand. Each of them was progressively brought together by new blocks. Today, a 'forest of skyscrapers' makes an urban continuity between Dubai and Sharjah. The same process of rapid urbanisation is being observed between the two emirates of Sharjah and Ajman. This domino effect from Dubai to Ajman will continue to extend towards Umm al-Quwain, the emirate north from Ajman, and even north of Ras al-Khaimah, though to a smaller extent.

Such spatial mobilities within the conurbation result in the return of some families back to Kerala. In fact, ordinary managerial staff, once allowed to bring their families, can't afford to stay if their wives do not provide a second salary. An increase in rents has followed the urbanisation process. Even if rents of flats decrease from Dubai to the northern city-states, there are additional expenditures. Migrants must buy a car because of the lack of public transport. Moreover, with longer distances between homes and workplaces, the time spent on transport is increasing. School fees and daily life expenses have also increased. In this context, the solution for qualified migrants could be to change jobs in order to get better wages and/or to be closer to their residence. This job mobility is allowed, but a no objection certificate (NOC) given by the employer is needed. But, tensions in the qualified labour market most often lead to a refusal on the part of the employer. Therefore, it is almost impossible to answer the increase of the cost of living with professional mobility.

Taking into account the difficulties regarding family reunification, two general trends emerge. The number of families with children gradually decreases from Dubai to Ajman. In fact, during the last years, Indian schools have registered a stabilisation in numbers in their pupils originating from the middle class. For childless young couples, it seems that the family reunification is still increasing slightly in the conurbation. The housing problem (cost of rent, long distance from jobs) is solved by flat sharing. In the Newspapers or small posters in Malayalam, stuck on Little Keralas' streets, one can see thousands of announcements such as 'Available sharing accommodation for Keralite couple/small family' or 'To let, 2-bedroom sharing for Keralite couple'. This flat sharing, well set up in Dubai and Sharjah, is spreading to Ajman and now to the northern city-states. The recent evolution of settlement strategies among Keralite migrants reveals the socio-spatial dynamics existing in the west coast cities of the UAE. The progressive slow-down or reduction in the number of middle-class expatriate families questions the relative opening up of the immigration policy of the country, launched from the 1990s onwards. Meanwhile, urban mobilities from the south to the north of the Dubai–Sharjah–Ajman conurbation have led to a socio-economic hierarchical organisation.

The east coast: new spaces for family settlements

Five main cities line up the 70 kilometres of seashore opened on the Arabian Sea. The most important is Fujairah, one of the seven city-states of the UAE. In the north, the city of Dibba is attached to the emirate of Sharjah for one part and to the emirate of Fujairah for another part. Between the two cities, Khor Fakkan is a territory of Fujairah emirate. In the south, Kalba and Khor Kalba are close to Oman state. Separated from the west coast by a desert mountain range, the east coast of the UAE is also a sparsely populated area. Its population, almost totally urban, is estimated to be around 200,000–240,000 inhabitants. Nevertheless, the proportion of Indian expatriates is more important than in the west coast, that is to say about one-third of the total population. As for the Keralites, if their proportion among Indian immigrants is taken in the national average, they represent about one-fifth of the total population.

Another specificity characterises the Keralite community: globally speaking, they have a better socio-economic position among the Indian expatriates compared to the west coast cities where it is the Gujarati community which occupies the top socio-economic position. In fact, the east coast cities are relatively poor. The lack of oil resources, the weakness of the industrial and services sectors, until recently, have reduced the presence of Gujarati businesses.

Therefore, with their administrative and managerial skills, the Keralites have taken the key posts since the first migration wave in the 1970s. So, even if the main foreign labour force is still composed of Keralites[3], an important minority are qualified. Consequently, the proportion of families here has been more important than elsewhere in the UAE. And, for the last 10 or 15 years, the family reunification dynamics has been increasing.

It is through the number of pupils in schools that we can appreciate the increase of the number of Keralite families. The Indian School of Fujairah opened in 1980. In 1995, the pupils in the school numbered about 500. Ten years later, they were 950. In 2010, around 1,400 pupils were registered. Around 85 per cent of the pupils in this educational institution are Keralites. Another example: Our Own School opened in Fujairah in 1988. In 2002, 1,200 pupils were registered. In 2007, they were 2,000. Since then, the number of pupils is still going up. Due to the fact that this institution provides an English syllabus, only half of the pupils are of Indian origin (a large majority are Keralites). A third school which offers the Indian (and Kerala) syllabus is Saint Mary's School in Fujairah. Like the others, the increase of pupils has been noticeable over the last 15 years.[4]

The development of these educational institutions reveals the socio-economic changes of the east coast of the UAE. 'Since 2007, there has been a rapid development of economic activities. The population is increasing. Traffic on roads and streets is more intense.' This comment of a Keralite entrepreneur in the construction sector, settled in 1984 in Fujairah, is followed by another one:

> The construction boom started in 2005 or 2006. It is the people [locals] from Dubai and Sharjah who started to invest in the sector. Indeed, it's a good business because the [immigrant] population is increasing and the cost of the plot of land and the construction is lower than in the west coast. The locals [from Fujairah emirate] are not wealthy enough to do that. They have the land and they sell it. Only five or six local families are well-off, the others are from the middle and lower classes.'

These investments in the construction sector are related to the economic growth of the region. For a few years, the Fujairah and Khor Fakkan harbours have become important hubs for oil and containers transport. Close to these harbours, industrial zones, like the Fujairah Free Zone, have been built. The development of these harbours is conducted by a joint venture between the Fujairah Port Authority and the Dubai Port Authority; for Khor Fakkan, it is a collaboration between the Fujairah emirate and the Sharjah emirate.

Many reasons explain the industrial development of the east coast. First, the seaside offers deep water harbours contrary to the Persian Gulf seaside. Second, they open onto the Oman Sea and therefore to Asia and its emerging countries. The cost of land and construction is also cheaper than on the West coast (about three times less in 2010). The harbours of Dubai are saturated for the containers. But, more fundamentally, the economic and maritime development of the east coast is linked to geopolitical issues. Constraints and risks at the Strait of Ormuz, such as density of traffic, transit taxes and military tensions, are avoided. Consequently, exchanges between the east and the west coasts are rapidly increasing. A new highway from Kalba to Sharjah/Dubai and further to Jebel Ali harbour is crowded with trucks carrying containers. A new pipeline has also been constructed.

The development of economic activities along the east coast of the UAE has led to an increase in immigrants, particularly those coming from the South Asia region. Together with the demand for unskilled or semi-skilled manpower, the need for qualified migrants has also increased. And the Keralite community has indubitable advantages. Therefore, for a decade, the third migration wave has brought more and more families. Internal migration flows are also noticed with the move of Keralite families from the west coast to the east coast; it is rarely professional mobility on the migrant's initiative. Rather it is due to the restructuring of enterprises or the setting up of new ones in the industrial and commercial zones along the east coast. Until now, the growth of the population has not questioned the family reunification dynamics. Rents and cost of living still allow middle-class families to stay. However, we start to notice some urban mobility from Fujairah to Kalba and even now to Khor Kalba where rents are cheaper. Is it the beginnings of a domino effect just like on the west coast? Will an east-side conurbation appear? Transport infrastructures are already completed and we can see new building areas emerging from the sand all along the coast. Then, in a short period of time, will these assist to the return of the more modest families back to Kerala?

Conclusion

Migratory strategies through family reunification reveal the socio-economic development within the different urban spaces of the UAE. In the Dubai-Sharjah-Ajman conurbation, with its strong commercial identity, the numbers of immigrant families are progressively decreasing or are moving to the urban margins which are naturally more distant. From this conurbation, two axes of development can be identified: the first one, to the north, towards the emirates of Umm-al-Quwain and Ras-al Khaimah, the second one, towards the east coast of the country. These urban spaces become then the new places of settlement of the most qualified Keralite migrants. The redefinition of family settlement strategies is related to the processes of metropolisation and globalisation. In the 'global city' of Dubai, the socio-spatial segregation of the immigrant population has been speeded up and diffused to other city-states. In this context, some families go back to Kerala despite an immigration policy which has become more flexible for family reunification.

The economic development of India also questions these settlement strategies of families. For some highly skilled migrants, the difference of salary between the two countries is now reducing. Moreover, the emergence of a consumer society in India, together with access to goods, services and housing with the same standards as in the Gulf, leads to a similar way of life. Therefore, despite a more favourable UAE policy for professional mobility – in order to retain the most qualified migrants – the increasing difficulties linked to cost of living may push more and more Keralite families to reconsider their stay in the host country.

However, things are different for a minority of well-off Keralite families. The commercial and business identity of the 'global city' has produced new forms of longer settlements among entrepreneurs and businessmen. It is obvious with the second generation which is born and brought up in the UAE.

Finally, another migratory strategy emerges among the most qualified migrants. The family reunification process and the time spent in the UAE are perceived as a temporary period before a re-emigration to the West (Percot and Nair 2011). It concerns highly skilled young couples migrating from Kerala or couples/bachelors from a second generation of migrants. The increasing value of their skills in the international labour market opens new opportunities in the most developed countries. To conclude, through the analysis of the spatial mobility and migratory strategies of Keralites, we witness an increasing complexity of international Indian migration which reflects the globalisation and metropolisation processes occurring today in the Gulf countries.

Notes

1 It is difficult to give precise figures due to the lack of reliable data on demographic issues.
2 Personal interview, January 2010.
3 The labour manpower has been more recently composed of Tamil and Telugu immigrants. This information is taken from interviews of two 'leaders' of the Keralite community. Settled in Fujairah since 1981 and 1984, the first one is managing the Fujairah ruler family businesses (Al Sharqi) and the second one is an entrepreneur in the building construction sector.
4 No precise data about the evolution of the number of pupils.

References

Alkobaisi, S. and S. Khalaf. 1999. 'Migrant's Strategies of Coping and Patterns of Accommodation in the Oil-rich Gulf Societies: Evidence from the UAE', *British Journal of Middle Eastern Studies*, 26(2) : 271–91.

Battegay A. 2005. 'Dubaï: économie marchande et carrefour migratoire. Etude de mise en dispositif', in A. Jaber and F. Metral (eds), *Mondes en mouvements. Migrants et migrations au Moyen-Orient au tournant du XXIe siècle*, pp. 271–91. Beyrouth, Lebanon: IFPO.

Beaugé, G. 1991. 'Les migrations au Moyen-Orient: tendances et perspectives', *Les migrations dans le monde arabe. ss dir de Beaugé G. et de Buttner F*, CNRS Edition, société arabes et musulmanes, 4 : 9–28.

Cadene P. and B. Dumortier. 2009. 'Les pays du Conseil de coopération du Golfe: à nouvelles tendances migratoires, nouvelles politiques?', *Maghreb-Mashrek*, 199 : 101–19.

Department of Economics and Statistics. 1987. *Report of the Survey on the Utilization of Gulf Remittances in Kerala*, Department of Economics and Statistics, Government of Kerala, Thiruvananthapuram.

Dumortier, B. and Marc Lavergne. 2002. 'Dubaï, ville du pétrole ou projet métropolitain post-pétrolier?', *Annales de Géographie*, 623: 41–59.

Janardhan, N. 2011. *Boom Amid Gloom – The Spirit of Possibility in the 21st Century Gulf*. Reading: Ithaca Press.

Marchal, R., F. Adelkhah and S. Hanafi. 2001. *Dubaï, cité global*. Paris: CNRS Edition.

Percot, M. and S. Nair. 2011. 'Transcending Boundaries: Indian Nurses in Internal and International Migration', in M. Percot and I. Rajan (eds),

Dynamics of Indian Migration. Historical and Current Perspectives, pp. 107–32. New Delhi : Routledge.

Rycx, J.-F. 2005. 'Le "sponsorship" peut-il encore canaliser les flux migratoires dans les pays du Golfe ? Le cas des Emirats arabes unis', in A. Jaber and F. Metral (eds), Mondes en mouvements. *Migrants et migrations au Moyen-Orient au tournant du XXIe siècle*, pp. 245–70. Beyrouth, Lebanon: IFPO.

Venier, P. 2003.*Travail dans le Golfe persique et développement au Kérala. Les migrants internationaux, des acteurs au coeur des enjeux sociaux et territoriaux*, Thèse de doctorat de géographie, Université de Poitiers, 497 pp.

———. 2009. 'Stratégies d'ancrage des immigrés kéralais (Inde du Sud) dans les villes des Emirats Arabes Unis', *Maghreb-Mashrek*, 199: 121–38.

———. 2011. 'Development of Entrepreneurial Initiatives in the UAE among Kerala Emigrants', in M. Percot and I. Rajan (eds), *Dynamics of Indian Migration. Historical and Current Perspectives*, pp. 165–94. New Delhi: Routledge.

Zachariah, K. C. and S. Irudaya Rajan.. 2007. Migration, Remittances and Employment. Short-term Trends and Long-term Implications, Working paper No. 395, Centre for Development Studies, Thiruvananthapuram, Kerala (www.cds.edu).

———. 2012. 'Inflexion in Kerala's Gulf connection. Report on Kerala Migration Survey 2011', Working paper No. 450, CDS, Thiruvananthapuram, Kerala (www.cds.edu).

Zachariah, K. C., E.T. MATHEW and S. Irudaya Rajan. 2003. *Dynamics of Migration in Kerala. Dimensions, Differentials and Consequences*. New Delhi: Orient Longman.

7

Revisiting the saga of Bangladeshi labour migration to the Gulf states

Need for new theoretical and methodological approaches

Rita Afsar[1]

Introduction

In recent years, migration has received policy focus as a viable livelihood option and as a major development mantra in many developing countries including Bangladesh, partly because of the increasing flow of remittances. Officially recorded remittances to developing countries have reached more than US$400 billion dollars approximately in 2012 and are expected to grow further to US$515 billion in 2015. Remittances help sustain growth and development in competitive global and ever expanding local markets and are both directly and indirectly linked to poverty reduction. According to the World Bank (2013), South Asia has emerged as the largest recipient of remittances in Asia in 2012 along with South East Asia due mainly to India's consistent top ranking along with the increased remittances flow to Bangladesh and Pakistan.

Between 1976 and 2012, more than 6 million Bangladeshi nationals migrated to the Gulf states, accounting for more than three-quarters of the total labour outmigration from the country. Remittances sent by migrants through official channels reached a record high level at US$14 billion in 2012, nearly two-thirds of which were generated by the sweat and blood of the temporary labour that had migrated to the Gulf states.

There are hundreds of studies and thousands of media stories on Bangladeshi labour migration to Arab countries. These studies and stories together highlighted different dimensions of migration such as context, causes, process and consequences. While some of the facts and findings encompassing these dimensions are well established, others are not so focused. Aspects such as wage differentials and attractions of the Middle East, exploitation of migrant workers (especially women in host countries), productive and non-productive use of remittances, links between migration and development, whether migration is beneficial for migrants and their families received disproportionately large attention in the media and in research.

However, there are complexities and nuances in migration decision-making, the process of implementation and recruitment, and in measuring the types of conditions and plausible factors associated with migration outcomes that have not received as much attention. This chapter presents a narrative of Bangladeshi labour migration to the Gulf states and identifies its distinct characteristics, established over time.

This chapter mainly analyses the complexities and nuances in migration decision-making, including implementation and recruitment processes that are not so well documented. Also, by using an innovative approach, it attempts to measure the multidimensionality involved in migration outcomes. The narrative draws largely on the author's empirical studies conducted in the early and late 2000s and also from the secondary literature.

Essentially, the chapter is divided into four parts. After this brief introduction, part two identifies some of the distinct characteristics of labour migration from Bangladesh to the Gulf states, based on a thorough review of the literature. It presents the inside story of the migration decision-making process by analysing causal and contextual factors involved in the process. It also highlights the important role played by migrants' social networks as well as recruitment agencies and sub-agents in inducing the crave for a 'bhalo' visa (one that would yield better work opportunities and higher incomes) and providing the necessary services for implementing the migration decision and channelling migration from the country's every nook and cranny to the Gulf states. By developing an innovative approach with the help of carefully chosen indicators, part four identifies the multiple dimensions involved in analysing migration outcomes and the plausible factors that influence those outcomes. It also presents the concluding remarks.

Characterising Bangladeshi labour migration to the Gulf States

Gulf states have generated the highest demand for Bangladeshi labour

According to official statistics, around 8.4 million Bangladeshi nationals migrated abroad for work, of which 6.5 million or more than three-quarters (77 per cent) went to the Gulf Cooperation Council (GCC) countries from mid-1976 till December 2012.[2] The corresponding figures for the most recent era (from 2000 to 2012) were recorded at 5.5 million and 4.2 million respectively, although the proportion of emigrants to the GCC countries (76 per cent) remained almost unchanged. Among the GCC countries, the Kingdom of Saudi Arabia (KSA) and United Arab Emirates (UAE) were the key players as their share of the total emigrants to the region ranged between 75 per cent and 80 per cent during the reference period. Also, outside the region, together these two countries exported almost two-thirds (59 per cent) of the total Bangladeshi migrants (Table 7.1).

Emigrants are young, lone migrants and largely ever married

Migrant workers in the GCC countries are a transient, contractual and disposable foreign workforce, who work for a specific duration in these countries, in which neither family reunification nor marriage with a local is allowed. This has transnationally split migrant workers from their families including spouse, children and/or other members (Rahman 2011; Yeoh, Graham and Boyle 2002). Occasionally, these contractual workers can visit their families, depending on the discretion of the employers to grant leave. Given that labour migration to GCC countries is transient in nature, there is predominance of lone male migrants in the stream of emigrants (Afsar 2009; Rahman 2011).

Like all other migration, labour migration to the Gulf states is age and gender selective. Empirical studies show that around three-quarters or more migrants from Bangladesh to Arab countries are under 30 years of age prior to migration. Also, the propensity to overseas migration increases nearly five times for young adults between the ages of 25 and 39 years, compared to either younger (15–24 years) or older (40 years and above) age groups (Afsar

Table 7.1 Bangladeshi migrants by country of employment over time, 1976–2012 and 2000–12

Period/Year	KSA	Kuwait	UAE	Qatar	Oman	Bahrain	GCC States	Malaysia	Singapore	Others	Total
1976–99	1285592	302692	331100	89998	213399	74964	2297745	385496	75503	151228	2909972
2000	144618	594	34034	1433	5258	4637	190574	17237	11095	3780	222686
2001	137248	5341	16252	223	4561	4371	167996	4921	9615	6433	188965
2002	163254	15767	25438	552	3927	5370	214308	85	6856	4007	225256
2003	162131	26722	37386	94	4029	7482	237844	28	5304	11014	254190
2004	139031	41108	47012	1268	4435	9194	242048	224	6948	23738	272958
2005	80425	47029	61978	2114	4827	10716	207089	2911	9651	33051	252702
2006	109513	35775	130204	7691	8082	16355	307620	20469	20139	33288	381516
2007	204112	4212	226392	15130	17478	16433	483757	273201	38324	37327	832609
2008	132124	319	419355	25548	52896	13182	643424	131762	56851	43018	875055
2009	14666	10	258348	11672	41704	28426	354826	12402	39581	68469	475278
2010	7069	48	203308	12085	42641	21824	286975	919	39053	63755	390702
2011	15039	29	282739	13111	135265	13996	460179	742	48667	58474	568062
2012	21232	2	215452	28801	170326	21777	457590	804	58657	90747	607798
2000–12	1330462	176956	1957898	119722	495429	173763	4254230	465705	350741	477101	5547777
% of total 2000–12	23.9	3.2	35.3	2.1	8.9	3.132119	76.7	8.4	6.3	8.599859	100
% of all GCC 2000–12	31.3	4.2	46.0	2.8	11.6	4.1	100				
1976–2012	2616054	479648	2288998	209720	708828	248727	6551975	851201	426244	478329	8307749
% of total 1976–2012	31.5	5.8	27.6	2.5	8.5	3.0	78.9	10.2	5.1	5.8	100

Source: Compiled and computed from BMET database, http://probashi.gov.bd/index,php?option=com_content&view=article&id=176&Itemid=220.

2009; Afsar et al. 2002). On average, migrant women (27 years) are younger than migrant men (28 years).

The majority of emigrants (between 60 and 67 per cent) are married and the rate of marriage increases to 75 per cent for migrants aged over 30 years (Table 7.1). Comparatively, the bulk of the emigrant women are ever married (80–90 per cent). By contrast, women migrant workers who have never been married constituted more than half of the ready-made garments (RMG) sector female workforce in Bangladesh (Afsar et al. 2002; Zohir, Salma and Majumder 1996). Higher prevalence of ever married women among the emigrant stream may be explained with the help of purity and pollution considerations, as argued by Afsar (2005) and Raghuram (2005). Marriage implies obligations and responsibilities for men and women, which in turn may induce migration. Half of the women migrants are divorced or widowed; unlike their married counterparts, these women tend to have greater responsibility with regard to family maintenance (Afsar 2009).

Conversely, the absence of an adult male, more particularly the male 'guardian', also enhances women's mobility, as they face fewer barriers and enjoy greater freedom in their decision to migrate than do the married women migrants (Afsar 2011). Escaping abusive marital relationships has also emerged as a persistent theme for women's migration. Feminist scholars have described this as 'autonomy of migration' (Mezzadra 2004).[3]

Disproportionately larger share of unskilled and semi-skilled categories among emigrants

Since the mid-1970s, there has been a predominance of low and unskilled workers (two-thirds of all emigrants), particularly to the GCC countries, amongst emigrants. The share of skilled workers remains almost stable at around one-third with some occasional fluctuations.[4] The professional group constitutes the smallest category and its share in the emigrant stream dropped from 4 per cent during 1976–99 to a fraction (1 per cent) between 2000 and 2012 (Figure 7.1). The preponderance of unskilled and semi-skilled emigrants may be contrasted with more than three times higher proportion highly educated Bangladeshi emigrants to countries of the Organisation for Economic Co-operation and Development (OECD),compared with those with low education (53.7 per cent and 16.6 per cent, respectively)in 2010–11 (Arslan C. et.al., 2014).

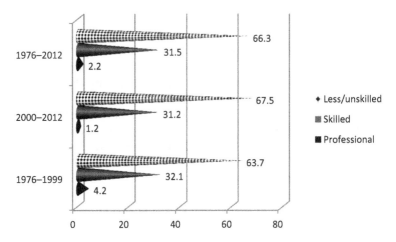

Figure 7.1 Relative share of emigrants by skill categories (cumulative)
Source: Computed from BMET database.

By contrast, more than one-third (35 per cent) of emigrants to the
GCC countries were either illiterates or had primary level of education and only over one-tenth (13 per cent) had completed high
school. On average, male and female emigrant workers had three
and seven years of education, respectively (Afsar 2005).

Cost factor not a deterrent to migration of poorer groups

Existing estimates suggest that over two-fifths of the emigrants to
GCC countries are from functionally landless families (Afsar et al.
2002; Rahman 2011), and nearly one-fifth of emigrants' families
earned below poverty threshold incomes (Afsar et al. 2002). This
clearly suggests that the pull of better employment opportunities
and wage differential are too high to defy options for overseas
migration, irrespective of income levels.

Further, it is argued that prospects for increased employment
in the host country's labour market for a given unemployment
rate is an important determinant of emigration (Mouhoud 2006).
Unemployment rate among emigrants prior to migration is much
higher – 15 per cent – as opposed to the national unemployment
rate of less than 5 per cent (BBS 2012). Higher unemployment may

be understood from the high concentration (44 per cent) of the youth (15–25 years) members among emigrants who were either students or unemployed.[5] Moreover, the unemployed category may also include those who have returned from abroad after their first-hand overseas job experience and are waiting for completion of formalities such as visa and work for the second assignment. This is because nearly two-fifths of emigrants had prior experience of overseas employment indicating that repeat migration is common among migrant labours (Afsar 2002).

Mouhoud also emphasises that income inequality in the home country is likely to increase emigration of poorer groups, while the opposite holds true for the richer ones. Between 1990 and 2005, the Gini-concentration ratio (measure of inequality in income distribution) increased by 46 per cent, from 0.276 to 0.404, in Bangladesh (Osmani and Latif 2013). Emigration thus may be viewed as an attempt to improve one's relative situation in comparison to one's familiar or social reference groups.

In the context of growing income inequality in Bangladesh, we may find the validity of Mouhoud's proposition in the consistently high trend in emigration of unskilled and poorer groups. Among the poor group, the propensity of emigration is higher among poorer women than poorer men.[6] Research shows that almost three-quarters of women domestic workers were living below poverty level prior to migration, compared with a little over one-quarter of women garment workers (27 per cent) and more than one-third (40 per cent) of male emigrant workers, using a dollar a day poverty line measure (Afsar 2005). Women migrants' poorer background is reflected in their landlessness, overwhelming dependence on a single earning member and lower overall family income compared with their male counterparts (Afsar 2009). Whether migrating to Dhaka or to the Gulf states, existing research suggests that women migrants tend to come from poorer backgrounds than do their male counterparts (Afsar 2003).

Larger flow of remittances from the GCC countries than from other regions

Remittances from the GCC countries have also increased significantly by 480.3 per cent from US$1502.43 million to US$7215.53 million between 2001–02 and 2010–11 (Bangladesh Bank 2012; GOB 2012), although the relative share of the largest remittances sending country, such as the KSA, plummeted by 17

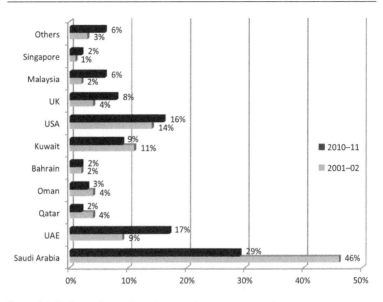

Figure 7.2 Relative share of remittances by source countries
Source: Afsar (2014).

per cent. Despite that, KSA retained its top ranking as the source country of remittances. On the other hand, the trend in the flow of remittances from the UAE, which occupies the second position, has been rising steadily over time (Figure 7.2). Consistent with their share of Bangladeshi migrant labour, the flow of remittances from this region has been the largest (almost two-thirds) compared to the other regions. Flow of remittances from the OECD countries and from other parts of the South East Asian region has been around one-quarter and almost one-tenth of the total flow, respectively, during this period.

Digging into causal domain: complexities and nuances of migration decision-making and the recruitment process[7]

Migration decision-making

The story of Bangladeshi labour migration highlights how migration decision-making is not as simple as ticking who makes the decision on what aspects of migration from a drop-down box. Rather, it is a multilayered and multidimensional process in which the context and causes that prompted the decision to migrate and the strategies to overcome barriers in the implementation of the migration decision often work simultaneously. Elsewhere, the author (Afsar 2009) observes:

> The search for a 'Bhalo' visa (one that would yield better work opportunities and higher incomes) often triggers migration irrespective of the economic standing of the migrants. On the one hand, over 70% of the migrants (both male and female) mentioned that they migrated to the Arab countries with the hope of getting better wages and a more secure life. On the other, nearly half of the men and one-fifth of the women migrants expressed that their decision to migrate was prompted in the context of severe economic difficulties they faced at home.

This clearly suggests that both push and pull factors do not necessarily work in a reverse cycle, rather they may often coexist and, simultaneously, may influence the migration decision-making process.

It should also be noted that push factors may not always be economic; they can also be social (marital discord, including divorce and desertion, family violence and drug abuse). On the other hand, ambition prompted largely by the demonstration effect of neighbours whose lives changed from 'rags to riches' arguably as a result of migration to GCC countries had also influenced many respondents to follow the same route. The following paragraphs present narratives that depict some of these dimensions which influence migration decision-making, and which have not attracted much attention in the international migration literature.

The push of low incomes, hunger and desperation: economic frontier

Harsh economic conditions and the lack of viable options for income generation in the home country often turn poor people into desperate risk takers. Over one-tenth (13 per cent) of the male migrants were the only earning members of their families. Also, more than two-thirds of the respondents were landless. When they experienced relentless economic pressures due to income crunch and insufficient food for the family, they decided to migrate. What is interesting to note here is that instead of giving up, these migrants had high hopes and confidence in their ability to earn higher incomes, even if they were in the most severe economic circumstances. The following is an example.

> Raisul (37 years) revealed his desperation due to his inability to produce enough paddy to feed his family for the entire year. Whatever he produced was consumed within 3–4 months and for the rest of the year, he had to work for other land-owning families in the village. However, he still did not manage to earn enough to cover the family's basic need for food nor could he meet the other expenses such as bearing the cost for children's education. As a result, three of his children could not study beyond primary level. (Afsar 2009: 12)

Many respondents also encountered a drop in income due to illness, death of the main breadwinner, loss in business, and a host of other factors, amongst which divorce and abandonment are critical for women. All these factors induced migration. Being isolated from traditional social ties and social protection including credit, crop insurance and other safety-nets, landless households have little capability or options to manage risks (Kuhn 2000). Box 7.1 illustrates the dimensions of income loss with the help of three case studies.

Box 7.1   Decline in income: multiple causes (cited from Afsar 2009)

Death of the main bread winner

Helal Miah (32 years), a young returnee said that his family had no land of their own to cultivate. Along with his father and brothers, he used to work as a *'kamla'* or agricultural labourer for the landholding neighbours. He earned between Tk. 100 and Tk. 200 for an entire day's work. Given the seasonality of rice production, he had agricultural work for three-quarters of the year and the rest of the year he worked as a construction labourer. Neither he nor his brothers had formal education. His family was always short of food. The situation worsened when his father died and all responsibilities of family maintenance fell on his shoulders. With little or no options to increase his income, he decided to migrate.

Loss in business

Before migration Aiyub Ali (38 years) had a hotel which was running at a loss. He started this business in partnership with one of his friends. He believed that his friend had misappropriated money that he remitted for investment when he had migrated overseas previously. Aiyub was frustrated, and he decided to migrate to KSA again to earn more money and make up the loss.

Family breakdown

Nazma (28 years) and her nine month old son were abandoned by her husband. She had no land and no earning member in the family. She migrated to earn enough income for her family's maintenance and for the child's welfare and education.

The debt trap

Economic hardships entangled some respondents into a debt trap. Nearly one-tenth (7 per cent) of the respondents – both male and female – decided to migrate when they saw no other option to get out of their indebtedness. For example, Matin (40 years) recalled how he struggled with his meagre monthly income of BDT 4,000–5,000 to support a family of eight members. In order to meet the family's daily basic needs, he started buying food and groceries such as rice, lentils, oil and soap on credit from a local grocer and gradually started sinking in the debt trap. Within a short time he owed BDT 20,000 to the grocer which was beyond his capacity to repay. Under the circumstances, he considered migration as 'the only way out'. The debt trap often exacerbates multiple vulnerabilities, especially for women, as may be seen from Box 7.2.

Box 7.2   The debt burden, illness of spouse and family violence (cited from Afsar 2009)

Jarina (33 years) was living with her husband and three little boys in an old house made of corrugated iron prior to migration. Her husband was a petty vegetable seller whose income, Tk.4000 per month – barely sufficient for the family's maintenance and children's education. Their situation worsened when her husband fell ill and Jarina borrowed Tk. 10,000 from the nearby Grameen Bank office to cover the medical expenses, against an instalment of Tk. 250 per week. Due to his illness, her husband could not sell vegetables every day and the income loss was adding to the family's misery. After a month her husband recovered and resumed his work, but the family expenses had multiplied, as they had to pay interests on the bank loan. This constant economic crunch created a disruption in their conjugal life. Her husband resorted to beating her quite frequently – twice or thrice a month. Even though she was illiterate, she thought of migration as a way to escape the abusive relation and increase her family's income.

Getting away from family discord and anti-social habits

Unhealthy habits, particularly drug addiction, can also spark migration. For example, Saburwas was 19 years old when he decided not to continue his studies anymore as he failed his high school examination. He was spending his idle time with his friends and was addicted to *ganja* (opium) and *Phensidyl* (cough syrup). He often fought with his parents for money to buy drugs. To rectify his behaviour, his father was anxious to engage him in some productive work and made necessary arrangements to send him abroad.

Demonstration effect of fellow villagers: emerging pull

The demonstration effect emerged as an important 'pull' factor. Rapid changes in the fortunes of the illiterate, semi-literate, unskilled and poor fellow villagers as a result of migration to Gulf countries often motivates their neighbours to take up international migration (Box 7.3).

Past experience and social networks

The other 'pull' factors that influenced the migration decision were previous migration experience as well as the presence of social networks in the destination country. Most of the migrants (over 90 per cent of men and 80 per cent of women) had one or more relatives abroad. Nearly half of the male migrants had previous experience of overseas migration themselves (Table 7.2), while for the majority (66 per cent) of women, it was their first migration.

Gender variation in the selection of destination

A marked gender variation can be observed with regard to the destination country. KSA was the major destination for more than 60 per cent of the male respondents. By contrast, for women migrants, destinations were more evenly spread between Kuwait, KSA and the UAE.[8] Due to its relatively liberal labour laws compared to other Gulf countries, women prefer Kuwait. Men, on the other hand, prefer KSA because of the strong social networks that have been established

---

Box 7.3   Demonstration effect: a 'pull' for overseas migration (cited from Afsar 2009)

Kamal Uddin (31 years) used to work in a small grocery shop with his father in a local market. In the *boro* season (mainly dry season), he grew potato, onion and other crops which he stocked and sold in the lean season. In this way he earned about Tk. 30,000–35,000 in a year. However, floods in the previous year damaged his crops and made his income unstable. Kamal also discovered that notwithstanding similar losses, his friend's family managed the same business smoothly with the help of the remittances sent by Musa (his friend). So, Kamal also decided to migrate in order to earn enough and restart his family business.

Table 7.2 Respondents who migrated before and/or have family members/relatives living abroad

Number of relatives abroad	Male	Female	All
No family members and/or relatives	4	3	7
One family member and/or relative	21	7	28
Two family members and/or relatives	16	3	19
Three or more family members and/ or relatives	4	2	6
All respondents	45	15	60
Migration experience			
First time migration	22	12	34
Second time migration	16	3	19
Third time migration	3	2	5
Over four times migration	4	0	4
All respondents	45	15	60

Source: Afsar (2009).

there over time and also because of the possibility of entering there on an Umrah visa,[9] which reduces the cost of migration. For example, Omar Faruque said that many of his friends and acquaintances went to KSA with an Umrah visa which reduced the cost of migration by more than BDT30,000. By contrast, to procure a 'free' visa[10] one has to spend more than BDT150,000. Given his financial situation, he decided to migrate by purchasing an *Umrah* visa. Also, migrants in KSA are estimated to generate between 20 per cent and 66 per cent higher incomes compared to those in the UAE and in Kuwait.

Many male migrants attached religious value to going to KSA. Latif, for example, was happy when he was offered a job in a leather company in KSA by a representative of the company, because he considered it as 'a rare opportunity to visit the holy city of Mecca and Medina' (Afsar 2009: 29).

Three stages between migration decision-making and recruitment

At least three stages have been identified between conceiving the decision to migrate and its materialisation through recruitment.

a. The first stage is marketing, in which a prospective migrant is hooked by the idea of a 'bhalo' visa from an informant, such as his/her expatriate family members/relatives, friends/fellow villagers or sub-agents working in the village or adjacent village. The respondents mainly understand that in order to work overseas, they needed a bhalo visa or a work permit for the proposed destination country. Relatives/friends or village acquaintances were the sources that informed two-thirds of the migrants about the possibility of work and a bhalo visa at the country of destination. Initially, the respondents received only sketchy information about the job such as wage range, broad type of occupation and, in some cases, a rough idea about the migration cost.

Nearly a quarter of the respondents obtained their overseas jobs and visas through sub-agents and private recruitment agencies. Migrants' choice of recruiting channels including sub-agents is largely influenced by the advice they receive from expatriate family members or relatives and/or other acquaintances. The majority of men and women procured visas from those recruiting agencies and sub-agents that were recommended to them by their social networks.

b. The second stage relates to transaction, when the informant purchases the visa and then declares the cost to the respondents, which seldom includes the detailed breakdown. While migrants became busy with managing finances to purchase the visa and cover the cost of the trip, the informant sends the work permit, with the help of a recruiting agency. The respondents generally make a lump sum payment to the *dalals* (sub-agents), and sometimes to the recruiting agencies, to cover the cost of the work permit, air fare and other fees.

Generally, I found the respondents had incomplete and vague information about type of visa, type of work, the working and living conditions, as well as other entitlements. Half of the sample migrants, both male and female, learned about the cost after purchasing the visa. Almost all female migrants and more than half of the male migrants had no information regarding the working conditions at the destination country (Figure 7.3), notwithstanding their official *Kafeel*-sponsored work visa. Less than one-third of the male migrants had information on the daily work hours. Only a solitary migrant had an idea about the weekly holiday on Friday.

With the exception of one, none of the respondents had attended the supposedly mandatory pre-departure briefing training run by the Bureau of Manpower Employment and Training

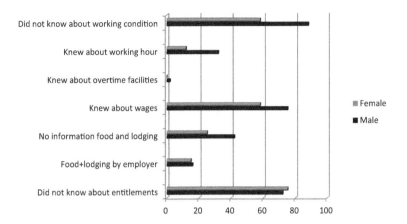

Figure 7.3 Information on working conditions and wages by gender
Source: Afsar (2009).

(BMET); they were not even aware of such a requirement. The recruiting agencies obtained attendance certificates from BMET on the respondents' behalf by offering extra money to the desk officer. Thus, a large majority of the respondents did not have any briefing prior to migration, while a few attended a 'mock' briefing programme run by the private recruiting agencies.

The issue is not limited to lack of necessary information alone but also pertains to the validity of whatever little information they have had on important entitlements such as wages, nature of the job, working hours and medical cover. One-third of the respondents reported lower wages and longer working hours than what they were informed by the recruiting agencies in the home country.

c. In the third stage, sub-agents and/or the recruiting agencies deliver services necessary for migrants to meet the formalities associated with the emigration process such as filling in passport forms, arranging for police clearance and health check-ups, and procurement of visa. In some cases, sub-agents also accompany their clients to the airport and help them meet all the necessary departure formalities.

Table 7.3 Types of services provided by the recruiting agencies and sub-agents

Lodging application for passport	Male	Female
Self	13	0
With the assistance of social network	4	2
Through sub-agent	22	8
Through an agency	4	2
Through a local journalist	0	1
Service provided by the recruiting agency		
Assisted to do medical check up	7	1
Made all necessary arrangements to get visa and flight	22	1
Service provided by the sub-agent		
Arranged the whole process (medical check-up, visa processing and flight arrangements) through an agency	7	14

Source: Afsar (2009).

All the female migrants, with one exception, met the necessary recruitment-related formalities with the help of sub-agents, as most of them had no formal education or previous migration experience (Table 7.3). A majority of the male respondents also used the services of recruiting agencies or sub-agents.

A large number of returned migrants reported that they obtained those services free of charge, which obviously helped the sub-agents to build goodwill. However, the author and others (Rahman 2011) found that a large part of the migration cost (more than three-quarters) is appropriated by recruiting agencies and brokers in home and host countries. Not surprisingly, therefore, in-depth interviews with the recruiting agencies reveal that the sub-agents generally receive between BDT10,000 and BDT60,000 as commission from these agencies on a case-by-case basis, which is inclusive of all types of services that they provide to clients. Sub-agents' proximity to rural migrants and the trust of the local people that they enjoy made them an indispensable sources which private recruiting agencies hire to recruit migrants. Some of the management staff of the recruitment agencies said: 'Without the Dalals it is impossible to run this business'; 'Villagers trust the Dalals'; 'Rural people do not know the recruiting agencies, do not believe the officials of the recruiting agencies but are ready to pay more to the Dalals, because they know them' (Afsar 2009).

Despite such familiarity, women and poor illiterate migrants still run the risk of becoming victims of bribery, forgery and cheating by both recruiting agencies and employers. As discussed in the next part, cheating influences migration outcomes.

Measuring migration outcomes: some useful indicators

In assessing migration outcomes, there are many grey areas and intangible gains and losses that are very difficult to quantify using the conventional cost-benefit ratio method. Moreover, it is important to include the non-economic dimensions of migration, such as job satisfaction and health and well-being, as indicators for measuring migration outcomes. Also, like migration decision-making, the positive and negative and/or mixed outcomes of labour migration can coexist. To capture these dimensions, elsewhere the author (Afsar 2009) developed an innovative approach with the help of various indicators, which are discussed ahead.

Overseas incomes vis-à-vis cost of migration

A simple comparison between the cost incurred in the process of migration and annual incomes of migrants after migration plus the amount of money remitted to home is helpful in understanding how many migrants have been able to offset the cost of migration and the time taken to repay the loan. Table 7.4 shows that nearly two-thirds (60 per cent) of the migrants earned enough to offset their migration costs within a year. More than half (53 per cent) remitted over 50 per cent of the migration costs back home each year. The duration of migration emerges as an important determinant of income and the size of the remittances (Figure 7.4). Incomes and remittances almost doubled when the duration of migration exceeded five years. Migrants' level of education does not appear to have any systematic relationship with their ability to earn more incomes overseas.

Figure 7.5 shows a wide various in outcomes across different occupational categories, from a positive balance of more than BDT260,000 for the single driver, to a negative balance of almost BDT98,000 for the three hotel boys. The other categories fall

Table 7.4 Distribution of migrants by annual income and remittances relative to the cost of migration

Income as % of migration cost	Respondent (%)	Mean duration (yrs)	Mean education (yrs)
Above 500%	13.3	10.7	4.8
Above 350%–500%	5.0	7.3	9
Above 200%–350%	16.7	6.7	4.9
Above 100%–200%	25.0	6.6	4.4
Below 100%	40.0	3.6	4.2
Total	60 (100)	6	4.7
Remittances as % of migration cost	Respondents (%)	Mean duration (yrs)	Mean education (yrs)
Above 350%	6.7	11.3	5
Above 200%–350%	8.3	10.4	6
Above 100%–200%	18.3	7.2	3.2
Above 50%–100%	20.0	7.8	5.3
Below 50%	46.7	3.2	4.7
Total	60 (100)	6.0	4.7

Source: Afsar (2009).

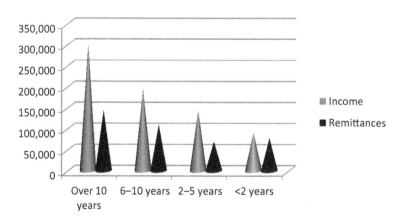

Figure 7.4 The respondents' average income and remittances (in BDT) by duration of migration

Source: Afsar (2009).

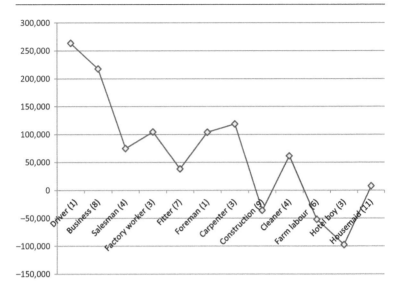

Figure 7.5 Difference between annual incomes and migration cost by types of occupation of migrants at destination

Source: Afsar (2009).

between these two extremes. Even though these figures must be treated with caution, given the small sample size and the probable recall bias, they serve to illustrate the wide diversity of migrants' experiences in terms of the financial gains and losses of migration. However, the figure also shows that the skill level of migrants and their capital and/or strength of social capital to start a business influence the level of overseas income.

Remittances, family incomes, liabilities and asset building

Research showed that more than 70 per cent of the households in Bangladesh received remittances (Orozco 2010). Migrants sent between 30 per cent and 56 per cent of their overseas income as remittances to their families in their home country (Afsar 2009; Afsar et al. 2002). Remittances have contributed between 61 per cent and 64 per cent of the households' income in Bangladesh (Afsar et al. 2002; Orozco 2010). The debt burden back home was another important determinant that often compelled a large number of recent migrants (between 40 and 60 per cent) to remit more by curtailing their daily maintenance costs (Afsar 2009; Afsar et al. 2002).

Studies on remittances-use pattern showed that building, construction, maintenance and repair of housing consumed between 10 per cent and 20 per cent, while another 10 per cent to 20 per cent is invested in the purchase of an important asset, such as land, in Bangladesh (Afsar et al. 2002; Murshid, Iqbal and Ahmed 2002).

After their return from the Gulf states, around 20 per cent of the migrants either joined their family business or started new ventures including grocery shops, fish farming and tailoring (Afsar 2009). However, a large majority of households receiving remittances owned less than two assets, which can make them vulnerable to external shocks, including a decline in overseas employment. Clearly, asset building has emerged as the key factor interlinking remittances with poverty alleviation.

Repayment of outstanding loans

Migrants considered their migration successful when they were able to repay their outstanding loans in the context of the huge loans and liabilities that they incurred to meet the cost of migration. Nearly two-thirds of the migrants were able to repay their outstanding loans, of which only 20 per cent of the respondents partially repaid. For nearly one-third of households, the remittances were not enough to repay the loan incurred prior to migration (*ibid.*). For them this was largely due to the fact that they had been cheated out of the expected wages by the private recruiting agencies, the sub-agents or their social networks.

Savings and investment in land, housing and other assets

Almost one-third of men and a quarter of women respondents invested remittances in purchasing land and/or housing. This usually served to compensate only partially for the assets they had sold off to finance their migration and hence needs to be assessed to measure migration outcomes. The author's (*ibid.*) estimates suggest that the average size of cultivable land declined to 10 per cent in the case of the male migrants. Women's investment in land was so small that it hardly improved their asset base. The loss of land was also partially offset by investment in business and the savings generated by 42 per cent of the respondents, including four women. Nonetheless, the lack of attractive and non-taxable investment options for returning migrants acts as a disincentive to productive investment.

Job satisfaction

Job satisfaction comprises another dimension of the migration outcome. As distinct from financial reward, 'job satisfaction' encompasses whether the migrants received their job-related entitlements, including timely payment of wages, holidays and medical expenses. Almost one-fifth of respondents expressed overall satisfaction with their migration mainly because they received these facilities. By contrast, a quarter of the respondents said that economic gains alone failed to satisfy them, mainly because they did not receive fair treatment and entitlements that had been promised prior to migration. For example, Motiur Rahman (39 years) was not satisfied as his 'supervisor was rude' and his employer gave him 'terrible food', even though he earned more than BDT140,000 annually and stayed overseas for seven years. By contrast, when migrants had good relations with their employer and/or supervisor, they enjoyed their work, even if they had to work long hours. For example, a few domestic helpers such as Farida (33 years) were highly satisfied as they considered their employers to be 'good'. Farida used to work 14–15 hours each day, but she was happy because there was no pressure from the employer or his family. She was given good food and her employer bore all her expenditures during her stay, including medical costs.

Health and well-being indicators

Ill-health and/or an accident can affect migration outcomes negatively. Of the quarter of respondents who did not have a rewarding migration experience, at least half suffered from an illness or an accident. This has not only created financial problems and drastically shortened their overseas stay, but also affected their post-migration situation (Box 7.4).

Box 7.4   Health conditions impact the migration outcome (cited from Afsar 2009)

Illness affects income

Jarina (33 years) fell ill on the job due to excessive workload and the bad quality food provided by her employer. Her employer took her to see a doctor, for which he deducted Jarina's two months' salary. Consequently, she only earned Tk. 157,000 from two years of overseas work, which was barely sufficient to cover her migration costs, not to talk of any productive investment on her return.

For Sadeq (40 years), things were even worse, as he was still suffering from the injuries he sustained as a result of physical abuse by his employer. He was deported to Bangladesh within a year of his migration. At the time of the interview he was very weak and still unable to work. He was fully dependent on his son and daughter to assist him in core activities and for sustenance.

Accident-induced indebtedness

Both Malek (34 years) and Khaleq (35 years) incurred huge debt because of their work-related accidents. Malek did not receive any compensation and Khaleq received less than 20% of the total cost. Although Khaleq was able to repay his loans by finding another job, Malek was laid off from his job and he returned home with no income and heavy debt burden.

Stress

Abul Hossain (26 years) got his first job only three months after arriving in KSA with a free visa. He did not have a valid work permit and his employer wanted to charge him 200 Riyals for one – money he did not have. So he was arrested by the police and jailed for 18 days. This stressful situation, including the conditions in jail, affected his health badly. As he had no money to pay for medical treatment, he had to depend on the charity of Saudi citizens. He did not benefit from migration at all and is now looking to migrate again through formal channels, so that he can repay his debts.

Marital and family breakdown

In the context of lone migration and the emerging transnationally split families, marriage, marital relations and the family situation need to be assessed as outcomes of migration. Elsewhere the author (Afsar 2011) wrote:

> Women migrant workers are likely to face increased personal and social costs compared to men, without adequate gender-responsive services (Afsar, 2009). For example, men may return to a stable family situation, whereas women may find disintegration of the family upon their return and their absence from home is often regarded as the cause of such disintegration. On marital relations between couples separated by distance literature has borne out mixed results. While some couples experience conflict and emotional distance, divorce and extra-marital affairs, others develop stronger emotional ties during their separation. In-depth case studies of return migrants from the Gulf countries shows that migration tends to increase marriage potential of male migrants in Bangladesh (Afsar, 2009). By contrast, a few female domestic workers experienced marital break-up. On the other hand, migration also gave women a little personal space outside parental control and the burden of household chores, and more freedom in selecting spouses and delaying marriage. There are also a few instances where a few women had left their first husband and married second time (Afsar, 2005).

Matrix to measure different dimensions of migration outcomes

By using the indicators discussed above, the author developed a matrix table, which helped her to assess and classify migration outcomes into three broad categories: positive, mixed and negative (Afsar 2009). In this process, by weighing the different dimensions of migration outcomes against a whole range of carefully chosen indicators, the overall impact of migration was classified as positive for more than half of the respondents (57 per cent) (Table 7.5). Of the remaining 43 per cent, the impact was assessed as mixed for half and the experience was, on balance, negative for the other half, meaning that losses the migrants incurred in the process of migration was greater than what they earned.

Cheating by own relatives and/or sub-agents or recruiting agencies on account of fraudulent contract, discrepancy between the promised job and the actual job, promised wage and actual wage,

Table 7.5 Migration outcomes: positive, negative and mixed

Positive outcomes	Male	Female	All
Respondents who sent remittances	40	12	52
Earned more income in a year than cost of migration	23	10	33
Repaid loans fully or partially	29	11	40
Able to generate savings	21	4	25
Became skilled	3	–	3
Bought land, repaired/ extended/constructed house	15	4	19
Satisfied with his/her migration experience	7	4	11
Negative outcomes			
Income was too low to offset migration cost	22	5	27
Did not have any income	1	3	5
Being cheated, exploited or not satisfied with migration experience	6	4	10
Did not gain anything but became indebted and lost out	11	4	15
Became sick, had problems with food, had an accident but not compensated	4	1	5
Family breakdown	–	4	4
Mixed outcomes			
Earned handsome income abroad yet dissatisfied with working conditions	7	2	9
Rewarding but cheated by employer and/or sub-agent and/or relative	4	2	6
Materially successful but did not receive compensation when suffered an accident while at work	3	–	3

Source: Afsar (2009).

and promised working conditions and actual working conditions emerge as important factors for failed migration. The other factors are ill health and accident. Conversely, the ability to earn more incomes overseas depends more on migrants' skill levels, the duration of migration, type of employer, bargaining power and strength of social networks at the destination, than on the type of visa and the channels of recruitment per se.

Concluding remarks

From the narrative of labour migration to the Gulf states, a set of new paradigms emerge which confront conventional wisdom. Some of these paradigms originate from the uniqueness of labour migration to the region, which include the brave move by the poorer people with low levels of education and skills to join the ranks of international migrants to change their lot in life. Understandably, they traverse through a steep path, which ultimately yields positive outcomes for some, while for others the result is negative or mixed.

What my respondents demonstrated through this process of migration is their unwavering will power and self-confidence, which emerges as an important dimension for the new generation migration theories to take into account. Such theories must also contextualise migration decision-making to generate a better understanding of the multidimensionality involved in this process, including the coexistence of push and pull factors and their interconnectedness. Similarly, the new generation migration theories are expected to develop methodological approaches to measure migration outcomes with different contours and dimensions.

Notes

1   The author gratefully acknowledges research assistance received from Ms Preetha- Haque, Queens College, Cambridge, UK.
2   The Gulf Cooperation Council (GCC) was established in Abu Dhabi on 25 May 1981. It comprises the 630 million acre (2,500,000 km^2) Persian Gulf states of the United Arab Emirates (UAE), State of Bahrain, Kingdom of Saudi Arabia (KSA), Sultanate of Oman, State of Qatar, and State of Kuwait. The GCC basically aims to promote coordination between member states in all fields to achieve unity.
3   For a detailed discussion, see Afsar (2011).
4   For example, on year by year basis, the share of skilled migrants in the total stream of emigrants was the highest in the years 2000 and 2005 (45 per cent each) and lowest in 2007 (20 per cent), 2001 (23 per cent) and 2011 (23 per cent).
5   Youth unemployment is higher (7.5 per cent) than the unemployment rate for people aged above 15 years in the country and students constitute more than one-third (37.3 per cent) of the youth labour force (aged 15–29 years) in the country (BBS 2012).
6   The average monthly family income of the male and the female emigrants was BDT6,842 and BDT4,098 respectively. The sample families' incomes were slightly higher than the rural and national averages recorded in the household expenditure survey (BBS 2006). Nearly two-thirds of the migrants' families were nonetheless earning less than BDT6,000 per month, which works out to roughly BDT30 per person per day, indicating that a large majority were below the poverty line (Afsar 2009). US$1 was around BDT69 in 2008 when the study was undertaken.
7   This section is heavily borrowed from the author's study in 2009 (Afsar 2009) that was largely based on recounting personal experiences of 45

male and 15 female migrants who had returned to the home country within a one year period prior to the survey.

8 However, macro data from official sources show that the relative share of the female migrants has been largest to the UAE (27 per cent), followed by KSA (15 per cent) and Kuwait (4 per cent) within the region, and Jordan (9 per cent) and Mauritius (4 per cent) outside the region from 1991 to 2012 (http://www.bmet.org.bd/BMET/viewStatReport.action?reportnumber=20, accessed on 31 August 2013).

9 Note that Umrah visa is not a work permit. Pilgrims come to KSA before Eid-ul-Azha to pay homage to the holy places of Mecca and Medina, which is known as Hajj. However, if a person wants to pay homage at any time of the year, he/she is allowed to do so. That pilgrimage is known as Umrah and the visa given is an Umrah visa.

10 This is a popular, legal but unofficial category of visa which allows a migrant to enter a GCC country for work under *Kafala* or sponsorship system but with no fixed *Kafeel* or sponsored-employer to offer paid work. While it gives migrants freedom to choose their own jobs in any sectors of the economy, it also makes them vulnerable to deportation as it is illegal to work in another sector or with other sponsor-employers than one's own (Shah 2008).

References

Afsar, R. 2003. 'Rapid Social Investigation on Policies, Mechanisms and Services and Issues of Migrant Women Workers of Bangladesh', a study sponsored and funded by UNIFEM under its Asia-Pacific Regional Programme for Empowerment of Migrant Women Workers, New Delhi, 21 September 2003.

———. 'Conditional Mobility: The Migration of Bangladeshi Female Domestic Workers', in Shirlena Huang, Brenda S.A. Yeoh and Noor Abdul Rahman (eds), *Asian Women as Transnational Domestic Workers*. Singapore: Marshall Cavendish Academic, Singapore National University.

———. 2009. 'Unravelling the Vicious Cycle of Labour Recruitment: Labour Migration from Bangladesh to the Gulf States', Working Paper 63, Geneva, International Labour Organization.

———. 2011. 'Contextualizing Gender and Migration in South Asia',*Gender, Technology and Development, Special Issue: Gender and Space: Themes from Asia*, 15(3): 389–410.

———. 2013. 'Remittances and Enterprise Development: Reflections from South Asia', in M. Rahman, Tan Tai Yong and A.K.M. Ahsan Ullah (eds) *Migrant Remittances in South Asia*. Hampshire: Palgrave Macmillan.

Afsar, R., M. Yunus and A.B.M.S. Islam. 2002. *Are Migrants Chasing after the Golden Deer?* Research Report Series, International Organization for Migration (IOM). Dhaka: UNDP.

Arslan, C. et al. 2014. "A New Profile of Migrants in the Aftermath of the Recent Economic Crisis", OECD Social, Employment and

Migration Working Papers, No. 160, OECD Publishing. http://dx.doi.
org/10.1787/5jxt2t3nnjr5-en.

Bangladesh Bank. 2012. *Bangladesh Bank Quarterly* January–March 2012,
9(3). Dhaka: Bangladesh Bank.

Bangladesh Bureau of Statistics (BBS). 2006. Preliminary report on Household Income and Expenditure Survey 2005, Ministry of Planning, Government of the People's Republic of Bangladesh.

———. 2011. *Preliminary Report on Household Income and Expenditure
Survey 2010*. Dhaka: Ministry of Planning, Government of the People's
Republic of Bangladesh.

———. 2012. *Statistical Yearbook of Bangladesh 2011*. Dhaka: Ministry
of Planning, Government of the People's Republic of Bangladesh.

El Mouhoud. 2006. 'International Migration, Globalisation and Development', Theoretical Note, in Issues in regulation Theory, No. 55,
June 2006.

Government of the People's Republic of Bangladesh (GOB). *Bangladesh
Economic Review 2012*. Dhaka: Economic Adviser's Wing, Finance
Division, Ministry of Finance.

Kuhn, R. S. 2000. 'The Logic of Letting Go: Family and Individual Migration from Rural Bangladesh', Working Paper Series 00–09, Labour and
Population Programme, Rand Corporation, Santa Monica.

Mezzadra, S. 2004. 'The Right to Escape', *Ephemera*,4(3): 267–75.

Murshid, K. A. S., K. Iqbal and M. Ahmed. 2002. *A Study on Remittances
Inflows and Utilisation*, Research Report Series. Dhaka: IOM, Regional
Office, South Asia.

Orozco, M. 2010. *Migration, Remittances and Assets in Bangladesh: Considerations about their Intersection and Development Policy Recommendation*, a report commissioned by the International Organisation for
Migration (IOM). Geneva: IOM.

Osmani, S. R. and M. A. Latif. 2013. 'The Patterns and Determinants of
Rural Poverty In Bangladesh: 2000–2012', Working Paper No. 18, Institute of Microfinance (InM), Dhaka.

Raghuram, P. 2005. 'Global Maid Trade: Indian Domestic Workers in the
Global Market', in Shirlena Huang, Noorashikin Abdul Rahman and
Brenda Yeoh (eds), *Asian Transnational Domestic Workers*. Singapore:
Marshall Cavendish.

Rahman, M. 2011. 'Does Labour Migration Bring About Economic Advan-
tage? A Case of Bangladeshi Migrants in Saudi Arabia', ISAS Working
Paper No. 135, Institute of South Asian Studies, National University of
Singapore, Singapore.

Ratha, D. 2007. *Leveraging remittances for development*. Washington,
D.C.: Migration Policy Institute, World Bank.

Sen, B. and Hulme, D. (eds). 2004. *Chronic Poverty in Bangladesh: A Tale
of Ascent, Decent, Marginality and Persistence: The State of the Poorest
2004/2005*. Bangladesh Institute of Development Studies and Chronic

Poverty Research Centre (CPRC), Institute of Development Policy and Management (IDPM), University of Manchester.

Shah, Nasra M. 2008. "Recent Labor Immigration Policies in the Oil-Rich Gulf: How Effective are they likely to be?" ILO Asian Regional Programme on Governance of Labor Migration Working Paper No 3, Bangkok: International Organization for Migration.

Sharma, M. and Zaman, H. 2009. 'Who Migrates Overseas and is it Worth their While? An Assessment of Household Survey Data from Bangladesh', Policy Research Working Paper Series: 5018, World Bank, Washington D.C.

Siddiqui, T. 2002. *Beyond the Maze: Streamlining Labour Recruitment Process in Bangladesh*. Dhaka: RMMRU.

World Bank. 2013. Migration and Development Brief 20, Migration and Remittances Unit, Development Prospects Groups, 19 April 2013.

Yeoh, B. S. A., E. Graham and P. J. Boyle 2002. 'Migrations and Family Relations in the Asia Pacific Region', *Asian and Pacific Migration Journal*, 11(1).

Zohir, C., C. Salma and P. Majumder. 1996. 'Garment Workers in Bangladesh: Economic, Social and Health Conditions', Research Monograph 18, Bangladesh Institute of Development Studies, Dhaka.

8

From rupees to dirhams

Labour migration from Nepal to the GCC region[1]

Neha Wadhawan

Introduction

South Asia is currently the dominant source of migrants to the Gulf Cooperation Council (GCC) countries (United Nations 2006). Migration from India, Pakistan, Sri Lanka, and Bangladesh to the Gulf region can be traced back over several decades and even centuries. However, migration from Nepal, a small landlocked country nestled in the Himalayas, to the GCC countries, namely Bahrain, Kuwait, Oman, Qatar, Saudi Arabia, and the United Arab Emirates (UAE), is a recent phenomenon when compared to other South Asian countries. Evidence of migration to India for work from Nepal suggests that labour migration is not a new trend in Nepal; for centuries people have migrated from Nepal to different parts of India for low-level informal sector jobs ranging from construction to domestic work. However, only since the 1990s did international labour migration from Nepal to countries other than India begin, mostly to the GCC countries and Malaysia.

Estimates suggest that around 40 per cent of the combined populations of the six Persian Gulf countries are composed of immigrants, with the proportion reaching 87 per cent in Qatar. The percentage of immigrants in the workforce is even higher, constituting at least 50 per cent in every country and reaching about 94 per cent in Qatar (Baldwin-Edwards 2011: 8–9). Despite a history that is over a quarter century old, Nepalis, as well as South Asians in general, have entered the Gulf labour market much later, which earlier hosted a larger number of Arab labourers from poorer countries like Egypt, Syria and Yemen as well as Palestinians. This arrangement was somewhat disrupted after the Arab-Israeli War of 1973, and more so after the 1990 Gulf War when the Yemenis and

Palestinians were seen as having sided with Iraq during the war.[2] Labour migration to the Gulf region from South Asia grew, with the citizens of the GCC countries largely involved in the public sector while foreign workers were employed in the private sector under the *kafala* system.[3]

Nepal, with an area of 147,181 square kilometres and a population of over 26 million, has nearly 2 million absentee workers living abroad (CBS 2011a). It is located in the Himalayas and bordered in the north by the People's Republic of China, and in the south, east and west by India. Nepal remains one of the poorest countries in the world, with a Human Development Index (HDI) of 0.463, placing it 157th out of 187 countries listed in the United Nations Development Programme's *Human Development Report 2013*.

While migration from all 75 districts of Nepal has been observed, the hills and mountainous zones of Nepal have witnessed large-scale outmigration due to extreme poverty and dependence on subsistence agriculture, coupled with very small landholdings, that are unable to provide food security in the region. As mentioned earlier, labour migration to India has been recorded over centuries, while labour migration to the Gulf region and Malaysia is a recent development. This chapter provides an overview of Nepali migration to the GCC region. It discusses available data on remittances and the contribution these make to the Nepalese economy. Based on an empirical study conducted in 2008–09 in Sindhupalchowk district in Nepal,[4] this chapter outlines case studies of migrant workers, both men and women, who have travelled beyond their country's borders in search of work. These case studies highlight the magnitude and reasons for migration and the conditions in which Nepali migrants work in the GCC region and earn a livelihood to support their families back home.

Migrating beyond India to the Gulf

Over the past couple of decades, the rate of migration to India has decreased with more and more Nepalis seeking employment opportunities elsewhere, especially in the Gulf region and Malaysia. The three Nepal Living Standards Surveys (NLSS) (1995/96, 2003/04 and 2010/11) show that the share of remittances received by households from India has declined over the years: 32.9 per cent of all remittances in 1995/96, 23.2 per cent in 2003/04, and just 11.3 per cent in 2010/11. This diminishing importance of India is because Nepalis have begun opting for newer and better-paying destinations (Sharma and Thapa 2013: 11).

The presence of porous borders and historical linkages across the subcontinent continue to attract labour migrants to India. Yet, about 1,000 people left the country every day in 2010 and early 2011 to destinations other than India. After June 2011, this number has risen to 1,500 people per day leaving for work to countries other than India (DoFE 2011). Table 8.1 shows the official number of migrant workers reported to be working in the GCC region in 2011–12. It is not surprising that Qatar has the highest number of Nepali migrants since it has the highest percentage of foreign workforce amongst the GCC countries. Women's migration to the Gulf region is also on the rise, with UAE and Kuwait attracting 2,260 and 5,357 women workers respectively, mostly for domestic work.

In 2009/10, about 294,000 Nepalese took government permission to work overseas. In the fiscal year 2010/11, 354,716 permits were issued to Nepalis who migrated for employment to countries beyond India for employment (DoFE 2011).[5] About 29 per cent of total households in Nepal have at least one member living abroad (CBS 2011a). It is estimated that around 3 million Nepalese are abroad, i.e. about one-third of the male population of working age. The scale of remittances is also staggering – they constitute a quarter of the income nationally and on average two-thirds of the income for remittance receiving households.[6] However, the official

Table 8.1 Number of Nepali migrant workers in GCC countries, mid-July 2011 to mid-January 2012

Country	Male	Female	Total
Qatar	59,392	453	59,845
Saudi Arabia	34,713	78	34,791
United Arab Emirates	31,311	2,260	33,571
Bahrain	3,327	300	3,627
Kuwait	6,146	5,357	11,503
Oman	1,721	252	1,973
Total	136,610	8,700	145,310

Source: Department of Foreign Employment, Nepal (www.dofe.gov.np), cited in Bajracharya and Sijapati (2012): 3.

numbers available with the Nepalese government and the estimates by experts based on various micro studies and representational surveys don't match.[7] The recruitment agencies estimate that about 40 per cent more people go out through irregular channels. This means that about 490,000 Nepalese have gone to work overseas in 2010/11, about the same number of young people that enter the Nepalese labour market annually.[8]

It was estimated that there were approximately 800,000 Nepalis in the GCC in 2005 (NIDS 2011) and it is likely that this number has increased since then. In 2010, Saudi Arabia, Qatar, the UAE, and Bahrain were ranked the third, fourth, fifth, and sixth, respectively, most common destinations for Nepalis leaving Nepal, behind only India and Malaysia (ibid.). Almost one-third of all households in Nepal received remittances from abroad in 2008, although, again, this is likely to have increased since then (ibid.). The value of remittances has been estimated at 24 per cent of the Nepali gross domestic product (GDP), accounting for more than revenues from tourism, exports and foreign aid combined (ibid.). It is also estimated that the largest share of remittances to Nepal is from the GCC countries, equalling 35 per cent of all remittances (Lokshin, Bontch-Osmolovski and Glinskaya 2007). Moreover, according to the Nepali Migrants to the GCC Countries Study (NMGCCS), 83 per cent of the sample drawn from Chitwan Valley planned to continue living outside Nepal, of which 33 per cent planned to go to another GCC country for work (Williams et al. 2012). Hence, the contribution of remittances from the Gulf is a vital factor spurring labour migration to the region and will continue to impact remittance flows in the future as well.

Legal instruments to govern international labour migration

In the face of a rapidly growing young population with rising expectations for higher standards of living, lack of employment or any economic opportunities at home, and an augmented labour demand both from the booming East Asian economies and the GCC countries, which were undergoing a construction boom, the Government of Nepal enacted a Foreign Employment Act of 1985. The Act licensed non-governmental institutions to export Nepalese workers abroad and legitimised certain labour contracting organisations. This encouraged large streams of international migration, including to the GCC countries, which had been confined to India prior to this date (Kollmair et al. 2006; Thieme and Wyss 2005). The Act was amended thrice – in 1992, 1998 and 2007 – and in 2007 itself a new Foreign Employment Act was enacted. Similarly, the Foreign Employment Rules came into force in 1999, and again in 2008 following the 2007 Act. However, none of these laws or the institutions established by these legislations deal with Nepalis going to India for work. The notion of 'foreign employment' and, to a very large extent, the notion of a 'foreign' destination itself is not attached to India (Sharma and Thapa 2013: 13).

The 1985 Act brought international migrants within the state's legal framework and opened the doors for organisations to register as recruitment agencies so that they can be regulated while earning from a very profitable business. While this was an attempt to ensure that international labour migration from Nepal was monitored, it increased the costs of migration several fold, which were transferred onto the poor migrant who would end up taking large loans and selling family land to meet the costs of the migration process. The later amendments were changes made to the earlier legislation to better manage and control foreign employment. The Foreign Employment Act 2007 was made to amend and consolidate the laws relating to foreign employment and reflects the government's effort to not only regulate the process but also take up a rights-based approach to migrant worker rights.[9]

The global financial crisis set in and the economic slowdown in 2008 resulted in the loss of several jobs, especially affecting immigrant workers across the world. Many Nepali workers lost their jobs and returned home from Malaysia and the Gulf region, in turn adversely affecting Nepal's remittance dependent economy.[10] After a new Constituent Assembly was elected in March 2008, ushering in political transition from a monarchical state to a federal republic following the end of a prolonged armed conflict between the Maoists and the Royal Nepal Army, some further initiatives have been taken. The Directive to Organise Nepali Domestic Workers 2010 and the Foreign Employment Policy 2012 were adopted and are positive steps but implementation remains lacking, primarily because of the political stalemate since 2010, the dissolution of the Constituent Assembly in May 2012, and the ensuing political atmosphere.

Impact of remittances in Nepal

Nepal is characterized by poor indicators of development such as the level of poverty (25 per cent), unemployment rate (17.4 per cent) and underemployment rates (32.3 per cent). Migrants' earnings help them and their families back home to survive in a country where poverty levels are high and lack of employment drives migration for work even today from all 75 districts of Nepal. Remittances are used primarily for consumption, education and health and contribute in particular to housing and social expenditure (e.g., religious rituals and marriage expenses). Some studies show that migration for work has contributed to almost 20 per cent of the decline in poverty in Nepal between 1995 and 2004 (c.f. Lokshin, Bontch-Osmolovski and Glinskaya 2007). Recent studies on migration and remittances include Seddon, Adhikari and Gurung (2001), Thieme and Wyss (2005), Kollmair et al. (2006); Adhikari and Hobley (2011) which highlight the crucial role of migrant remittances in the Nepalese economy. Nearly four-fifths of all Nepalese households are essentially farm households, as of the total 4.25 million households, 3.36 million constitute agricultural holdings (CBS 2006). Labour migration is an important source of remittances, a major contribution to household income in an economy where a majority of the population continues to survive on subsistence agriculture.

The share of remittances in total household income has increased for the past two decades; it is possible to say that this phenomenon has accompanied Nepali migration to the GCC region. The share of remittances in total household income among recipients was 26.6 per cent in 1995/96, which increased to 35.4 per cent in 2003/04 (CBS 2004). Further data from NLSS III (CBS 2011b) indicate there has been a major increase in households receiving remittances (rising from 31.9 per cent in 2003–04 to 55.8 per cent in 2009–10). Over this period, total remittances to Nepal increased from 35 billion to 208 billion Nepali rupees.[11]

Nationally per capita remittance income has increased from Rs 625 (1995/96) to Rs 2,100 (2003/04) to Rs 9,245 per year (2010/11). The NLSS III survey indicates that 79 per cent of remittances are used for daily consumption and only 2.4 per cent is invested for capital formation, 7.1 per cent for paying loans, 3.5 per cent for education, and 4.5 per cent for household property (Adhikari and Hobley 2011: 20). This is also reflected in the data available on remittances which account for a substantial 21.6 per cent of Nepal's GDP, according to the latest remittance estimates generated by the World Bank (2010). It is not only the volume of migration that has changed but also the type of migration, with a shift away from India as the dominant migration destination to a more diversified set of destinations (NIDS 2010; Seddon, Adhikari and Gurung 2001). Until 1981, India was the only destination for Nepalese workers, except for a few who joined the British army and some who moved to other countries. But now migration to the Gulf States and Malaysia has dramatically increased (Adhikari and Hobley 2011).

Case studies from Sindhupalchowk

There is no data on Nepali migrant workers by ethnicity or age group, nor is there data on the flow of remittances by gender. Over the past few decades, however, it can be observed that it is not only upper-caste groups or early migrant communities like the Gurungs, Magars and Thapas who have migrated out to international destinations in search of work, but smaller indigenous communities like the Tharus and Tamangs who have also migrated beyond South Asia have in search of work.

While official figures of Nepalis seeking foreign employment in destinations beyond India became available from the fiscal year 1993/94 onwards, gender-segregated data became available only after the fiscal year 2006/07 (Sijapati and Limbu 2012: 22). Figures from the Department of Foreign Employment (DoFE) show that a mere 3 per cent of the total individuals receiving permits for foreign employment in 2010/11 were women. The 2011 census, on the other hand, indicates that females comprise 13.3 per cent of the total absentee Nepalis, while, according to the Nepal Migration Survey (NMS) 2009, 10 per cent of the total migrants are females (the last two figures, of course, include those going to India as well). Sijapati and Limbu (ibid.) argue that while all these sources make it clear that females migrate for work in less numbers than males, it is also important to note that figures obtained from the DoFE could be an underestimation because of the illegal channels that Nepali women use to reach Gulf countries, given the barriers that the government has placed on female migration, most notably the ban on female migration to these countries in 1998, which was partially lifted in 2003 and done away with only in 2010. The author's research findings in 2008–09 show that a large majority of women migrants from the area migrated for domestic work to the Gulf despite the ban. Migration for domestic work did not decrease with the ban; in fact, several domestic workers migrated through India to the Gulf to avoid detection.

During fieldwork conducted in 2008–09 in Sindhupalchowk, the author interviewed several return migrants from the Gulf including those aspiring to migrate for employment to the GCC region. Sindhupalchowk is a district located in the central development zone, north of Kathmandu valley, and is dominated by the Tamang community. The data presented ahead was collected during fieldwork conducted in a village in Sindhupalchowk district which is located close to Nepal's northern border. A household census of the village was conducted to collect data on socio-economic characteristics of the households, including landholding pattern, consumption items owned, remittances, process of migration, etc. The author recorded detailed interviews of both men and women migrating to the Gulf for work. This section presents case studies based on migrants' work experience in the Gulf region and their future aspirations.

Men from Sindhupalchowk district have been migrating for construction work to India since the 1940s. Later, they found jobs as cooks and helpers in restaurants as well as homes in Delhi and Calcutta. Some men from the village had migrated to the Gulf as cooks and drivers. Since 2005, there has been a shift in migration patterns with women taking the lead in migrating as domestic workers to the GCC countries and Lebanon. While men were away for most of the year, for two years sometimes, they would return annually, bringing back some part of their earnings. Man Singh Pakhrin (55)[12] explains:

> There was no school in this part of the hills, so going to school was out of the question. I went as a construction worker on the Bomdilla pass border roads in Assam in the 1970s. We earned 20 rupees a week and after spending on food and drinks to survive the cold, there was not much savings left to take back home. We travelled in groups to avoid being robbed by bandits in the jungles. Nowadays, young men and women go to Dubai and earn in US dollars and dirhams! It is risky because of the high visa costs and corrupt agents but they earn more than they can ever dream of earning in India. We walked over the mountains and travelled some part by bus or train but the youth travel in airships these days!

It is evident that migration to the GCC region holds the promise of better earnings and an opportunity to live and work in a large city. The migration process is expensive but travel has become convenient and comfortable. However, stories of abuse and disappearances abound in the region and people are aware that high earnings come at the cost of life sometimes.

Suke Tamang, a driver working in Dubai till March 2009, had lost his job and had returned to the village with his earnings when I met him. He narrated his experience to me.

> I worked as a driver for an Indian company in Dubai. I lost my job as the company fired several workers in the past few months. I tried looking for a job but my visa had expired since I no longer hold a job and I had to come back. I have heard horror stories of men in labour camps, living in cramped quarters with no drinking water or proper places to urinate. There are several Nepali men who have lost their passports or they have been taken away by agents and employers. Many Nepalis are stranded and can be found outside the Nepali Embassy trying to return home.

Mala Tamang (45), who had returned from Kuwait in September 2008, told me about her experience as a domestic worker.

> I have seen all kinds of people and have worked in Bahrain and Kuwait. My earlier employers in Bahrain in 2002 were very nice and they looked after all my needs and got me medical treatment when I was unwell. They left and I came back to Delhi and went again to Kuwait in 2005. I faced many hardships while I was there. They took away all my belongings, my passport and phone numbers so that I could not contact anybody. I worked 16 hours a day and they gave me very little to eat. The lady in the house would abuse me often and even beat me with a stick. I ran away and went to the embassy for help. I was lucky as I managed to escape but many other Nepali women are stuck in the Gulf without any help.

The household census in the sample village revealed that women remit three times the amount remitted by men. Migrant women domestic workers were always expected to remit. Male migrant workers reported that they tried to save but sometimes the money got stolen and, in other instances, they could not save as it was spent on alcohol and other consumption expenditure. Female migrants, especially domestic workers, do not have to incur living costs in the GCC countries. At the same time, women migrant domestic workers are more prone to abuse, both sexual and physical, at their workplace since it is a private household located in a foreign country. Working hours are usually not defined and these workers are not allowed to step out of the employer's house in most cases. Some domestic workers who had returned from the Gulf reported that in most cases the employers took away their passports and contact numbers of relatives. This was done in order to prevent the worker from running away from the employer's house and prevent him/her from contacting relatives to get help.

Let us take the case of Kanchi Pakhrin, a 19-year-old Tamang girl from Sindhupalchowk. I interviewed her brother Prakash Pakhrin (25) in the village in April 2009 and he told me:

> Kanchi first went to Delhi with my father in 2003 to replace my sister Usha, who was getting married. She worked with a Korean family in Gurgaon, near Delhi, for four years and earned INR7,000. After the Korean family left, she migrated through an agent based in Delhi and we were told that she was working as a domestic worker in Dubai and was promised USD400 per month but we have not received any money since and have no news of her whereabouts. The agent's phone is switched off and I have no idea how to contact her or inquire about her welfare. I just hope she will return home safe one day.

The interesting aspect which must be taken into consideration here is that migration for domestic work from Nepal to the Gulf countries has been banned now for several years. Yet the census data revealed that most women migrant domestic workers were headed for the Gulf countries. During in-depth interviews it emerged that India was the transit country for them to reach the Gulf. This migration was carried out through illegal agents and touts, located in Nepal and India, who charged huge sums of money to facilitate the illicit process. As discussed earlier, the legal provisions regulating international labour migration had increased the costs of migration, especially for the male migrant worker, and so migrating to India via porous borders was a much preferred channel, as it involved lesser paperwork and the opportunity of earning a livelihood while waiting for the visa and other relevant documents.

The largest employment sector available to migrants across gender from this village was domestic work. Out of a total of 110 migrant women recorded in the selected village, as many as 83 migrant women workers from the village had migrated for paid domestic work. This was despite the fact that migration of women to the Gulf region for domestic work was banned during the field survey (2008–09). Of the remaining migrant women, 16 of them had migrated for higher education or had accompanied a male relative to the city for better studies, in addition to helping with domestic duties for her own family at the destination. Only three migrant women workers were employed in the construction sector and had migrated to Kathmandu and Delhi with their husbands. The survey also recorded that two women workers were employed in beauty parlours and another two were employed in the carpet weaving industry in Kathmandu.

Conclusion

A gendered analysis of international labour migration to the GCC region reveals interesting patterns. While national legislation and the nexus of legal and illegal recruitment agencies has resulted in making the process expensive and precarious for male migrant workers, they at least have access to varied forms of employment. On the other hand, women's migration for domestic work has boomed despite various restrictions being placed against it. The migration of women to Kuwait, Qatar, Saudi Arabia, and the UAE was completely outlawed in 1998, and was allowed only for the 'organised' sector from 2003 onwards. The ban was lifted in 2010, but another was imposed in 2012, prohibiting all women under 30 from going to the aforementioned Gulf countries as domestic workers.

A ban on migration for domestic work does not reduce such movements, in fact it further exacerbates the conditions under which migrant women workers move in search of work. In Nepal, the ban on migration for domestic work to the GCC countries has led women to rely on unregistered recruitment agents who channel such migrants through illegal means and charge higher fees to facilitate the process. With the more recent ban on women under 30 migrating for domestic work, extra charges are levied by agents for the passport-making process as fake age documents are used. This study revealed that since the 1998 ban, the migration of domestic workers to the GCC countries has not decreased. On the contrary, migration for domestic work from Nepal has increased multifold, without any reliable data to substantiate the numbers, and continues unabated as these agents send domestic workers to the Gulf countries via India. Consequently, the channel of migration to these countries via India has become a popular one and seems to be the only alternative. India has affected a similar ban, further limiting their access to justice in the transit country, destination country and in Nepal in case of any labour violations and abuse.

Recruitment agencies play a crucial role in the process of migration for domestic work and hence must be studied carefully to contribute to a comprehensive understanding of this process. There is a need for careful regulation since there is a very thin and fuzzy line distinguishing trafficking or forced migration and migration by choice to international destinations via these agencies. Let us take the case of Lebanon to explain this issue. Philippines and Sri Lanka banned their domestic workers from migrating to Lebanon in 2002 due to harassment and abuse faced by a majority of workers and complaints being filed with their respective embassies. This led to recruitment agents looking for new source locations in poor developing countries and opening up the market for Nepali and Madagascan domestic workers to work in Lebanon. Nepal finally banned migration for domestic work to Lebanon in December 2009. Hence important aspects relating to regulation of working conditions and ensuring safe migration are international issues which must be dealt with in coordination with other labour-sending countries.

Over all, men and women migrant workers have inadequate information about the destination countries in the Gulf region. Potential labour migrants face financial problems which lead them to migrate without adequate skills and training about expectations and work culture in the destination country before departure. Other reported issues relate to discrepancies in wage fixation before and after departure. Working conditions in the destination countries are usually poor for both regular and irregular migrants resulting in poor health, abuse of human rights, high HIV prevalence rates, forced labour, and trafficking as a result of incomplete official papers and passports.

Despite all the drawbacks, higher currency exchange value, the possibility of employment and the search for a better future ensures the popularity of the Gulf region as a destination for migrant workers from Nepal. Future legislation at the national-bilateral and regional-international level must aim at regulating and monitoring the entire process of migration to safeguard migrant workers' rights, commencing with recruitment agencies without burdening the migrant worker with burgeoning costs and bureaucratic red tape. The recent national elections in Nepal held on 19 November 2013 will hopefully lead to the end of the long-standing political stalemate in the country and gain momentum towards creating an efficient system to protect migrant workers' interests within Nepal and beyond.

Notes

1   The author wishes to thank Prof. P.C. Jain for his insightful comments on the chapter. An earlier version of this chapter was presented at the Gulf Studies Seminar at the India Arab Cultural Centre, Jamia Millia Islamia, New Delhi on 29–31 January, 2013.
2   Rahman (2010) and Colton (2010) cited in Sijapati and Limbu (2012: 28).
3   Under the kafala system, a migrant is sponsored by an employer and assumes full economic and legal responsibility of the employee during the contract period. Nepalis in the Gulf also come under this same system. See also Bajracharya and Sijapati (2012), for a detailed discussion on the kafala system with reference to Nepali workers in the Gulf (available at www.ceslam.org).
4   The author conducted a household census in a sample village in Sindhupalchowk followed by detailed interviews with migrants and non-migrants in the Village Development Council (VDC) region as part of her doctoral fieldwork for her unpublished thesis titled 'Globalisation, Gender and Migration: The Political Economy of Domestic Work', Jawaharlal Nehru University, New Delhi.
5   Department of Foreign Employment, Government of Nepal (2011).
6   Data from Ministry of Labour and Transport Management and IoM (2010), report titled 'Foreign Labour Migration and its Impact on Nepalese Economy, Kathmandu', cited in Adhikari and Hobley (2011: 12).
7   For some studies estimating migration rates to the Gulf, please see Kollmair et al. (2011) and Williams et al. (2013).
8   Data from Ministry of Labour and Transport Management and IoM (2010), report titled 'Foreign Labour Migration and its Impact on Nepalese Economy, Kathmandu', cited in Adhikari and Hobley (2011: 12).
9   Chapter 2, 'National Instruments Guiding Labour Migration in Nepal', in Sijapati and Limbu (2012: 25–68) provides an exhaustive overview of national legislation relating to labour migration in Nepal.

10 There is no official figure on the number of migrant workers who actually returned home from overseas with or without having finished their contracts but newspaper reports and informal conversations with recruitment agents and migration experts during the field study point to the numbers being substantially large.
11 The value of a Nepalese rupee was pegged to the Indian rupee in 1993 at a rate of 1.6 Nepalese rupees = 1 Indian rupee. Currently, 1 USD is equivalent to approximately 100 Nepalese rupees.
12 All names of respondents mentioned in this chapter are fictitious in order to protect their identity.

References

Adhikari, J. and M Hobley. 2011. "Everyone is Leaving – Who will Sow our Fields? The Effects of Migration from Khotang District to the Gulf and Malaysia", Swiss Agency for Development and Cooperation (SDC), Kathmandu.

Bajracharya, R. and B. Sijapati. 2012. The Kafala System and Its Implications for Nepali Domestic Workers, CESLAM Policy Brief, No. 1, March, http://www.soscbaha.org/publications/download/finish/1/79.html (last accessed on November 1, 2013).

Baldwin-Edwards, M. 2011. Labour Immigration and Labour Markets in the GCC Countries: National Patterns and Trends, Research Paper No. 15, Kuwait Programme on Development, Governance and Globalisation in the Gulf States, March.

Central Bureau of Statistics (CBS). 2004. Government of Nepal, Nepal Living Standards Survey 2003/04, Vols 1 and 2, Kathmandu.

———. 2006. *Agricultural Census of Nepal*. Kathmandu: CBS.

———. 2011a. *Preliminary Findings of Census 2011*. Kathmandu: CBS.

———. 2011b. *Preliminary Findings of NLSS III*. Kathmandu: CBS.

Department of Foreign Employment (DoFE). 2011. 'Labour Migration for Employment', Department of Foreign Employment, Government of Nepal,

Kollmair, M., S. Manandhar, B.P. Subedi and Thieme, S. 2006. 'New Figures for Old Stories: Migration and Remittances in Nepal', *Migration Letters*, 3(2): 151–60.

Lokshin, Michael, Mikhail Bontch-Osmolovski and Elena Glinskaya. 2007. 'Work-related Migration and Poverty Reduction in Nepal', Working Paper 4231, World Bank Policy Research, Washington D.C.

Nepal Institute of Development Studies (NIDS). 2011. *Nepal Migration Year Book 2010*. Kathmandu, Nepal.

Seddon, D., J. Adhikari and G. Gurung. 2001. *The New Lahure. Foreign Labour Migration and Remittance Economy of Nepal*. Kathmandu: NIDS.

Sharma, Sanjay and Deepak Thapa. 2013. 'Taken for Granted: Nepali Migration to India', Working Paper No. 3, Centre for the Study of Labour

Mobility (CSLM), http://www.ceslam.org/docs/publicationManagement/Migration_Nepal_India.pdf (accessed on 3 November 2013).

Sijapati, Bandita and Amrita Limbu. 2012. *Governing Labour Migration in Nepal: An Analysis of Existing Policies and Institutional Mechanisms.* Kathmandu: CSLM, Himal Books.

Thieme, Susan and Simone Wyss. 2005. 'Migration Patterns and Remittance Transfer in Nepal: A Case Study of Sainik Basti in Western Nepal', *International Migration*, 43(5): 59–96.

United Nations (UN). 2006. International Migration and Development, Report of the Secretary-General, Sixtieth Session of the UN General Assembly, Agenda Item 54(C), UN, Washington, DC.

United Nations Development Programme (UNDP). 2013. Human Development Report, The Rise of the South: Human Progress in a Diverse World, New York.

Williams, N., A. Thornton, D.J. Ghimire, L.C. Young-DeMarco and M. Moaddel. 2013. 'Nepali Migrants to the Gulf Cooperation Council Countries: Demographics, Behaviours and Plans', in M. Kamrava (ed.) *Migrants in the Gulf Coopereation Council Countries*. New York: Columbia University Press.

World Bank, 2010. 'Outlook for Remittance Flows 2010–2011', Migration and Development Brief, World Bank,Washington, DC.

Part III

Impact of migration

Chapter 9

Bangladeshi labour migration to Saudi Arabia

Md Mizanur Rahman

Introduction

The 1973 oil boom and the subsequent undertaking of an unprecedented number of development projects in the Gulf Cooperation Council (GCC) countries led to an extremely rapid increase in the demand for foreign labour (Arnold and Shah 1986; Eelens, Schampers and Speckmann 1991; Shah and Menon 1999). As a result, people from relatively labour-surplus but capital-poor countries of Maghreb, Mashreq and South and South East Asia have joined the labour markets of the GCC countries since the early 1970s (Shah 1994; Simel and Smith 2004). Over the decades, the GCC countries (Saudi Arabia, Qatar, Kuwait, Oman, Bahrain, and the UAE) have emerged as a relatively permanent destination for migrant workers. In 2008, migrant workers were estimated to form nearly 77 per cent of the total labour force in the GCC countries (Baldwin-Edwards 2011: 9; Winckler 2010: 12).

Labour migration to the GCC countries is temporary in nature, although the migration phenomenon is almost permanent in the Gulf society. This is because temporary labour migration has a structural role to play in the region's economy (Asis and Piper 2008: 426). Migrant workers in the GCC countries are hired under the *kafala* system for a specific duration. Additional measures such as not permitting the family reunion, not allowing marriages with locals and not tolerating procreation outside wedlock ensure the transiency of migrant labour in the Gulf. The GCC member countries follow an almost similar policy when it comes to hiring, retaining and deporting migrant workers (Kuptsch 2006; Rahman 2011b; Shah 2008). This common migration policy in the Gulf countries has forced migrant workers and their families (spouse, children and extended family members) to live under 'transnationally split' (Yeoh, Graham and Boyle 2002) conditions, with provision of physically visiting home countries during discretionary annual leave.

Since migrants and their families live under 'transnationally split' conditions, migrants remit back home to support family members who are left behind. As a result, labour migration is seen more as a livelihood strategy, whereby millions of left-behind families are maintaining better living standards in their home countries (Asis 1995; Asis, Huang and Yeoh 2004; Hugo 2002; Oda 2004; Pago 2008). The widely shared viewpoint is that temporary migration brings about economic advantage for migrants and their families (Hugo 2003; Schiller 2010). However, this description of temporary migration hides the subtle and complex considerations that provoke temporary migration and determine its course in the migration process. This is because potential migrants and their families in Asia are often presented with the opportunity to engage in migration that depletes family economic resources.

The popular assumption that temporary migration brings about economic advantage often links income risks and capital constraints in low-income countries. However, the opportunity for temporary employment in a high-income country does not necessarily translate into economic advantage for migrants and their migrant families in a low-income country. This is because the economic theory that explains migration in terms of income risks and capital constraints does not adequately take into account the risks and costs borne by migrants and their families in the contemporary migration process. To understand the economic advantage of labour migration, we need to consider the risks that a migrant is exposed to and the implications it carries for the migrant family's economy. This is an overly neglected aspect of labour migration research. This research attempts to close the gap in existing knowledge.

This research examines the nexus between emigration and emigrant family's economy by highlighting the undercurrent of the risks in the emigration process. This study draws from the experiences of Bangladeshi migrant families whose members are working in Saudi Arabia. Saudi Arabia is chosen for this study because it is the largest destination for Bangladeshi migrant workers and the largest remittance-source country for Bangladesh.

The next section presents the theoretical and conceptual issues relating to international labour migration and family dynamics followed by a brief discussion on the data sources for this study. The section on data sources provides the trends and patterns of Bangladeshi migration to Saudi Arabia. This is followed by a discussion of the kafala system under which migrant workers are invited to work in Saudi Arabia. An analysis of the economic costs of migration, the economic benefits of remittances, and the implications of these costs and benefits on family economic resources follows. The final section gives a summary of the findings of the study and discusses policy implications.

Theoretical and conceptual issues

Economic theories often address the economic causes and consequences of labour migration for migrants, their families and communities (Stark 1991; Straubhaar 1988; Taylor 1999; for an overview, see Martin 1991 and Massey et al. 1998). For instance, the neoclassical microeconomic model of individual choice views international labour migration as a sum of individual cost-benefit decisions undertaken to maximise actual income or expected income through international movement (Borjas 1989; Todaro 1976). However, in developing countries it is not the individuals but the families that mobilise resources for migration, and take charge of receiving and allocating remittances (Grasmuck and Pessar 1991: 15). Confronted with the inherent dilemma of who makes the decision in developing countries, the 'New Economics of Labour Migration (NELM) emerges with fresh insights to complement the neoclassical economic approach' (Stark 1991).

The NELM regards migration for work as a family decision and explains the migration decision by going beyond economic variables like the income differential between two countries. In NELM, migration is seen as a response to income risks and failures in a variety of local markets, for example, credit, crops and future markets in the developing countries (ibid.). This new theoretical perspective sees individual migration as a broader family strategy. Precisely, the NELM focuses on the family rather than the individual as the decision-making unit and paves the way for linking individual migrant behaviour with expectations of and obligations towards family members left behind, a phenomenon that was previously treated separately in the migration literature (Lauby and Stark 1988; Stark 1991).

Financial remittance (hereafter remittance) is the much cited link that theorists of new economics of labor migration always present as a case in point. The NELM recognises that in the developing world, markets for capital, the future and insurance are often absent, imperfect or inaccessible. In order to self-insure against risks to income, production and property, or to gain access to scarce investment capital, the family sends one or more members overseas for work. In other words, international migration is seen as a strategy for risk minimisation and capital accumulation (Stark 1991). Although the above discussion theoretically explains the rationale for migration from labour-abundant but capital-poor countries to labour-scarce but capital-rich countries, it does not account for the undercurrent of risks that migrants are exposed to in the migration process.

Temporary migration of labour is not necessarily free from risks and actual migration does not always minimise the risk of income and contribute to capital accumulation. This is because a migrant often commences an international trip for work by incurring large debts and risking personal savings and valuable family assets that undermine the family income and aggravates income risks and capital constraints. The major spheres of risks include the migrant worker programme under which migrants are hired, the recruitment procedures they undergo and the economic costs of migration they incur in the migration process. The migrant worker programme, popularly called the kafala system, is plagued with provisions/practices of lack of proper 'job contract', breach of contract in the midst of migration, limited horizontal and vertical mobility across different sectors of economy, and inadequate legal mechanisms for upholding workers' rights (Baldwin-Edwards 2011; HRW 2006, 2008, 2009; Simel and Smith 2004).

Migrant networks and recruitment agencies adapt to the changing practices of recruitment to funnel migrant workers to the GCC countries and the constellations of interests at different points create conflicts and contradictions throughout the recruitment process (Gamburd 2000; Rahman 2011a). Finally, the economic costs of migration usually refer to the expenses that migrants incur in the recruitment process. In some predominantly male migrant-sending countries such as Bangladesh and Pakistan, the term 'economic costs of migration' is widely used, while in some predominantly female migrant-sending countries such as the Philippines and Indonesia, the terms 'recruitment fees' and 'placement fees' are usually used instead of the economic costs of migration.

This is because sponsor-employers often pay for women's migration, especially in domestic worker migration and deduct the advance payment from the monthly salary of female workers when working with the sponsor-employers in the destination country (Lindquist 2010; Rahman and Lian 2009; Wilcke 2011). A key difference between the migration of men and women in Asia is that men must generally pay a fee to the recruitment agency prior to departure, while women do not usually pay (Rahman 2011a). Recently, Johan Lindquist elaborates the gendered differentiated patterns of recruitment by showing that while capital flows 'down' in the migration of women, for the migration of men capital flows 'up', from the migrant to the recruitment agency and sponsor (Lindquist 2010). As a result, the critical issue in the migration of men is precisely paying the economic costs of migration.

Apart from the migrant programme, recruitment process and economic costs involved, other spheres of risks such as working and living conditions, wages, access to remittance services and health care also have the potential to influence the economic experiences of migrant families. Therefore, we need to scrutinise labour migration as a process with all its intricacies so that the spheres of potential risks embedded in the migration process and the implications of exposure to these risks are fairly incorporated in the analysis. What I am suggesting is that there is a need to study the temporary migration of labour as a process with its complexities so that potential victimisation and exploitation that migrants experience in the migration process are taken into account. In doing so, we need to scrutinise some key aspects of temporary migration such as labour migration policy, migrant recruitment, the economic cost of migration, remittances, and the implications of the latter two on family economic dynamics.

In line with the theoretical development, scholars have widely reported the relationship between emigration and family in Asia (Asis 1995, 2000, 2003; Gunatilleke 1992; Hugo 2002; Zlotnik 1995). The existing literature provides profound insights into the functional and structural changes that take place within a family under conditions of migration. These include moderate changes in headship and gender roles; upward social mobility; successful adjustment in the absence of male or female migrants; improved education, health care and quality of life; left-behind women taking on roles previously assumed by the men; left-behind children learning to be more independent and so on (Asis, Huang and Yeoh 2004; Gamburd 2000; Parreñas 2005; Rahman 2009; Semyonov and Gorodzeisky 2005; Zachariah Mathew and Rajan 2001).

Thus, the existing studies enhance our understanding of the broader implications of migration on family dynamics and guide us to deepen our analysis further on other prominent aspects of family dynamics such as family economic dynamics. Temporary migration affects family economic dynamics in at least two ways: one is the outflow of indispensable family resources to meet the expenses incurred in the migration process (referred to as the 'economic cost of migration') and the other is the transfer in cash (or kind) from migrants to their non-migrating families in the countries of origin (referred to as the 'migrant remittances'). Both economic costs of migration and migrant remittances thus affect family economy in the migration process. In studying the implications of emigration on family economic dynamics it is therefore imperative to shed light on both the outflow of family economic resources and the inflow of remittances to the family.

Data sources

This research is based principally on the Bangladesh Household Remittance Survey (BHRS) conducted in 2009. The BHRS collected information from a nationally representative sample of 10,926 migrant households. The BHRS was implemented by the International Organization for Migration (IOM) in Dhaka with financial support from the Department for International Development (DFID, United Kingdom (UK)). Unlike the small-scale surveys (e.g. small migrant worker surveys or village case studies) that delimit the scope of research and retard the generalisability of the study, the strength of the representative survey lies in its ability to generalise the study and elucidate the findings with confidence. In addition to the survey data, the study also draws from qualitative interviews of prospective migrants, returnees and members of migrant households in Bangladesh conducted in the second half of 2009.

The BHRS covered migrant households across the country through a nationally representative sample from all seven administrative divisions of Bangladesh.[1] The districts of the seven divisions of the country were divided into two strata, with one stratum consisting of 'More Concentration of Migrant' (MCM) households and the other stratum consisting of 'Less Concentration of Migrant' (LCM) households'. Following this, clusters were formed with one or more *mauza*s (closely synonymous with a village), depending on the cluster's size as set in terms of number of general households. These clusters were selected independently from each stratum using the Probability Proportional to Size (PPS) method of selection. The total sample was made up of 457 clusters (i.e. 257 from MCM districts and 200 from LCM districts). All households in every selected cluster were listed, identifying only the migrant households. Household listings were done by taking a complete census of the households in each of the clusters. This involved visiting every household in the designated area.

In the survey, a migrant household has been defined as a household that had at least one of its members living/working abroad for a period of at least one year at the time of the survey. The selection of the migrant household was made independently of their current status (e.g. regular or irregular) in the country of destination. The head or other responsible member of the household was interviewed in the survey. The survey covered a wide range of migration issues encompassing socio-economic background, processing and economic costs of migration, working and living conditions, remittances, and impact of remittances on households. The survey comprised 4,427 migrants who were working in Saudi Arabia. Therefore, this study represents the experiences of these 4,427 migrants and their families. Given the nature of the survey and the number of cases, the study is expected to produce much needed insights into the interface between emigration and family economic dynamics in the Bangladesh-Saudi Arabia migration corridor.

Bangladeshi migration to Saudi Arabia

Saudi Arabia, the sacred land of Islamic devotion to Muslims from all around the world, is also the largest temporary migrant-worker receiving country in the Middle East. Like other GCC countries, labour migration to Saudi Arabia started after the 1973 oil price hike. The growth of foreigners in Saudi Arabia was steady and remarkable: 4.63 million foreigners in 1992, 5.25 million in 2000, and 8.42 million in 2010 (Fargues 2011: 12). Despite the presence of the highest number of foreigners, unlike other GCC countries, foreigners in Saudi Arabia have never surpassed the local population. Nevertheless, 31 per cent of the total population belonged to foreigners in Saudi Arabia in 2010 (*ibid*.: 13). Broadly, foreigners can be categorised as low-skilled or high-skilled professional migrants. The majority of foreigners are low-skilled migrants, working in construction, manufacturing, services, agriculture, and domestic sectors and living in camps with other co-workers or in owners' residences (in the case of domestic workers).

Saudi Arabia is a popular destination for Bangladeshi migrants. The official record of labour migration flows to the GCC countries was initiated by the Bureau of Manpower, Employment and Training (BMET) in 1976. According to BMET, the formal recruitment of Bangladeshi labour to Saudi Arabia started in 1976 with only 217 migrants. The total number of migrants who went to Saudi Arabia for work between 1976 and 1980 was nearly 20,000; between 1981 and 1990, approximately 300,000; between 1991 and 2000, about 1.18 million; and between 2001 and 2013, around 1.3 million (Figure 9.1). In total, over 9 million Bangladeshi migrants sought overseas employment between 1976 and 2013 and of these migrants nearly 2.8 million joined the labour market in Saudi Arabia. Bangladeshi migrants from Saudi Arabia remitted over US$30 billion to their families between 2000 and 2013 (Figure 9.2).

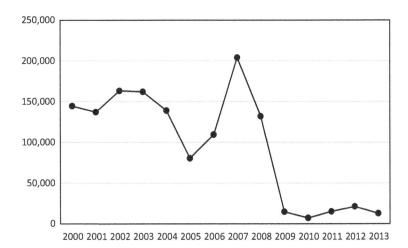

Figure 9.1 Trends of Bangladeshi migration to Saudi Arabia, 2000–13

Source: The Bureau of Manpower, Employment and Training (BMET) data, retrieved on 15 June 2014.

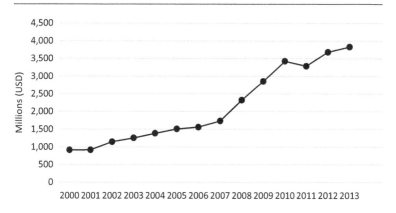

Figure 9.2 Trends of remittances from Saudi Arabia to Bangladesh, 2000–13

Source: BMET, Ministry of Expatriates' Welfare and Overseas Employment (MEWOE) and Bangladesh Bank (BB). BMET and MEWOE information was retrieved on 15 June 2014.

Kafala system and recruitment of labour to Saudi Arabia

Labour recruitment in Saudi Arabia and other GCC countries is governed by the kafala or sponsorship system (Baldwin-Edwards 2011; Colton 2010; De Bel-Air 2011; Longva 1999; Shah 1994).[2] Under this system, a migrant is sponsored by an employer who is a GCC citizen. The kafeel, i.e. the employer-sponsor, assumes full economic and legal responsibility for the employee during the contract period. A kafeel may be an individual, a placement agency or a company/ institution. The system works such that the migrant worker can only work for a kafeel for a specific period of time. Kafeels often hold the worker's passport and other travel documents. Foreign workers are not allowed to marry or be involved in sexual relationships with locals. However, professional foreigners (expatriates) can marry locals, but citizenship is not guaranteed and local men enjoy greater privileges over local women when it comes to international marriage and citizenship issues.[3] The overall emphasis of the kafala system is control and to ensure 'flexibility' to fluctuations in the labour market.

The kafala system has given birth to the so-called 'visa trade', a multimillion dollar industry in the Gulf (Shah 2008). The visa trade involves the sale of a work visa. In the UAE, for instance, a work visa for an Indian is sold for around US$2000 (or AED 7,500)[4] (*ibid.*: 9). The scale of visa trading is so massive that the Saudi labour minister reported that 70 per cent of the visas issued by the government were sold on the black market (*ibid.*). The kafala system has been met with much criticism over the years. It has been accused of encouraging corruption, visa trading and the importation of more workers than can be accommodated by the labour market (Colton 2010, De Bel-Air 2011; Shah 2010). Since the system generates lucrative incomes for local sponsors, governments in the Gulf countries have so far failed to stop visa trading, notwithstanding the genuine interests, in part, of the Gulf governments to stop the practice.

Recruiting agencies and migrant networks play a critical role in the recruitment of other South Asian migrants to the Gulf countries (Arif 2009; Gamburd 2000; Gunatilleke 1991; Osella and Osella 2000; Shah and Menon 1999; Zachariah, Mathew and Rajan 2001). Both actors are also involved in the recruitment of Bangladeshis to Saudi Arabia. In the recruitment system assisted by a recruiting agency, the process involves the following episodes and actors. A recruiting agency in Saudi Arabia places a 'demand letter' to its counterpart in Bangladesh. The recruiting agency in Bangladesh then searches for prospective migrants and asks them to submit the required documents (passport, pictures, biographic information and partial payment) to begin the process. The recruiting agency in Bangladesh relies heavily on intermediaries called sub-agents, who act as mediators between a prospective migrant and a licensed recruiting agent. These sub-agents help prospective migrants find jobs and help agencies find prospective workers in a more timely fashion. Sub-agents charge fees to recruiting agencies for their services.

Once the potential migrant submits all documents to the sub-agent, the sub-agent passes the documents to the recruiting agency for further action. Upon receiving the documents from the sub-agents, the recruiting agency in Bangladesh contacts its counterpart in Saudi Arabia for visa processing. The potential kafeel then secures the visa from the relevant authority in Saudi Arabia and sends it to the recruiting agency in Bangladesh. It usually takes a few weeks from the submission of documents to the kafeel in Saudi Arabia to the delivery of the work visa to the recruiting agency in Bangladesh. The recruitment procedures described here are not specific to the Bangladesh-Saudi Arabia corridor; similar recruitment procedures are noticed in other GCC destinations for Bangladeshi migrants. In fact, migrant workers from other South Asian countries also go through similar recruitment procedures for the Gulf countries (Arif

2009; Arnold and Shah 1986; Gamburd 2000; Gunatilleke 1992; Oda 2004).

As migration matures, many potential migrants learn more about the process of migration and the way to seek alternative services for jobs in Saudi Arabia. Instead of finding jobs with agencies, many potential migrants seek jobs arranged with a kafeel in Saudi Arabia through personal networks. A working visa arranged through personal networks is called '*Urro* visa' in Bengali or 'flying visa' in English, so called because it flies directly from a migrant broker in Saudi Arabia to a prospective migrant in Bangladesh. In other words, it bypasses local recruiting agencies and their sub-agents (for details, see Rahman 2011a). Arranging a 'flying visa' usually proceeds as follows. A migrant broker finds a job for a friend or relative usually with his/her kafeel or the kafeel's network of friends and relatives. After successfully identifying a potential kafeel, the migrant broker arranges the required documents and passes them to the potential kafeel for a work visa. Once a work visa is procured, the migrant broker sends it to the potential migrant in Bangladesh.

Apart from the 'flying visa', there is another type of visa called the 'free visa' (Rahman 2011a). Although there is no official category of visas called 'free visas' in the Gulf countries, the term is widely used among migrant communities. Pakistani migrants call it '*azad*' (free) visa in Urdu. This unofficial category of visas allows a potential migrant to enter a GCC country for work under the kafala system, but the sponsor-employer (kafeel) who officially sponsors the migrant does not offer paid work. Instead, a free visa holder finds a job on his own, but by working for an employer other than his kafeel, the migrant workers become illegal and vulnerable to deportation.

As discussed earlier, visa trading generates additional incomes for kafeels, thereby driving irregular recruitment practices in Saudi Arabia. The problem exists whether workers are recruited under general work visa, flying visa or free visa. However, it is the free visa that exposes migrants to job insecurities and deportation. Such a recruitment practice denies migrant workers of the very basic right of work and deprives them of earning, which motivated them to work overseas. Moreover, since recruitment practices are shaped by a constellation of vested interests at different points in the system, they increase the economic costs of migration, which means that migrants will need longer time to recover their recruitment expenses. The next section discusses this issue in detail.

The economic costs of migration to Saudi Arabia

The economic cost of migration involves not only the actual financial costs of migration but also the embedded costs, that is, the sources of arranging the financial cost of migration and their potential impact on family economic dynamics. To secure a job in Saudi Arabia, a potential migrant is required to pay part of the financial costs, which is often about one-fourth to one-half of the total cost, to the middlemen/sub-agents in advance. The remaining amount is usually paid in several instalments depending on the progress of the visa application. All dues are payable for the recruitment agency-mediated recruitment before a prospective migrant flies to Saudi Arabia. However, in the migrant broker-initiated recruitment some exceptions may happen, especially when prospective migrants are close relatives of migrant brokers.

After paying the recruitment-related fees, migrants have to wait for some time before they can actually leave for Saudi Arabia. The waiting time between the first payment and the departure for Saudi Arabia should not ideally take more than three months. As discussed earlier, the issuing of a working visa in Saudi Arabia and transferring it to the recruiting agency or the prospective migrant in Bangladesh should not require more than a few weeks. Of the surveyed migrants, around 57 per cent of migrants received the work visa and flew to Saudi Arabia within three months. However, 11 per cent waited between three and five months while 32 per cent had to wait between six and 13 months, or even longer. On average, a migrant had to wait around 5.22 months to complete the recruitment procedures in Bangladesh. This is because sub-agents often manipulate the waiting time for profit out of migrants' initial payments.

Since the demand for visas is higher than the supply of visas, potential migrants are forced to make extra payments to secure a job placement, generating additional revenues for sub-agents. For migrants, advance payment and the delaying of recruitment increases the cost of migration as they often borrow from moneylenders at a higher interest rate and this undermines the family economy as such sources of funds put pressure on family incomes. Once prospective migrants initiate the recruitment procedure with the first instalment, they cannot cease the recruitment and claim repayment of the full amount. This exposes potential migrants to victimisation and exploitation, even in the country of their origin.

This study maps out three important aspects of the economic costs of migration, namely the sources of funds, the contribution of multiple sources to the needed funds, and disbursement of financial cost of migration as formal service fees and intermediary fees. The average cost of migration to Saudi Arabia was in BDT206,058[5] or USD3,000.[6] The Bangladesh government set BDT84,000 (USD1,230) as a maximum recruiting fee for migrants going to the Gulf countries and Malaysia (Martin 2010: 12). However, financial transactions between the prospective migrant and the recruiting agency are not strictly monitored by the government agencies. As a result, the government-set fee has hardly any influence on the actual cost of migration.

The average cost of migration to Saudi Arabia (BDT206,058 or USD3,000) was an amount that was virtually beyond the personal savings of migrants. Most migrants had to rely on multiple sources to accumulate the funds for migration. The major sources of securing funds, by frequency of occurrence, were as follows: selling land (27 per cent), mortgaging land (23 per cent), taking a loan (72 per cent), and disposing other family assets such as livestock and jewellery (19 per cent). Only 9 per cent of migrants used personal savings to meet the expenses of migration. The study also outlines the contribution of each source to the total cost of the migration project. Of the total cost, 24 per cent were sourced from the selling or mortgaging of land, 52 per cent came from loans and other sources such as contributions from in-laws and dowry, and selling of family assets (e.g. livestock and jewellery) constituted nearly 20 per cent. Around 4 per cent were derived from personal savings.

Considering the high cost of migration, this study further investigates the major areas of expenses in the recruitment process to offer a glimpse into the distribution of economic costs across different service providers. The study divides the economic costs of migration into: (*i*) formal service fees that include government fees, passport fees, wage earners' contributions and other relevant mandatory service fees in Bangladesh and (*ii*) mediators' fees that include fees charged by intermediaries and recruiting agencies for their services. The former accounts, on average, for about 24 per cent of the total cost, and the remaining 76 per cent represent intermediaries' fees.

It is important to note that regardless of the channels of recruitment, intermediaries' fees also include kickback fees inherent in the economic costs of migration to Saudi Arabia.[7] The bulk of the intermediaries' fees actually goes to the recruiting agencies or sponsor-employers on the Saudi side (see also, De Bel-Air 2011; Gardner 2010). Although the Bangladeshi media often blames the recruiting agencies in Bangladesh for the exorbitant fees, they are in fact making a tiny profit while the bulk of the profit goes to the other side of the recruitment end which deserves more in-depth investigation.

Considering the enormous costs of securing an overseas work contract, potential migrants need to tap different sources to raise the needed amount. To invest in migration, migrants sell off family assets, borrow from moneylenders who charge high interest rates, and exhaust the savings of migrants and their family members. The migration project can undermine family economy in two ways. First, it hampers regular family incomes because income-generating assets, such as land, livestock and the like are sold or mortgaged to raise money for recruitment-related fees. Second, the loans constrain the family's resource use. To ascertain some of the impact of migration on family economic dynamics, this study examines the size of landholdings and loan status at the time of survey.

Land is a crucial income contributor and status marker in South Asia (Oda 2008). Nearly 50 per cent of the surveyed migrant households sold or mortgaged land to repay migration expenses, which means that these households have been deprived of regular incomes from land. Additionally, the landownership pattern is very polarised in Bangladesh. Rapid population growth and the inheritance law have led to fragmentation of land over time and the number of landless households is over 50 per cent in Bangladesh (Monsur 2008). In the survey, nearly 42 per cent of households had no agricultural land, that is, they were landless. The remaining 58 per cent may be considered marginal landowners as they own certain amount of agricultural land. On average, they owned approximately 181 decimal of agricultural land, which is much lower than the minimum land a rural household requires for subsistence for a family of five members in Bangladesh (Bertocci 1972).

Apart from landholdings, 72 per cent of migrant households took out loans from moneylenders (69.05 per cent) and non-governmental organisations (NGOs) (2.75 per cent). At the time of the survey, nearly 61 per cent of migrants had outstanding loans to repay; the average loan amounted to BDT157,057 or USD2,286 (USD1=BDT68.68). More than 77 per cent of the migrants were working in Saudi Arabia for a period of three years or longer, and yet the majority of migrant households were still saddled with sizable debt. It is important to note that the interest rate for migration loans is different from other types of loans such as those for agriculture, business, weddings, and festivals (Rahman 2009). Since migration is perceived to yield high returns, money-lenders charge up to 7–10 per cent interest per month or roughly 100 per cent interest per year. If the interest is compounded, the debt will double in less than a year and triple in less than two years.

In the decision to seek overseas employment, there is indeed a trade-off between the possibility of higher incomes and the destruction of the existing family economy. Many choose migration with the hope that remittances can compensate for the potential collapse of the existing family economy. Whether the hope that they have pinned on remittances is realistic is discussed in the next section.

Inflows of remittances to migrant families

We have so far seen the outflow of family resources and its implications on family economy. Remittances are the most tangible benefit that labour migration generates for migrants and their families. However, the amount and frequency of remittances are important variables for the economic well-being of the migrant families. The amount of remittances is contingent on the monthly incomes of the migrants overseas. Therefore, this study investigates the monthly remuneration of migrants in Saudi Arabia. On average, the monthly remuneration of the migrants was BDT18,723 or USD273. While this amount is several times higher than what a job in Bangladesh would have offered, if the monthly salary is estimated against the economic costs of migration, which was on average BDT206,058 or USD3,000, a migrant requires roughly 11 months to recoup his/her financial cost of migration if other expenses are controlled.

This chapter presents inflows of remittances and family economy in three phases. First, it presents the average amount of remittances for each transfer and the frequency of remittance transfers in a year. Second, the study maps out major areas of use of remittances such as family expenses, repayment of loan, medical and education expenses, and income generation. Third, it discusses the implications of remittances on remittance-receiving families in terms of food, education and income. On average, migrants remitted approximately four times a year. The average amount of each transfer was BDT22,258 or USD324. If average remittances and frequency of remittances are calculated, a migrant household received around USD1,296 in a year. Given the annual flow of remittances to migrant households, a migrant needs roughly 2.31 years to recover the actual financial cost of migration if other expenses are controlled. In actual fact, it takes migrants more than 2.31 years to repay loans because of the deficit of family incomes.

This study also explores who migrants usually remit to and who manages the remittances in households. According to the survey, on average, 31 per cent of migrants remitted to their spouses (i.e. wives) – note that nearly 32 per cent of migrants were married. Interestingly, 55 per cent of migrants remitted to their fathers – 67 per cent of migrants in the sample were unmarried. The remaining migrants remitted to other members of the family such as sisters and brothers and, in some cases, to close relatives. The flow of remittances between migrant husbands and left-behind wives vis-à-vis migrant sons and fathers is an area where an in-depth study is required. The management of remittances, especially when migrant workers (remitters) are away, is critical to understanding intra-household relations and its gendered outcomes. In terms of making decisions about management of remittances, 71 per cent of recipients revealed that they made the decision themselves, 2 per cent of recipients made the decision as instructed by the migrants overseas, 5 per cent of recipients who were not family members (migrant in Saudi Arabia remitted to outside family members) made the decision themselves, and 22 per cent of migrants and their recipients mutually decided how to manage remittances. The latter was predominantly recipients who were wives of migrants, hinting at improved gender relations between the wife at home and the overseas-based husband.

The use of remittances is an important indicator for family economic dynamics. Migrant families used the funds for a myriad purposes such as basic expenses (food and clothing), purchasing land or property, repayment of debts, savings, construction of house, marrying off a brother or sister, education, medical treatment, religious festivals (e.g. Eid-ul-Fitr and Eid-ul-Azha), purchasing cattle and so on. The five major areas of use of remittances are family expenses, followed by loan repayment, medical treatment, education and local income generation. Around 88 per cent of households used remittances to meet their family's basic expenses, 31 per cent used remittances for loan repayment, 22 per cent for medical treatment, 19 per cent for education, and 18 per cent for local income generation.

In addition to economic purposes, remittances were also used for religious festivals (6 per cent) and marrying off brothers or sisters (1.31 per cent). Nearly 6 per cent of households saved a part of their remittances for future use. The use of remittances in the above fields suggests that migrant households prioritised expenses according to local requirements. For instance, it may seem unproductive to spend hard-earned remittances for religious festivals or marrying off siblings. However, the social expectation of migrant households in the communities of origin and local perceptions about development (such as capacity to marry off grown up sisters) are important for migrant households that they cannot overlook them in the communities they live in and claim honour and prestige (Gamburd 1995; Rahman 2009). Therefore, there is a need to incorporate the local meaning of development in the broader migration and development debate.

Remittances showed some visible impact on the migrant families in terms of food consumption, education, and local income generation. Around 74 per cent of families reported having improved food consumption and nearly 67 per cent of families reported having enhanced educational opportunities. However, the role of remittances in income generation was mixed: nearly 27 per cent of migrant families reported an increase in incomes through establishing new sources of income, investing or expanding existing sources of income and making deposits in banks/buying stocks or savings certificates. However, given the extent of landlessness and indebtedness, it is not surprising to see the low use of remittances in income generation.

Conclusion

This study has addressed the attendant risks in the temporary labour migration process and its implications for migrant family economy in the Bangladesh-Saudi Arabia migration corridor. The study particularly highlights the nature and extent of risks that migrants are exposed to in the migration process. The NELM explains migration as a response to risks of incomes and failures to local markets. The catchy phrases that theorists often use to explain the initiation of migration in the developing world is 'risk-minimising' and 'capital-accumulating' strategy. The study has argued that international migration for work is not necessarily free of risks and that actual migration does not always contribute to capital accumulation. This study has shown that migrants often undertake international migration, incurring large debts and exhausting personal savings and family assets that undermine families' incomes and aggravate income risks and capital constraints.

The research examined labour migration as a process by high-lighting the key aspects of recruitment, economic costs of migration, incomes, and remittances, and implications of economic costs and remittances on family economy. In the context of recruitment, this study has identified two areas where migrants are exposed to victimisation and exploitation. One is the delaying of recruitment by intermediaries that increases the economic cost of migration, and the other is the provision of free visas for migrant workers, which can prevent migrants from working in Saudi Arabia.

The issue of the economic costs of migration not only exposes migrants to victimisation and exploitation but also undermines the family economy. The study has shown how the financial costs of migration expose migrant families to risks of losing local incomes and incurring debts. In terms of the implications of remittances on family economy, the study reports that 74 per cent of migrant households enjoyed improved food consumption, 67 per cent enjoyed enhanced educational opportunities, and 27 per cent experienced increased incomes because of inflows of remittances to family economy. The receipt, control and management also have implications for family relationships, especially between husbands and wives.

At the policy level, this study has identified three areas that require policy intervention. First, specific policy intervention is required to stop labour migration under the free visa category. Second, the financial cost of migration is excessively high and government may consider imposing restrictions on maximum recruitment costs and also the enforcement of these measures. Third, the government may introduce soft loans for all applicants for overseas jobs so that prospective migrants will not be overly burdened by excessive interest rates. This will also help retain existing regular income flows to households and enable them to benefit from remittances.

By providing gainful employment to around 8 million migrants, mainly from South Asia, South East Asia, Maghreb and Mashreq regions, and allowing them to remit around USD29 billion in a year (as in 2010[8]), Saudi Arabia is indeed making a vital contribution to the socio-economic transformation taking place in migrant-source countries throughout the region. This contribution by Saudi Arabia deserves more recognition from the sending countries. However, the high economic cost of migration and the reports of maltreatment of migrant workers in Saudi Arabia are also a matter of concern for many sending countries (for details, see HRW 2008). Therefore, there is a need to adopt policy measures to ensure the fair treatment and welfare of migrant workers in Saudi Arabia. As a host country, the burden of improving the status of migrant workers principally lies with Saudi Arabia. Furthermore, Saudi Arabia is the birthplace of a great religion that enshrines and promotes core human values including fair treatment and this also puts much hope for immediate attention.

Research on migration and its implications on family economy in the South Asia-GCC migration corridor is an understudied area and much work is required to understand the risks that migrants and their families assume in the migration process. This study should be seen as an initial attempt in conceptualising emigration and family economy, and building on it can further the analysis of migration and family economy.

Notes

1   Bangladesh is divided into major administrative regions called divisions and each division is further split into districts. In total, there are seven divisions and 64 districts in Bangladesh.
2   I have explained elsewhere about the kafala system and recruitment in the GCC countries. Please see Rahman (2011a).
3   Based on various issues of *Gulf News*, a leading news source for Gulf countries, http://gulfnews.com/news/gulf/uae/visa/scheme-should-not-include-arab-women-say-gcc-nationals-1.295400; http://gulfnews.com/news/gulf/saudi-arabia/wedding-costs-force-saudis-to-look-for-brides-overseas-1.646907 ; http://gulfnews.com/opinions/columnists/foreign-marriages-don-t-blame-it-on-the-dowry-1.679794; http://gulfnews.com/news/gulf/uae/general/national-women-demand-equal-rights-as-men-1.222720 (accessed on the 20 December 2011).
4   AED: United Arab Emirates dirham.
5   BDT: Bangladeshi Taka.
6   All Bangladeshi currency (BDT) figures were converted into USD in early 2010. The exchange rate was USD 1= BDT68.68.
7   For details on the visa trade, see De Bel-Air (2011) and Shah (2008), and also *Gulf News*, 13 April 2004.
8   Zawya, leading business intelligence on the Middle East and North Africa, http://www.zawya.com/story.cfm/sidZAWYA20110908030328/Foreigners_in_Saudi_remitted_over_29bn_in_2010 (accessed on 12 September 2011).

References

Arif, G. M. 2009. 'Recruitment of Pakistani Workers for Overseas Employment: Mechanism, Exploitation and Vulnerabilities', Working Paper No. 64, International Labour Organization, Geneva.

Arnold, Fred and Nasra M. Shah (eds).1986. *Asian Labor Migration: Pipeline to the Middle East*. London: Westview Press.

Asis, Maruja M. B. 1995. 'Overseas Employment and Social Transformation in Source Communities: Findings from the Philippines', *Asian and Pacific Migration Journal*, 4(2–3): 327–46.

———. 2000. 'Imaging the Future of Migration and Families in Asia', *Asian and Pacific Migration Journal*, 9(3): 255–74.

———. 2003. 'International Migration and Families in Asia', in Robyn Iredale, Charles Hawksley and Stephen Castles (eds), *Migration in the Asia Pacific: Population, Settlement and Citizenship Issues*. Celtenham: Edward Elegar.

Asis, Maruja M. B. and Nicola Piper. 2008. 'Researching International Labor Migration in Asia', *The Sociological Quarterly*, 49: 423–44.

Asis, Maruja M. B., Shirlena Huang and Brenda S.A. Yeoh. 2004. 'When the Light of the Home is Abroad: Unskilled Female Migration and the Filipino Family', *Singapore Journal of Tropical Geography*, 25(2):198–215.

Baldwin-Edwards, Martin. 2011. 'Labor Immigration and Labor Markets in the GCC Countries: National Patterns and Trends', *LSE Global Governance*, 15 (March): 1–73, http://www2.lse.ac.uk/government/research/resgroups/kuwait/documents/Baldwin-Edwards,%20Martin.pdf (accessed on 8 December 2011).

Bertocci, Peter J. 1972. 'Community Structure and Social Rank in Two Villages in Bangladesh', *Contributions to Indian Sociology*, VI: 19–52.

Borjas, George J. 1989. 'Economic Theory and International Migration', *International Migration Review*, 23(3): 457–85.

Colton, Nora Ann. 2010. 'The International Political Economy of Gulf Migration', *Migration and the Gulf*, The Middle East Institute, Washington, DC.

De Bel-Air, Françoise. 2011. 'Reforming the Sponsorship (Kafala) in the GCC Countries: What Socio-political Stakes? The Case of Saudi Arabia'. Conference paper presented at Workshop 12, *Migration in the Gulf*, Gulf Research Meeting, University of Cambridge, 6–9 July.

Eelens, Frank, T. Schampers and J.D. Speckmann. 1991. *Labor Migration to the Middle East: From Sri Lanka to the Gulf*. London: Kegan Paul.

Fargues, Philippe. 2011. 'Immigration without Inclusion: Non-nationals in Gulf State Nation Building'. Conference paper, 2011 Gulf Research Meeting, University of Cambridge, 6–9 July.

Gamburd, Michele Ruth. 1995. 'Sri Lanka's "Army of Housemaids": Control of Remittances and Gender Transformations', *Anthropologica*, 37(1): 49–88.

———. 2000. *Transnationalism and Sri Lanka's Migrant Households: The Kitchen Spoon's Handle*. New Delhi: Vistaar Publications.

Gardner, A.M. 2010. *City of Strangers: Gulf Migration and the Indian Community in Bahrain*. London: Cornell University Press.

Grasmuck, Sherri and Patricia R. Pessar. 1991. *Between Two Islands: Dominican International Migration.* Berkeley: University of California Press.

Gulf News. 2004. 'Illegal Visa Trade still Flourishes', 13 April, http://gulfnews.com/news/gulf/uae/visa/illegal-visa-trade-still-flourishes-1.319255 (accessed on 20 December 2011).

Gunatilleke, G. (ed.). 1991. *The Impact of Labor Migration on Households: A Comparative Study in Seven Asian Countries.* Tokyo: UNU Press.

Hugo, Graeme J. 2002. 'Effects of International Migration on the Family in Indonesia', *Asian and Pacific Migration Journal*, 11(1): 13–46.

———. 2003. *Migration and Development: A Perspective from Asia*, IOM Migration Research Series, No. 14. Geneva: International Organization for Migration.

Human Rights Watch (HRW). 2006. *Building Towers, Cheating Workers: Exploitation of Migrant Construction Workers in the UAE*, Human Rights Watch Report, Volume 18, No. 8(E), Human Rights Watch.

———. 2008. *"As if I am not Human": Abuses against Asian Domestic Workers*, Human Rights Watch Report (July), New York: HRW.

———. 2009. '*The Island of Happiness: Exploitation of Migrant Workers on Saadiyat Island, Abu Dhabi*, Human Rights Watch Report, New York: HRW.

Kuptsch, Christiane (ed.). 2006. *Merchants of Labor.* Geneva: International Labour Organization.

Lauby, J. and O. Stark. 1988. 'Individual Migration as a Family Strategy: Young Women in the Philippines', *Population Studies*, 42(3): 473–86.

Lindquist, Johan. 2010. 'Labour Recruitment, Circuits of Capital and Gendered Mobility: Reconceptualising the Indonesian Migration Industry', *Pacific Affairs*, 83(1): 115–27.

Longva, A. N. 1999. 'Keeping Migrant Workers in Check: The Kafala System in the Gulf', *Middle East Report* 29(211): 20–2.

Martin, Philip. 1991. 'Labor Migration: Theory and Reality', in D. Papademetriou and P. Martin (eds), *The Unsettled Relationship: Labor Migration and Economic Development.* New York: Greenwood Press, pp. 27–42.

———. 2010. 'The Future of Labour Migration Cost', in *World Migration Report 2010.* Geneva: International Organization for Migration.

Massey, Douglas S. et al. 1998. *Worlds in Motion – Understanding International Migration at the End of the Millennium.* Oxford: Clarendon Press.

Monsur, Sadman Khaled. 2008. 'Landlessness and its Impact on Economic Development', *Star Campus*, 2(86): 7–8.

Oda, Hisaya (ed.). 2004. *International Labor Migration from South Asia.* Tokyo: Institute of Developing Economies.

———. 2008. 'The Impact of Labor Migration on Household Well-being: Evidence from Villages in the Punjab, Pakistan', in H. Sato and M.

Murayama (eds), *Globalization, Employment and Mobility: the South Asian Experience*. New York and Tokyo: Palgrave and IDE-JETRO, pp. 39–69.

Osella, F. and C. Osella. 2000. 'Migration, Money and Masculinity in Kerala', *The Journal of the Royal Anthropological Institute*, 6(1): 117–33.

Pajo, Erind. 2008. *International Migration, Social Demotion and Imagined Advancement: An Ethnography of Socioglobal Mobility*. New York: Springer.

Parreñas, Rhacel Salazar. 2005. *Children of Global Migration: Transnational Families and Gendered Woes*. Stanford, CA.: Stanford University Press.

Rahman, Md. Mizanur. 2009. *In Quest of Golden Deer: Bangladeshi Transient Migrants Overseas*. Saarbrucken: VDM Verlag.

———. 2011a. 'Recruitment of Labor Migrants in the GCC Countries: The Case of Bangladeshis', Working Paper No. 130, Institute of South Asian Studies, National University of Singapore.

———. 2011b. 'Bangladeshi Migrant Workers in the UAE: Gender-differentiated Patterns of Migration Experiences', *Middle Eastern Studies*, 47(2): 395–412.

Rahman, Md. Mizanur and Lian Kwen Fee. 2009. 'Gender and the Remittance Process: Indonesian Domestic Workers in Hong Kong, Singapore, and Malaysia', *Asian Population Studies*, 5(2): 103–27

Schiller, Nina Glick. 2010. 'A Global Perspective on Migration and Development', in Glick Nina Schiller and Thomas Faist (eds), *Migration, Development and Transnationalism: A Critical Stance*. Oxford: Berghahn Books.

Semyonov, Moshe and Anastasia Gorodzeisky. 2005. 'Labor Migration, Remittances and Household Income: A Comparison between Filipino and Filipina Overseas Workers', *International Migration Review*, 39(1): 45–69.

Shah, M. Nasra. 1994. 'Arab Labor Migration: A Review of Trends and Issues', *International Migration*, 32(1): 3–27.

———. 2008. 'Recent Labor Immigration Policies in the Oil-Rich Gulf: How Effective are they likely to be?' ILO Asian Regional Programme on Governance of Labor Migration Working Paper No 3, International Organization for Migration, Bangkok.

———. 2010. 'Building State Capacities for Managing Contract Worker Mobility: The Asia-GCC Context', in *World Migration Report 2010*. Geneva: International Organization for Migration.

Shah, M. Nasra and Indu Menon. 1999. 'Chain Migration through the Social Network: Experience of Labor Migrants in Kuwait', *International Migration*, 37(2): 361–82.

Simel, Esim and Monica Smith (eds). 2004. *Gender and Migration in Arab States: The Case of Domestic Workers*. Geneva: International Labour Organization.

Stark, Oded. 1991. *The Migration of Labor*. Oxford: Basil Blackwell.

Straubhaar, Thomas. 1988. *On the Economics of International Labor Migration*. London: Verlag, Bern und Stuttgart: Paul Haupt.

Taylor, J. E. 1999. 'The New Economics of Labor Migration and the Role of Remittances in the Migration Process', *International Migration*, 37(1): 63–88.

Todaro, Michael P. 1976. 'Internal Migration in Developing Countries: A Review of Theory, Evidence, Methodology and Research Priorities', A WEP Study, International Labour Office, Geneva.

Wilcke, C. 2011. *Domestic Plight: How Jordanian Laws, Officials, Employers and Recruiters Fail Abused Migrant Domestic Workers*. New York: Human Rights Watch.

Winckler, Onn. 2010. 'Labor Migration to the GCC States: Patterns, Scale, and Policies', in *Migration and the Gulf*, Middle East Institute, Washington, DC.

Yeoh, Brenda S. A., Elspeth Graham and Paul J. Boyle. 2002. 'Migrations and Family Relations in the Asia Pacific Region', *Asian and Pacific Migration Journal*, 11(1): 1–11.

Zachariah, K. C., E. T. Mathew and S. Irudaya Rajan. 2001. 'Social, Economic and Demographic Consequences of Migration on Kerala', *International Migration*, 39(2): 43–71.

Zlotnik, Hania. 1995. 'Migration and the Family: The Female Perspective', *Asian and Pacific Migration Journal*, 4(2–3): 253–71.

Sri Lankan migration from Sri Lanka to the Gulf

Female breadwinners and domestic workers

Michele Ruth Gamburd

Introduction

Since 1976, increasing numbers of Sri Lankan guest workers have migrated to the Gulf Cooperation Council (GCC) countries. For 30 years, female domestic workers have formed the single largest category among these migrants. The author, a cultural anthropologist, has done research since 1992 in a village in southwestern Sri Lanka. Her research provides the qualitative data in this chapter (Gamburd 2000, 2003, 2005, 2008a, 2009). Using ethnographic sources and statistical information, this chapter provides a brief overview of Sri Lankan migration to the Middle East.[1]

A brief history of migration in the Indian Ocean region provides context for the recent trend of transnational labour. When discussing international migration, several issues call for attention. The first is the common conception of push and pull factors: why are people willing to leave their own country, and why do they seek work in a particular destination? The chapter examines the economic realities at household, national and global levels that push Sri Lankan workers abroad, as well as the forces that pull them to the Gulf as temporary sojourners with few economic or political rights. It details the process of getting a job abroad and explores some workers' experiences in the international labour market. Turning the gaze back to Sri Lanka, the chapter considers the social benefits and costs of migration, focusing in particular on consequences for the social structures (gender relations and household organisation) that facilitate migration, and the effects that migration has on these structures. The chapter concludes with consideration of likely future trends in Sri Lankan labour migration.

The history of Sri Lankan migration to the Gulf

Several waves of Sri Lankan migration have taken place since the country gained independence in 1948. Beginning in the mid-1950s, economic and social pressures have sent wealthy, educated, English-speaking émigrés to Europe, Australia, Canada, and the United States (US). Ethnic violence, which surged into civil war in 1983, spurred an outmigration of Tamil-speaking Sri Lankans from the north and east and augmented the return of Tamil plantation workers to south India from Sri Lanka's central highlands (Bass 2013). These Sri Lankans have set up permanent communities in their destination countries.

In contrast with these permanent emigrants, since 1976 a significant and growing number of Sri Lankan guest workers have journeyed to the Gulf in a pattern of cyclical labour migration. The current pattern builds on a long history of interconnections in the region; South Asian populations have dispersed throughout West, South and South East Asia for millennia along the rich and dynamic Indian Ocean trade routes (McGilvray 1998; Nichols 2008: xii). In earlier times, South Asia formed the centre of economic and cultural activity, with the Arabian Peninsula relatively marginal in importance. Since the discovery of oil in the Gulf in 1930, and especially since the oil boom in the early 1970s, the regional balance of power has changed. As petroleum has flowed out of the Gulf, money has flowed in. The resultant development has brought millions of guest workers to the Gulf to realise the oil-producing countries' plans for modernisation and development. These workers come from dozens of countries in Asia and beyond, and they bring with them a wide variety of skills and experience.

The Sri Lankan Bureau of Foreign Employment (SLBFE), the government's main administrative body regulating labour migration, estimates that half a million Sri Lankans worked abroad in 1994. The number doubled to one million in 2003, and by 2010 had increased to 1.9 million (SLBFE 2012: 194). Most Sri Lankan labour migrants (91 per cent), both male and female, journey to the Gulf, with four countries (Saudi Arabia, the United Arab Emirates or UAE, Kuwait, and Qatar) absorbing over 80 per cent of Sri Lanka's guest workers (*ibid.*: 14). With 1.9 million Sri Lankans (over 9 per cent of the island's 20 million people) in West Asia, Sri Lanka's well-being is closely tied to policies and events in the Gulf.

Economic decision-making in migrant households

Why are people willing to leave Sri Lanka to work elsewhere? The answer lies in economic necessity. Locally available jobs are mostly poorly paid and temporary, particularly for women. Although transnational domestic workers earn only an average of US$100–US$120 a month while abroad, this is more than double the median monthly per capital income for Sri Lanka (a bit less than US$40 in 2006 [DCS 2007: 28]). A transnational domestic worker earns between two and five times what rural women could earn working in Sri Lanka, and such wages equal or exceed the wages earned by most village men. Migrant men can also earn higher wages abroad than in Sri Lanka.

Several studies suggest that each migrant supports four to five members of his or her family (Jayaweera, Dias and Wanasundera 2002: 1; Weerakoon 1998: 109). The SLBFE estimates that in 1993, migrant labourers made up 9 per cent of the total number of employed Sri Lankans. By 2003, the figure stood at 14 per cent, and by 2010 it had jumped to 25 per cent (SLBFE 2012: 194). A significant and growing percentage of Sri Lankan families are thus directly dependent on Gulf remittances.

Families often see migration as a good strategy to procure money for one-time large-scale purchases. Most migrant women state that they wish to buy land and build a house. They calculate that they can earn US$4,000–US$5,000 to accomplish this goal by working for four or five years in Saudi Arabia, Kuwait or the UAE.

In addition to securing better housing, women's motives for migration usually include getting out of debt, supporting their family's daily consumption needs, educating their children, providing dowries for themselves or their daughters, and starting small businesses (Gamburd 2003). Participants in the decision-making process (undergone repeatedly for migrants who return several times to the Gulf) weigh financial necessity and household improvements against separation, incursion of loans and alternate arrangements for childcare.

National and global economic and political context

Many idiosyncratic factors motivate individuals' migration choices, but all decisions take place within national and global economic and political contexts. Despite its many development advantages and its high ranking in health, education and other social indicators, Sri

Lanka carries a high debt burden. One cause of Sri Lanka's difficult economic circumstances is the recently concluded ethnic conflict, which from 1984 to 2009 often spoiled the atmosphere for international investment, dampened enthusiasm in the tourist market and drove the government of Sri Lanka deeply into debt for the purchase of military equipment. Development loans have also contributed to international debt (IPS 2008: 21).

Designed to reduce the national debt, neo-liberal policies and structural adjustments have been imposed from outside and adopted voluntarily. These programmes open the economy to international investment while simultaneously curtailing government spending on price subsidies, health care, education, and social security networks. These economic decisions have led to financial hardship for the poorer segments of Sri Lanka's population (estimated at 25–39 per cent of the people), among whom unemployment and underemployment is high, especially for women (Central Bank 2003: 9; Ruwanpura 2000: 3). As it becomes more difficult to make a living locally, poor people see labour migration as an increasingly viable and attractive option. Sri Lanka's transnational migrant workers come disproportionately from this poorer segment of society.

Migration not only alleviates unemployment among the nation's poor, it also provides hard currency with which Sri Lanka repays its international debts. In many developing countries, migrants' remittances exceed both foreign direct investment and money coming into the country as grants and loans (Eversole 2005; Sassen 2002). The Government of Sri Lanka is very pleased to have migrants' remittances because these bring hard foreign currency into the country. Remittances help the balance of payments: foreign debts and military purchases must be repaid in hard currency, such as that from the Gulf countries, rather than in the Sri Lankan rupee, which is a soft currency prone to inflation and devaluation.

Migrant labourers' remittances contribute significantly to Sri Lanka's foreign exchange earnings. In 2011, total remittances stood at SLR569 billion or roughly US$ 5.2 billion; 59 per cent of this total, SLR335 billion or US$3 billion came from the Gulf (SLBFE 2012: 183). In generating foreign earnings, in 2011, private remittances come first (over 48 per cent), followed by Sri Lanka's large garment industry (40 per cent) and the export of tea, rubber and coconut (*ibid.*: 184). The country has a great financial stake in the remittances generated by migrant labourers, particularly those working in the Gulf.

Migrants registering with the SLBFE and travelling through the international airport come from most districts in Sri Lanka, though in the years up to and including 2011 few have come from the territories in the north that were for many years held by the insurgent Liberation Tigers of Tamil Eelam (LTTE). Low numbers of migrants also originate in the tea country or the far southeast. The greatest flow of migrants comes from Colombo district, followed by the districts of Gampaha, Kurunegala, and Kandy (*ibid.*: 45). Complex patterns in distributions of migrants' gender and skill level appear in comparisons between rural and urban areas and between areas dominated by different religious and ethnic groups.

The national economic context in Sri Lanka provides ample push factors for migration, but what exactly pulls these guest workers to the Gulf? The answer is oil, and the money made from its sale in the international market. The Organization of Petroleum Exporting Countries (OPEC) raised the price of oil in 1973, and money began to flow into West Asia (Gardner 2010; Longva 1997). Foreign labourers soon followed the money. In 1976, labourers from Sri Lanka started to go to West Asia, with men working as heavy machinery drivers, masons, carpenters, and electricians, providing labour for a construction boom. Since then, ever-increasing numbers of guest workers have flooded into the Middle East from Sri Lanka and many other countries.

As part of a newly affluent and leisurely lifestyle, households in the Middle East soon began to employ domestic servants, and the early 1980s saw the beginning of female labour migration from Sri Lanka. Women go abroad predominantly as domestic servants, although some also work in garment factories. During the last 25 years, the majority of migrants have been women. In 2005, two-thirds (800,000) of the estimated stock of overseas contract workers were women (SLBFE 2006: 57). By 2011 females made up only 48 per cent of the Sri Lankans departing for foreign employment (SLBFE 2012: 3); the lower percentage reflects rapid growth in male migration during the past 10 years. The high representation of women reflects the demand for particular workers in the Middle East. There are also jobs for men (such as chauffeurs, gardeners, grocery stock boys, and air conditioner technicians), but these are scarcer, and therefore more expensive to procure.

Sri Lanka is deeply dependent on migrant labour and on the continued well-being of the Gulf nations. This dependence was graphically illustrated in 1990, when Iraq invaded Kuwait. Around

100,000 Sri Lankans and countless guest workers from other countries were employed in Kuwait at the time (MacLeod 1991; Miller 1991). The invasion caused international chaos. People fled to Jordon and Saudi Arabia, and thereafter returned home. Many arrived back in Sri Lanka with only the clothing on their back, and the country lost their remittances while also having to support the returnees.

Government policies and labour relations in main destination countries

Guest workers form a crucial aspect of local economies in the GCC countries, which include Bahrain, Kuwait, Oman, Qatar, Saudi Arabia, and the UAE. Most GCC countries have a de facto dual labour market, with well paying, non-strenuous, public sector jobs created for 'nationals' and poorly paying, difficult, low-status, private sector jobs performed by foreigners (Khalaf 1992: 65–6; Vora 2013: 13; Winkler 2005: 100). Overall, foreigners make up an estimated 40 per cent of the population of the GCC countries and constitute 70 per cent of the workforce; foreign representation in the workforce rises significantly higher in Kuwait (82 per cent), the UAE (90 per cent) and Qatar (90 per cent) (Kapiszewski 2006: 4; Khalaf and Alkobaisi 1999: 272; Leonard 2003: 133).

Dependence on guest workers worries government officials in the Gulf, and the GCC states have implemented policies to minimise the perceived threat. Most governments have instituted labour force 'nationalization' plans to reserve employment in certain sectors for citizens of the country, achieving the most success in public sector jobs (Addleton 1991; Looney 1992). In addition, stringent policies control workers on a number of fronts. The sponsorship system (*kafala*) serves as a primary mechanism of control. Workers are tied in the host country not to the state but to an individual employer or sponsor (*kafeel*), who assumes responsibility for that worker during his or her sojourn in the country (Gardner 2010: 20, 58). The worker can remain legally in the country only as long as he or she works for this sponsor. In addition, there are restrictions on length of stay, strict regulations prohibiting workers from changing jobs, and difficult-to-meet criteria for bringing in family members (Khalaf 1992: 72). For wealthy professionals, regulations restrict the ability to own land and businesses. It is nearly impossible for foreigners to obtain citizenship in the Gulf; even members of South

Asian communities that have been based in the Gulf for generations are vulnerable to deportation and other forms of displacement
(Gardner 2008). All of these factors function to keep guest workers' stays short, temporary or informal (Khalaf and Alkobaisi 1999:
294; Longva 1997). Thus most Sri Lankan sojourners do not intend
to settle – and indeed are forbidden from settling – in the Gulf.

Neither citizens nor guest workers have many legal rights or protections in the Gulf. GCC states provide ample economic and social
services to their citizens; in many countries, basic services such as
health care and education are provided for free or at low cost, and
housing and utilities such as water, sewage and electricity are free
or highly subsidised (Gardner 2010: 44). Citizens pay no taxes. But
the political systems are not democratic, and ordinary people have
little or no say in the governance of the country (Winckler 2010:
10). Guest workers have even less political freedom; unions are not
allowed, and troublemakers are sent home. In addition, workers have
few legal protections (Rahman 2010). In many GCC countries in the
mid-2000s, labour laws covered male labourers but did not protect
domestic workers in private households.[2] Those laws that did exist
were not always enforced against middle- and upper-class employers.

Diplomats from labour-sending countries can and do intercede
for their citizens in the event of a crisis, but the Sri Lankan state
is constrained in its ability to safeguard its citizens working in the
Gulf (Gamburd 2009). Diplomatic visas are limited in number, consular offices and embassies are expensive to maintain and labour
welfare officers have large caseloads.[3] In addition, foreign diplomats lack the authority to enforce contracts, demand the payment
of back wages or correct unsuitable working conditions. The power
to inspect worksites and police labour codes lies with the Ministry of Labour in the host countries, but these government organs
are often understaffed; furthermore, host country officials are not
obligated to protect foreign citizens, and may not be motivated to
defend foreigners at the cost of local businesses.

The Sri Lankan state faces conflicting goals in mediating disputes
between workers and sponsors in host countries. On the one hand,
remittances are a primary source of foreign exchange, and making
sure that workers receive their wages augments the inward flow of
funds. On the other hand, advocating too energetically for labourers' rights could sour the market by making Sri Lankans 'difficult' to
employ, thus leading sponsors to recruit workers from other countries. Under these circumstances, Sri Lanka has adopted a mixed

strategy. Diplomatic missions often shelter and repatriate labourers in crisis; despite benefiting from guest workers' cheap labour, most host countries take little responsibility in these cases. Sri Lanka has also negotiated labour agreements with host countries and has cautiously explored the possibility of multilateral agreements with other labour-sending nations. In a context in which labour law operates nationally but the labour market operates transnationally, labour-sending nations cannot easily or effectively protect their citizens working abroad.

Identity politics in a segmented labour market

In addition to the bifurcation between public-sector jobs for citizens and private sector jobs for guest workers, GCC labour markets are further segmented: employment sectors in various countries are dominated by people of particular ethnicities and nationalities. For example, Pashtuns from Pakistan and Afghanistan make up the majority of taxi drivers in Dubai (Nichols 2008), Filipinos work as concierges and run beauty parlours in Bahrain (Nagy 2008), and Indians, Pakistanis and Bangladeshis do the majority of the construction work in the Gulf (Gardner 2010). These divisions have arisen due to historic connections between particular manpower recruiting agencies in host and sending countries, coupled with chain migration patterns whereby individuals bring their friends, relatives and countrymen to a particular employer, industry or destination country and thereby acquire a reputation of being the 'natural' community to do a particular sort of job.

Gender is another key element in allocating employment. From 1988 until 2007, women have made up the majority of Sri Lanka's labour migrants; in the mid-1990s, they accounted for 75 per cent of migrant flow (SLBFE 2012: 3). Although a few Sri Lankan women find employment in garment factories in the Gulf, roughly 85 per cent worked as domestic servants in 2011 (ibid.: 6). Sri Lankan women share this market niche with women from Indonesia and the Philippines. Several other countries also send smaller numbers of female domestic servants to the Gulf. Racial, ethnic, religious, and national stereotypes predetermine wages. For example, in the UAE in 2004, housemaids from the Philippines were paid more than those from Indonesia, Sri Lanka, Ethiopia, and Bangladesh, in that order; and sponsors paid job agencies more for recruiting Muslim than non-Muslim employees (Gamburd 2009).

Male guest workers in the Gulf come from not only Sri Lanka but also India, Bangladesh, Pakistan and a large number of other countries. Guest workers labour in construction and agriculture, and the GCC imports cleaning and maintenance crews, road workers, drivers, office workers, shop clerks, nurses, doctors, engineers, technicians, and teachers. In recent years, Sri Lankan officials have actively encouraged male migration. These male guest workers fill a diversity of roles, and skilled and unskilled labourers have made up roughly equal percentages of Sri Lanka's male migrants (each roughly 40 per cent) from 1994 until 2011 (SLBFE 2012: 10).

Of the Sri Lankans working in the Gulf, less than 2 per cent are members of the professional, cosmopolitan, diasporic elite with business interests in the area, and 6 per cent are middle-level or clerical workers (*ibid.*: 8). Over 90 per cent are skilled, semi-skilled or unskilled labourers or housemaids (male and female members of the transnational proletariat). These Sri Lankans work, remit money and plan to return home once they have accomplished their financial goals.

Getting a job abroad

There are two ways for Sri Lankan women to get a job abroad. One is to work through job agencies (which the SLBFE refers to as 'registered sources'); the other is to work through informal connections (which the SLBFE refers to as 'direct sources').

Women procure jobs through registered agencies as follows. When a sponsoring family in the Gulf wants to hire a domestic servant, they go to a job agency. The agency in the Gulf is in touch with job agencies in labour-sending countries. In Sri Lanka, a woman interested in working as a housemaid gets in touch with a job agent, sometimes through a local sub-agent. The woman fills out an application for a job, and the Sri Lankan agency sends this information to collaborating agencies abroad. When a sponsor in the Gulf selects the woman's application, the two job agencies arrange for the woman to get a passport and a visa, undergo preliminary job training, take a medical test, pay for SLBFE insurance, and purchase an airline ticket. The woman flies to the host country, and the receiving agent delivers her to her employers. Most women go abroad on two-year contracts. The labour contracts are written in English and Arabic, languages in which most housemaids are not highly literate.

In the late 1990s, Sinhala-Buddhist women paid job agents US$300 to procure a job (Gamburd 2000: 68). Muslim women often went abroad without paying fees. These fees reflected demand in the Middle East, where sponsors paid US$400 for a non-Muslim housemaid and US$800 for a Muslim housemaid (*ibid.*: 62). The fees paid by the sponsors supposedly covered all the women's expenses, with a signing bonus for Muslim women, but extralegal charges whittled the Muslim women's bonus down to nothing and add extra charges to be paid out of pocket by the non-Muslim women. Most migrant women did not have enough cash on hand to pay the agent. Since the prospective migrants were poor and had no collateral to offer for a loan, banks refused to lend to them. Women turned to informal moneylenders, who charged high rates of interest. Migrants often paid back twice what they borrow; having taken US$300, women often repaid a moneylender US$600 (*ibid.*: 82). Because women made on average US$100 a month, they worked for half a year to pay for their job placement.

Because of the expenses involved with agency jobs, both domestic servants and sponsors preferred to arrange overseas employment through a second, less formal strategy: 'ticket jobs'. A sponsor interested in hiring a servant talked with friends or relatives to find out if any of their housemaids knew someone in Sri Lanka who was interested in working abroad. If they found a suitable person, the sponsor arranged a ticket and visa for the new housemaid, who flew to the Gulf without the aid of an agency. The recipient of a 'ticket job' usually paid US$200 to the housemaid who arranged the job (*ibid.*: 71). This fee came out of the arriving housemaid's first two months' wages, so she did not need to borrow from a moneylender. The providing housemaid often waived the fee for close friends and family members. Such direct source jobs were cheaper for the sponsors too; they paid only the airfare and the charges for procuring a visa.

Labour conditions abroad

Sri Lankans working abroad face a variety of labour conditions depending on their skills and qualifications. As noted above, nearly half of Sri Lanka's labour migrants are women working as domestic servants. In much of the global north, migrant transnational domestic workers meet the needs of the global 'care deficit'. As women in the north move into the workforce, they seek market proxies to perform domestic labour, often hiring women from less developed countries to perform these services (Ehrenreich and Hochschild 2002: 11). In contrast, in the Gulf transnational domestic servants free their sponsors for leisure, supporting a socially significant lifestyle. Employing domestic servants has become a necessary element of household status in the Gulf (Longva 1997). For example, 90 per cent of households in Kuwait employed at least one domestic servant in the late 2000s (Ahmad 2010: 27).

In Sri Lanka, migrant domestic servants are referred to as 'housemaids', even though these women's duties often exceed the narrow technical limits of the term. Migrant domestic servants may perform a variety of functions for their sponsors, including cooking, polishing, dusting, vacuuming, sweeping, cleaning, laundering and ironing clothing, washing the cars, looking after children and elders, and taking care of pets, domestic animals and gardens. Some homes have only one domestic servant; others have several.

Although some women live independently of their sponsors, particularly in Jordon and Lebanon (see Frantz 2009: 55; Smith 2010: 380), most housemaids live in servants' quarters in their employers' residences. Throughout the world, live-in female servants have less autonomy and lower salaries than do women with part-time or live-out arrangements (Lan 2003; Rahman, Yeoh and Huang 2005: 255). In the Gulf, domestic servants are often confined to the houses where they work, and are not allowed by employers (or by local gender norms) to travel alone or to associate freely with people outside the sponsor's family. Contracts often specify the number of hours of work and days of holiday, but in practice housemaids are on call at all hours of the day, particularly during the Ramadan fasting period. They often report working for 16 or more hours a day, and they rarely receive days off. Sponsors justify these restrictions by noting that they minimise the opportunities for employees to steal from or gossip about their employers, or to get into trouble. Many Sri Lankan women report that they value the 'protection' offered to their reputation by this work situation (Gamburd 2000), but isolation can also lead to abuse and exploitation (Human Rights Watch 2007, 2008).

Male migrants usually pay higher agency fees than do female migrants, but their salaries are also greater. Because Sri Lankan men work in a wide range of skilled and unskilled positions, their work situations are more varied than those of housemaids. Many labourers live in barracks near their worksites, or in neighbourhoods of crowded, run-down buildings (Gardner 2010). Men have more chance to socialise with their countrymen and to get to know people from other countries than do female domestic workers. But because men's working hours are usually long and their days off are few, men's sociability revolves around their worksite.

Sri Lankan professional-level, middle-level and clerical workers socialise with fellow countrymen and with members of the wider professional expatriate population. Relatively few in number, Sri Lankan professionals tend to integrate into the wider English-speaking expatriate population, networking with peers from India and other South Asian nations.

Workers encounter a number of difficulties while in the Gulf. The types of complaints most often received by the SLBFE in 2010 include breach of contract (3,158), non-payment of wages (2,875), lack of communication (1,689), physical and sexual harassment (2,073), sickness (1,837), and not being sent back home after the completion of the contract (797) (SLBFE 2012: 87). Comparing the total number of complaints (just over 14,704) with the total departures during 2010 for foreign employment (267,507) shows that fewer than 6 per cent of departing migrants (and fewer than 2 per cent of the total estimated stock of overseas migrant workers) file complaints each year (*ibid.*: 3).

The relatively small number of complaints does not, however, reflect the totality of troubles encountered by migrants. The numbers reflect only the situations reported to consular offices and the SLBFE. Both men and women often borrow money to pay the agency fees to obtain their jobs abroad. These workers are thus virtually tied to their employment until they can pay back their debts. Due to the difficulty of changing sponsors while abroad, workers often accommodate to adverse labour conditions in order to keep their jobs and wages (Khalaf and Alkobaisi 1999: 274). Workers bear many minor and some major problems, and solve others informally rather than reporting them to the authorities. Migrant activists and advocates estimate that as many as 20 per cent of migrant workers encounter difficulties with their employment; of these problems, less than a quarter are addressed through official channels.[4] Instead, migrants activate social networks and unofficial support structures to solve problems and weather crises while abroad.

The system does contain some protections for migrant women. For those who go abroad on 'agency jobs' and run into trouble, host country agents will in theory find other sponsors for housemaids or send them home free of charge during the first three months. But the agencies lose money through failed placements. Job agents therefore often seek to keep women in unfavourable situations until the three-month period has passed, after which the woman has to pay her own airfare home. Women who go abroad on 'ticket jobs' can appeal to the housemaid who arranged the employment, but she too is in a relatively powerless situation and cannot provide much help. Women feel, however, that going abroad on a 'ticket job' is safer than trusting an agency, because the contact housemaid can learn something about the host family before deciding whether she thinks they would make good employers. Women who run into untenable situations can call the agency, the police or the Sri Lankan consular office for help, but cannot count on effective support from any of these sources.

At the end of a two-year contract, the housemaid and the sponsor may agree to continue the employment relationship. In this case, the sponsor will pay for the domestic servant to fly home for a month's vacation and then return to the Middle East. If either housemaid or sponsor wishes to terminate the relationship, the housemaid will return to Sri Lanka, and both migrant and sponsor are free to set up a relationship with other parties. Housemaids who return repeatedly to the same household are envied. They usually have safe work environments, they often get a raise when they return for repeat contracts, and they do not have to spend money (on job agencies and moneylenders) each time they go abroad. In addition, appreciative employers may reward loyal servants with gifts of goods and money. Housemaids who work repeat contracts abroad report that they have come to love their sponsors' families as much as their own.

Social consequences of migration for families left behind

Despite the uncertainties in the Gulf, the difficult and dirty work and long absences from family and friends, migrants still eagerly pursue jobs abroad. They do this, they say, for the sake of their families. Migrant workers who earn less than a particular threshold cannot bring their families with them to the Gulf, and thus most Sri Lankan guest workers are separated from their family members for the duration of their contract. These lengthy absences, particularly of migrant mothers, create a number of social challenges. And as families adjust to migration, family structures and gender relations shift and change.

The family is a key institution supporting migration. Decisions about migration are made collectively, and family members often enable migration in a number of ways. Relatives in the extended family may find jobs for each other abroad. Migrants often pay fees to manpower recruitment agencies, and family members are instrumental in gathering the money or providing collateral for loans.

Family structures facilitate migration; reciprocally, migration has altered family structures. Most Sri Lankan female migrants come from the 20–49 age group (SLBFE 2012: 77). Surveys from the 1990s and early 2000s indicate that at that time migrant domestic workers had six to nine years of schooling, were married, had two or more children, and had not otherwise worked outside the home (Eelens, Mook and Schampers 1992: 6; Gunatillake and Perera 1995: 43, 160; Jayaweera, Dias and Wanasundera 2002:11). When such women leave for extended periods of time, households have to make alternative arrangements to cover the domestic duties these absent members used to perform. This is especially important when women leave behind young children. In these cases, fathers take over some of the domestic duties, but most often a grandmother or other female relative provides primary childcare (Gamburd 2008a). Migration strengthens extended families by actively reinforcing kinship bonds through the exchange of goods and services within the family.

In conditions of poverty, the extended family serves as an insurance policy, cushioning people from economic hardship. Poor women often share with kin the care of children and elders. The intensive, exclusive mothering found in middle-class nuclear families is not the norm in much of the world (Nicholson 2006). Instead, different people take on the bundle of duties considered as 'motherhood'. This fragmentation of motherhood allows women to work outside the home or even outside the country while others take over necessary household tasks.

Although poor Sri Lankan women have always worked, a dominant ideal of motherhood suggests that women should be in the home with their children. Migrant mothers often run up against this image and face accusations that they have 'abandoned' their children to work abroad. Women pragmatically counter this charge, saying that they have not gone abroad for personal satisfaction or pleasure. Instead, they have worked and suffered to improve conditions for their families, especially their children. Husbands and wives agree that providing food, shelter and education for children is the primary parental duty. Which parent earns money and which one nurtures is less important; the job must get done by someone. When a mother can more easily find lucrative employment, nurturing may fall to the father.

As women move into the wage labour market, the value of domestic service changes. Duties women once did for free, at home, they now do abroad for money. This quantitative remuneration for domestic duties makes clear that housework, or women's work, is real work and holds a waged value. Domestic service also clearly demonstrates how absurd it is to try to split the domestic from the public sphere.

As women receive wages, their power within the household increases. Women who have missed their children's childhood want to have something concrete to show for their years away. They are therefore committed to achieving the goals they set for their migration, which in many cases means buying land and building a cement house with a tile roof. Women gain power in the village and the family by making decisions about how to spend their money.

As women work abroad and gain more say in consumption choices, men also experience a shift in their household duties and gender roles. In particular, women's work abroad challenges the ideal of the male breadwinner. Women have always worked, but their extended work outside the country can create a crisis of masculinity. In particular, men feel awkward taking over the domestic duties in their wives' absence. Men with steady jobs who provide for the family while the women earn money for a one-time large-scale purchase are not as threatened, particularly if a female relative has taken over household chores. But men who substitute for their absent wives can feel diminished. Pressure to conform to unattainable gender norms, combined with continued poverty, can drive men to turn to one readily available avenue to reinforce their masculinity: alcohol use. A common stereotype predicts that a migrant women's husband will eat, drink, waste her money, and forget to repay the moneylender. But research reveals that most husbands deal much more responsibly with their duties on the home front (Gamburd 2008b). In the face of long-term female migration, local gender stereotypes are changing, though slowly. Women are gaining some power and authority, they are not gaining as much empowerment from their wage-earning as one might expect. And men are still uncomfortable with the 'stay-at-home dad' role, despite pragmatic arguments in its favour.

Migration affects not only household structures and gender relations, but other village statuses including class and wealth. Formerly poor households use migrants' remittances to buy land, build new houses, start businesses, educate their children, and provide large dowries for their daughters. As new money rolls in, it puts older class hierarchies in flux.

In many migration streams, migrants absorb cultural traits from abroad. Which host country they visit makes a difference in this regard. For example, Sri Lankan returnees often construct new houses with their earnings. Migrants who have been to the Gulf construct standard Sri Lankan homes with cement block walls and tile roofs. In contrast, migrants who have worked in Italy construct houses with distinctly Italian architectural styles (Brown 2011). The key to this difference is the extent to which migrants are offered the opportunity to integrate in the host country. Working-class migrants in the Gulf are at best offered the opportunity to join a family as a servant. They are not offered a desirable place in the wider society, and thus their orientation remains towards their Sri Lankan family and culture. In contrast, many migrants who journey to Italy do so with the hope of settling there. Current trends suggest that the next generation of Sri Lankan labour migrants will contain more men, that migrants will leave at younger ages and before marriage, that they will journey to destinations other than the Gulf, and that they will aspire to emigrate rather than sojourn abroad.

What might the future hold?

In the future, care of children and the aged will become a more significant issue than it is at present. Sri Lanka is currently undergoing a demographic transformation from a pyramid-shaped population structure with many younger people and few elders, to a columnar population structure characteristic of most developed nations (de Silva 2007; World Bank 2008). This demographic shift may eventually curtail migration or prompt the burgeoning of collective elder care arrangements such as old folks homes or assisted living facilities. As the percentage of elders increases in the society, there will be fewer members of the subsequent generations to look after them. In the future, prospective migrants may have to decide whether to work abroad and earn money for their family, or to remain in Sri

Lanka to look after their elders (Gamburd forthcoming). But as long as the Gulf continues to export petroleum to an oil-hungry world, migration from Sri Lanka to West Asia is likely to continue.

The Government of Sri Lanka has a lot at stake in transnational labour migration. In the past few years, legislators have proposed several migration-related initiatives, ranging from an effort to ban the migration of women with children under the age of five to an effort to raise the minimum wages for migrant domestic workers from US$100 to US$200 a month. Neither initiative has been successful; the courts shot down the first as a violation of women's fundamental rights, and job agents protested the second saying that host countries would turn to labourers from other countries if Sri Lanka implemented its proposal (Gamburd 2005: 100). Due to Sri Lanka's weak international position, the government has not been effective in providing more than the minimal safety and well-being of migrant workers abroad. True changes in this respect will only flow from international labour organisations, multilateral efforts between labour-sending countries and collaboration with labour-receiving countries (Gamburd 2009).

Changes will also flow from the internal evolution of household structures. After 30 years of labour migration, Sri Lankan villages are now sending a second generation of migrants abroad. In part due to the hard work of migrant parents in providing childhood opportunities, the second generation has different aspirations and ideals. These youngsters are generally better educated than their mothers and fathers. And while the older generation sent mostly women abroad, the second generation is sending both men and women. These young migrants go abroad before they are married, or at least before they have children. The young women have higher aspirations than to work as housemaids. The young men are working as heavy machinery drivers or other semi-skilled labour. This generation hopes to work not in the Gulf but in other developing or developed countries such as Korea, Malaysia, Singapore, and Italy, with more opportunities for entrepreneurship and advancement (Gamburd 2008a; Wanasundera 2001). Migrants who go to Italy have few expectations to return permanently to Sri Lanka. This may prove difficult for the older generation, the caretakers who looked after their grandchildren while the first generation of migrants was abroad. If the youngsters leave Sri Lanka for good, taking their nuclear families with them, who will look after the elders? The next 10 years may bring interesting changes for family structures and larger national and regional economic dynamics.

Notes

1 In this chapter, 'the Middle East', 'West Asia', and 'the Gulf' are used interchangeably to refer to a varied and diverse region with many cultural traditions. This rich complexity gets lost in many Sri Lankan accounts of migration, where migrants are said to work in 'Arabia', 'the Middle East', or merely 'abroad'.

2 Regarding Saudi Arabia, see Hugo (2005: 83) and regarding the UAE and Kuwait, see Leonard (2003: 134, 153). Information on the UAE is courtesy L.K. Ruhunage, Counsellor (Employment and Welfare), in a personal interview, Consulate General of the Democratic Socialist Republic of Sri Lanka, Dubai, UAE, 11 November 2004,.

3 L.K. Ruhunage, Counsellor (Employment and Welfare), personal interview, 11 November 2004, Consulate General of the Democratic Socialist Republic of Sri Lanka, Dubai, UAE.

4 David Soysa, interview, Migrant Services Centre, Dehiwela, Sri Lanka, 3 February 2004.

References

Addleton, Jonathan S. 1991. 'The Impact of the Gulf War on Migration and Remittances in Asia and the Middle East', *International Migration*, 29(4): 509–26.

Ahmad, Attiya. 2010. 'Migrant Domestic Workers in Kuwait: The Role of State Institutions', *Viewpoints: Migration and the Gulf*, pp. 27–8. Washington: Middle East Institute.

Bass, Daniel. 2013. *Everyday Ethnicity in Sri Lanka: Upcountry Tamil Identity Politics*. New York: Routledge.

Brown, Bernardo. 2011. 'Indifference with Sri Lankan Migrants', *Ethnology*, 50(1): 43–58.

Central Bank. 2003. *Central Bank of Sri Lanka Annual Report 2002*. Colombo: Central Bank of Sri Lanka.

de Silva, W. Indralal. 2007. *Beyond Twenty Million: Projecting the Population of Sri Lanka 2001–2081*. Colombo: Institute of Policy Studies.

Department of Census and Statistics (DCS). 2007. *Household Income and Expenditure Survey – 2006/07*. Colombo: Department of Census and Statistics.

Ehrenreich, Barbara and Arlie Russell Hochschild (eds). 2002. *Global Woman: Nannies, Maids, and Sex Workers in the New Economy*. New York: Henry Holt.

Eelens F, T. Mook, and T. Schampers. 1992. 'Introduction', In F. Eelens, T. Schampers and J.D. Speckmann (eds), *Labor Migration to the Middle East: From Sri Lanka to the Gulf*, pp. 1–25. London: Kegan Paul International.

Eversole, Robyn. 2005. '"Direct to the Poor' Revisited: Migrant Remittances and Development Assistance', in L. Trager (ed.), *Migration and Economy: Global and Local Dynamics*, pp. 289–322. Walnut Creek, CA: Altamira Press.

Frantz, Elizabeth. 2009. 'Of Maids and Madams: Sri Lankan Domestic Workers and their Employers in Jordon', in Nicole Constable (ed.), *Migrant Workers in Asia: Distant Divides, Intimate Connections*, pp. 45–66. London: Routledge.

Gamburd, Michele. 2000. *The Kitchen Spoon's Handle: Transnationalism and Sri Lanka's Migrant Housemaids*. Ithaca: Cornell University Press.

———. 2003. 'In the Wake of the Gulf War: Assessing Family Spending of Compensation Money in Sri Lanka', *International Journal of Population Geography*, 9: 503–15.

———. 2005. 'Lentils There, Lentils Here: Sri Lankan Domestic Labor in the Middle East', in Shirlena Huang, Brenda S.A. Yeoh and Noor Abdul Rahman (eds), *Asian Women as Transnational Domestic Workers*, pp. 92–114. Singapore: Marshall Cavendish.

———. 2008a. 'Milk Teeth and Jet Planes: Kin Relations in Families of Sri Lanka's Transnational Domestic Servants', *City and Society*, 20(1): 5–31.

———. 2008b. *Breaking the Ashes: The Culture of Illicit Liquor in Sri Lanka*. Ithaca: Cornell University Press.

———. 2009. 'Advocating for Sri Lankan Migrant Workers: Obstacles and Challenges', *Critical Asian Studies*, 41(1): 61–88.

———. 2015. 'Migrant Remittances, Population Ageing, and Intergenerational Family Obligations in Sri Lanka', in LanAnh Hoang and Brenda Yeoh (eds), *Transnational Labour Migration, Remittances and the Changing Family in Asia*. London: Palgrave.

Gardner, Andrew M. 2008. 'Strategic Transnationalism: Indian Diasporic Elite in Contemporary Bahrain', *City and Society*, 20(1): 54–78.

———. 2010. *City of Strangers: Gulf Migration and the Indian Community in Bahrain*. Ithaca: Cornell University Press.

Gunatillake, Godfrey and Myrtle Perera (eds). 1995. *Study of Female Migrant Worker* (sic). Colombo: Marga Institute (Sri Lanka Centre for Development Studies), World Bank, and Ministry of Policy Planning and Implementation.

Hugo, Graeme. 2005. 'Indonesian International Domestic Workers: Contemporary Developments and Issues', in Shirlena Huang, Brenda S.A. Yeoh and Noor Abdul Rahman (eds), *Asian Women as Transnational Domestic Workers*, pp. 54–91. Singapore: Marshall Cavendish.

Human Rights Watch. 2007. *Exported and Exposed: Abuses Against Sri Lankan Domestic Workers in Saudi Arabia, Kuwait, Lebanon and the United Arab Emirates*, New York: Human Rights Watch.

——— 2008. *"As if I am not Human": Abuses against Asian Domestic Workers in Saudi Arabia*. New York: Human Rights Watch.

Institute of Policy Studies (IPS). 2008. *Sri Lanka: State of the Economy 2008*. Colombo: Institute of Policy Studies.

Jayaweera, Swarna, Malsiri Dias and Leelangi Wanasundera. 2002. *Returnee Migrant Women in Two Locations in Sri Lanka*. Colombo: CENWOR.

Kapiszewski, Andrzej. 2006. 'Arab Versus Asian Migrant Workers in the GCC Countries'. Paper presented at the United Nations Expert Group Meeting on International Migration and Development in the Arab Region, United Nations Secretariat, Beirut, Lebanon, 15–17 May 2006.

Khalaf, Sulayman N. 1992. 'Gulf Societies and the Image of Unlimited Good', *Dialectical Anthropology*, 17: 53–84.

Khalaf, Sulayman and Saad Alkobaisi. 1999. 'Migrants' Strategies of Coping and Patterns of Accommodation in the Oil-Rich Gulf Societies: Evidence from the UAE', *British Journal of Middle Eastern Studies*, 26(2): 271–98.

Lan, Pei-Chia. 2003. 'Negotiating Social Boundaries and Private Zones: The Micropolitics of Employing Migrant Domestic Workers', *Social Problems*, 50(4): 525–49.

Leonard, Karen. 2003. 'South Asian Workers in the Gulf: Jockeying for Places', in Richard Warren Perry and Bill Maurer (eds), *Globalization under Construction: Governmentality, Law, and Identity*, pp. 129–70. Minneapolis: University of Minnesota Press.

Longva, Ahn Nga. 1997. *Walls Build on Sand: Migration, Exclusion, and Society in Kuwait*. Boulder: Westview Press.

Looney, R.E. 1992. 'Manpower Options in a Small Labour-Importing State: The Influence of Ethnic Composition on Kuwait's Development', *International Migration*, 30(2): 175–200.

MacLeod, K. 1991. 'Third World Pays Price of War: Fallout from Gulf Conflict Rocks Economics of Poor Nations', *Toronto Star*, 2 April.

McGilvray, Dennis B. 1998. 'Arabs, Moors, and Muslims: Sri Lankan Muslim Ethnicity in Regional Perspective', *Contributions to Indian Sociology*, n.s. 32: 433–83.

Miller, J. 1991. 'Displaced by Gulf War: 5 Million Refugees', *New York Times*, 16 June.

Nagy, Sharon. 2008. 'Searching for Miss Philippines Bahrain: Possibilities for Representation in Expatriate Communities', *City and Society*, 20(1): 79–104.

Nichols, Robert. 2008. *A History of Pashtun Migration, 1775–2006*. Oxford: Oxford University Press.

Nicholson, Melanie. 2006. 'Without their Children: Rethinking Motherhood among Transnational Migrant Women', *Social Text*, 24(3): 13–33.

Rahman, Anisur. 2010. 'Migration and Human Rights in the Gulf', *Viewpoints: Migration and the Gulf*, pp. 16–18. Washington: Middle East Institute.

Rahman, Noor Abdul, Brenda S.A. Yeoh and Shirlena Huang. 2005. '"Dignity Overdue': Transnational Domestic Workers in Singapore', in Shirlena Huang, Brenda S.A. Yeoh and Noor Abdul Rahman (eds), *Asian Women as Transnational Domestic Workers*, pp. 233–61. Singapore: Marshall Cavendish.

Ruwanpura, Kanchana N. 2000. *Structural Adjustment, Gender and Employment: The Sri Lankan Experience*. Geneva: ILO.

Sassen, Saskia. 2002. 'Global Cities and Survival Circuits', in Barbarah Ehrenreich and Arlie Russell Hochschild (eds), *Global Woman: Nannies, Maids, and Sex Workers in the New Economy*, pp. 254–74. New York: Henry Holt.

Smith, Monica. 2010. 'Erasure of Sexuality and Desire: State Morality and Sri Lankan Migrants in Beirut, Lebanon', *The Asia Pacific Journal of Anthropology*, 11(3–4): 378–93.

Sri Lankan Bureau of Foreign Employment (SLBFE). 2012. *Annual Statistical Report of Foreign Employment – 2011*. Battaramulla, Sri Lanka: Research Division, Sri Lanka Bureau of Foreign Employment.

——— 2006. *Annual Statistical Report of Foreign Employment – 2005*. Battaramulla, Sri Lanka: Research Division, Sri Lanka Bureau of Foreign Employment.

Vora, Neha. 2013. *Impossible Citizens: Dubai's Indian Diaspora*. Durham: Duke University Press.

Wanasundera, Leelangi. 2001. *Migrant Women Domestic Workers: Cyprus, Greece and Italy*. Colombo: CENWOR.

Weerakoon, Nedra. 1998. 'Sri Lanka: A Caste Study of International Female Labor Migration', in S. Sta. M. Amparita, J.J. Balisnono, R. Plaetevoet and R. Selwyn. (eds), *Legal Protection for Asian Women Migrant Workers: Strategies for Action*, pp. 97–118. Makati City, Philippines: Ateneo Human Rights Center.

Winckler, Onn. 2005. 'Was It Worth It? A Reexamination of the Cost/Benefit Balance of the Inter-Arab Labor Migration', Paper presented at the conference 'Transnational Migration: Foreign Labor and Its Impact in the Gulf', Bellagio, Italy, 20–24 June 2005.

——— 2010. 'Labor Migration to the GCC States: Patterns, Scale, and Policies', *Viewpoints: Migration and the Gulf*, pp. 9–12. Washington: Middle East Institute.

World Bank. 2008. *Sri Lanka: Addressing the Needs of an Aging Population*. Report No. 43396-LK. Human Development Unit, South Asia Region. Posted 28 May 2008, http://go.worldbank.org/I14DRI6CS0 (last accessed on 15 November 2008).

Choosing a profession in order to leave

Migration of Malayali nurses to the Gulf countries

Marie Percot

Introduction

When, in the mid-1970s, Indian nurses started to be hired for newly built hospitals in various Gulf countries, it was an unexpected opportunity for the most adventurous of them to gain previously unimaginable good wages. Nearly 40 years later, thousands of young girls, predominantly Christians from Kerala, fill up the nursing schools all over India, the vast majority of them acknowledging the intention of migrating abroad after graduation. Nowadays, their ambitions are no longer confined to a job in the Gulf countries since many other opportunities are to be found in Western countries such as Australia, New Zealand, the United Kingdom (UK), etc.

Hence a nursing diploma is now considered as a passport opening the world not only to the nurse herself, but also to her relatives. Families encourage this female migration, since it is consciously regarded as a privileged opportunity to increase social mobility. The migration opportunity has consequently partly changed the status of nurses, which used to be rather low in India. It has also been a chance for these young nurses to set up life strategies, based on the experience of older migrants. Migration to the Gulf is most often considered as an intermediate step before further migration to the West, but following the development of a Keralese diaspora in most Gulf states and, more recently, the economic crisis in the West, the Gulf is also more and more considered as a place where it is possible to enjoy a comfortable life. Lately, some migrant nurses and their husbands are even leaving the West to resettle in a Gulf country.

This chapter deals with the evolution of this specific migration and its remarkable sociocultural consequences during the last four decades. Having first presented the familial and social background of the migrant nurses, I outline and analyse some exemplary cases. I then explain the evolution of this specific migration of qualified women during the past decades and the evolution which has taken place in the life of Keralese nurses in the Gulf. In a last part, I compare the conditions of life of migrant nurses in the Gulf and in the West, showing how and why the Gulf is more and more regarded as a good opportunity.

This chapter is based on research started in 2001, with nearly two years of ethnographic fieldwork in Kerala, Delhi and Mumbai, in the United Arab Emirates (UAE) and Oman, as well as in Ireland, one of the latest countries to have recruited Indian nurses. I have been able to interview more than 300 women (nursing students, migrants or ex-migrants) and have been invited to stay with 15 nurses' families (in Kerala, Muscat, Dubai, and Dublin) with whom I am still in touch through either phone or Facebook. Interviews were also conducted with nurses' husbands, members of the extended family, as well as with nursing school principals or hospital directors.

Nurses' background and migration's strategies

Most Malayali nurses come from low middle-class or middle-class families: the father is most often a farmer employing a few agricultural labourers and/or he works as a petty clerk. Most nurses belong to the first generation in their family who has been able to attend higher studies and the first women of their family to work in a salaried job (Percot and Nair 2011). Until the middle of the 1980s, stipends were given for nursing studies. In a context where salaried jobs for women was developing in Kerala and was more and more accepted socially, nursing was a good option for not so wealthy families to insure a job opportunity for their daughters. Later, the increasing migratory opportunities lead to a growing number of candidates to this profession and to the blossoming of private nursing schools. However, families managed to pay, considering that their investment will surely be covered by their migrant daughter's remittances.

The first generation of migrants constituted of married women in their 40s. With time, younger and younger women started to leave, to the point that, nowadays, nurses migrate as soon as they have got the two years of experience required by recruiting countries. Indeed, for parents, migration of a daughter who is still single presents some advantages. First, they beneficiate from her remittances until her marriage after which their daughter will be able to save for her own dowry.[1] In addition,

a migrant nurse gives to her future husband a way to migrate himself, whether it is by legal family reunification in Western countries, or, in the Gulf countries, by first getting a 'visiting visa' which afterwards is easily transformed into a working visa. This opportunity actually often plays a role in reducing the dowry amount asked for by the groom's family. Nowadays, families can even pretend to more prestigious sons-in-law: a few decades ago, the latter were generally blue collars (mechanics, electricians. . .); today, most of them are degree-holders.

Even if the choice of nursing as a profession is not an individual decision of these young women, they however find their own interest in this choice and often push their families to let them take this path. They, first and foremost, want to have a professional career and not remain like their mothers as 'housewives'. Second, their student years (most often far from their family home) and their first years as professionals in an Indian metropolis are unanimously considered as liberating. They find themselves free from social control that all these young women describe as too strongly burdening them in their native town or village. All these young women are also well aware that, once married, migration will de facto free them from the tight control of the extended family, particularly from the authority of a mother-in-law. Almost all of them praise the model of the nuclear family, a model which is still not the norm in their social milieu. At last, like male migrants, they share the ambitions attached to migration: discovering other countries, climbing the social ladder, but also gaining more professional and individual experience.

Nowadays, most young nurses' final goal is migration to a Western country (whether it is the United States of America [USA], UK, Australia, or New Zealand). They consider this to be more prestigious than migrating to a Gulf country. But, at the same time, they also look for certain advantages: easier family reunification, free and better education for their young children, the possibility to invest in a house abroad and, very importantly, another citizenship with which displacement will be easier than with an Indian passport. Such things are not possible in a Gulf country. Yet, to reach a Western country is more difficult since it requires altogether more capital and additional diplomas (IELTS in all cases, NCLEX-RN[2] for the USA). One thus more often observes a step-by-step migration, starting with a first sojourn to a Gulf country. However, this step to the Gulf may last for long: by default, if one has not been able to pass the required exams or gather enough capital; by choice, if the couple has succeeded enough in the Gulf and choose not to venture further.

A new generation of migrant nurses

In an average Malayali family, there will be a brother in Saudi Arabia, another one in Dubai, a sister in Kuwait, an uncle in Canada, an auntie in the UK and maybe some cousins in the States or Australia . . . So, we Malayalis feel a little bit as if the world was ours and that Kerala was only the centre of it!

This was stated by Joey, another young nursing trainee, trying to explain why she was so keen to go abroad that she chose this profession against her parents' will: 'I want to see the world, I want to travel, I want to learn new things. What chances do I have to do that if I become an accountant or if I got an MBA?'

The story of Teresa, 34 years, is another example of this new generation of Keralese migrant nurses. She has the same social background as Joey, and almost all the nurses I met for this study had very similar family backgrounds. Her father is a farmer (owning of 2 acres of farmland for growing commercial crops), her mother is a housewife, her sister is married, a housewife herself, and her brother is working in Dubai. Older than Joey, she has already accomplished some of her goals. She actually found a job in a government hospital (where you get the best salaries) in Muscat immediately after completing two years of work in an Indian hospital. Her brother paid Rs 70,000 for her migration expenses, which was given to a 'travel agency' which provided the contract, plane ticket and visa. She then got married two years later. She is an exception in that she married a man she met through one of her friends, having a 'love marriage', while almost all young Keralese – including migrant nurses – still follow the tradition of 'arranged marriage'. Teresa says that after four years of work and saving she has been the one to put aside the biggest part of the money earned and been able to buy all the gold jewellery given as dowry to the in-laws. Six months later, earlier than planned by the young couple, she was pregnant (she 'forgot' to take her contraceptive pill) and resigned after three months to return to Kerala. She used the time of her pregnancy to prepare for the exams necessary to get a nursing job in the West, eventually taking the exams which she passed with flying colours.[3] But since the capital of the couple was not large enough to pay for travel and visa fees (partly because they made several trips between Oman and Kerala), she returned to the Gulf, Abu Dhabi this time, leaving behind her newborn baby to the care of a sister of her husband, who was himself still working in Muscat. Three months were needed to save the money required to repay the travel agency and four more months to save the money needed to go to USA. Teresa was able to save the all her salary, since she chose to live in the hostel of the Abu Dhabi hospital and provided food free of charge. The couple then left for New Jersey, where she obtained a contract with a big hospital. This time, they took the child with them. Teresa went on to have more children and get American citizenship. Having specialised in oncology, she later got a better professional opportunity in Qatar where the family has now moved.

It is worth observing that Teresa's husband, Nirmal, who works in the tourism sector, is himself a pure product of the migration culture of Kerala. His parents met in Libya, where both of them used to work'. His mother was a nurse and because of her profession they were able to reach Germany in the late 1970s with the help of Protestant missionaries. During his childhood, Nirmal was living between Germany and Kerala (where a paternal uncle used to take care of him), while his sister stayed with the parents in Düsseldorf and eventually married a German. Nirmal's parents today hold German citizenship. Like many Indians, he is polyglot, fluent in six languages. But Nirmal and Teresa thought at first that it would be better for them to live in the US, in particular when they imagined the future of their children. They later changed their mind for two reasons. First, with American citizenship it would be easy for their children to go back to the USA for higher education once they were grown up. At the same time, they do not want their children to become alienated to their own culture. So settling in a Gulf country, because of the existence of a Malayali diaspora and of the geographical proximity with the home country (allowing more frequent sojourns in Kerala), seems to be a better option now, economically as well as socially.

In January 2004, I was invited to the wedding of Swaya, a 25-year-old nurse, who was just returning after working in Saudi Arabia for three years. She had been working there in a small hospital in Dammam where she got a contract at the same time as two of her best school friends from nursing school. Their stay in Dammam had been quite difficult, involving financial deception, since the contractor[4] who had got them the job 'forgot' to specify, first, that he was taking 30 per cent of their salaries and, second, that there were no paid holidays for this three-year contract. So they stayed in Saudi Arabia for three years without coming home. Conditions must have been harsh, since all the nurses of their hospital went on strike three times. Nevertheless, the three young girls, even if they were not entirely happy about this country and its people, also keep good memories of their job in a very modern hospital and of their life in the hostel where they used to live. In particular, they like to tell stories of the happy parties that their Filipino colleagues would organise regularly. In a certain way, these first years of migration seem to have been like an extension of the life they had when they were studying and living together in their Delhi nursing school. Yet, the three of them decided not to renew the Saudi contract, though it would have been possible.

Like her two friends, Swaya is a Hindu Ezhava. I first met her one week before her wedding when one of her friends invited me to visit her to see the dowry jewellery (nearly 400 grams of gold in the form of bangles, necklaces and a belt). Swaya affirms that her family offered a dowry of Rs 250,000. Her father is a part-time account-ant clerk in the local administration. He earns Rs 3,000 and, in addition to his regular work, runs a farm of 3 acres. But Swaya has two sisters who are still to be married and only one brother who works in an Indian shop in Fujairah. Swaya's groom, 33 years old, lives by himself in Saudi Arabia where he has been working for the last seven years as an engineer with an American oil company. She has met him only twice because he came back from the Gulf only ten days before the wedding. Swaya worries a little bit because he was not very talkative during their two meetings, but her friends comfort her, saying that he must be shy and that a man living alone in Saudi Arabia for so many years can only have lost the habit of chatting with women. However, Swaya wanted to follow him as soon as possible and to continue working there and therefore follow the courses for the NCLEX that she had just started in Kerala. 'I hope he will allow me to do so', she says, because she would very much like to live in the West: Australia, the USA or the UK, she does not care where. Her friend insists: 'She is right. You can't spend your life in Saudi. Those Arabs are not good people; you have no freedom there. It's OK to start, but after a few years, it's better to try another place'. But they are not so sure that the future husband 'will allow' a move, since he has such a good job there. On the wedding day, the husband, a fat man who does not smile easily, does not really seduce the friends of Swaya and they worry a little bit: the groom's young sister is leaving for Chennai to study and somebody would have to take care of the widowed mother; they fear that this role of caregiver would fall on Swaya, since the groom has not said clearly that he intends to take his new wife with him and that he is going back to the Gulf after one week. It seems that there is no way to ask the question directly to the husband or to any in-laws.

Two months later, Swaya had indeed left to join him in Jeddah. The in-laws did not hesitate for long to make their choice between the potential salary of their new daughter-in-law and the necessity of somebody taking care of the mother, who now lives with a nephew. According to her friends, who chat with her through Internet, Swaya had already told her husband about her plans for the West and the idea of the Green Card seemed to appeal to him, but he is still not convinced he will get a job corresponding to his qualification in the West as he did in the Gulf. Three years later, the couple finally left for Ireland. However, as Swaya's husband feared, he has not found a job corresponding to his qualification. They may go back to some Gulf country as soon as they get Irish citizenship, most probably in 2016.

New generation, new aspirations

From these examples, very representative of the new generation of migrant nurses or candidates for migration, different important aspects of migration can be gleaned. First, one observes that for all these young women migration is a clear and evident objective. This has to be understood in the wider context of the massive migration from Kerala to the Gulf countries (Zachariah, Kannan and Rajan 2002). Moving to another country, at least for a few years, is a goal that many Malayalis – and more generally Indians – consider as highly profitable. Indian cinemas as well as literature, which depict again and again Indians in-between two countries and two cultures with all the conflicts, happiness, freedom or contradictions engendered by migration, largely reflect this tendency. The young nurses or nurses-to-be are well aware of all these aspects and consciously follow this path. For them, to become a nurse is, first of all, *the* passport for this way of life, a fact that all the principals of nursing schools acknowledge. One of them attests:

> More than 90 per cent of our students do choose this job because their plan is to work abroad. It is a problem for us because we know very well that [the] vocation for caring is not their first interest and we worry about the quality of the nurses we are actually training. It is also a problem for Indian hospitals because we have a large turnover in our staff as so many nurses are ready to leave at any moment [. . .] On the other hand, this migration phenomenon has a good impact on the way this profession is now considered, socially speaking [. . .] We nowadays have students from social categories that used to be very rare before these migration opportunities, like young Hindus or even Muslim girls, and we think that it's just the beginning (. . .) The stigma on this profession is disappearing little by little with each new opportunity appearing abroad.[5]

Actually, Indian nurses have been working in the Gulf, and in much smaller proportion in the West, for nearly 40 years now, giving time to the new generation to set up a planned strategy based on the experience of the pioneers. In India, and more especially in Kerala, women in migration are a minority, but for the young nurses it does not seem to appear as an adventure as it can be for unqualified women, vulnerable to every sort of exploitation (Varghese and Rajan 2011). As qualified recruited staff, nurses know that their conditions of work and life in the Gulf or anywhere abroad will be quite good and that the bad experiences, like false contracts or harassment, are rather uncommon when it comes to nursing. Being a nurse in India, they are sure to find a job but with salaries as low as Rs 2,500 at the beginning. If they reach the Gulf, their salaries may directly rise to Rs 70,000, a very enviable position when most of the other workers there earn only three to four times more than in Kerala.

Status, dowry and wedding

For young migrant nurses, saving a little bit of money and seeing other countries (which they are often eager to do) is not the only ambition which propels them to migrate. In fact, their migration plans also have much to do with social status and marriage prospects, like it appeared in the story of the young girls I gave as examples. In the past, the marriage opportunities for young single nurses or nurses-to-be were not very satisfying, particularly in the hypergamic tradition that prevails in India. Jenna, a 50-year-old nurse (whose 'just married' niece has settled in Australia with her husband after a few years in Dubai), explained to me:

> Twenty years ago, there was no respect for nurses. People were gossiping because we have to touch men in our job and they used to give us a bad reputation. When I got married, my mother-in-law told my husband that I should resign for the dignity of the family [. . .]. But today nursing is a job where there is no unemployment and, most of all, [one] that allows you to go to the Gulf or to America itself. So even good families are now looking for nurses as a bride. In my generation, a nurse was lucky to marry a technician as I did; today they can even marry a lawyer, as my niece did.[6]

Shoba George (2005: 152), in a study undertaken on Indian nurses who have migrated to USA, partially confirms this opinion, saying that 'girls with a good family background are in such demand that they get "booked up" while still in school'. The recent 'attraction' for nurses can also be checked out in the matrimonial advertisements of Indian newspapers or specialised Internet sites where the phrase 'nurse wanted', namely 'nurse working in the Gulf will be preferred' appears regularly.

The chance to get 'a good husband' is an issue that came up again and again in the discussions I had with the young nurses. To be 'in high demand' has another consequence that all of them are pointing out: it allows them to reduce the price of the dowry asked by the future in-laws because, after the wedding, the earnings of the bride, as an actual or potential migrant, will supplement the in-laws' income. Actually, a migrant nurse brings not only more money, but she also offers a way for her husband to migrate. The migration chain has thus started and other members of the in-laws' family may follow this path. Another advantage of marrying a migrant nurse in the Gulf is her ability to borrow money if she is employed in a government hospital. This money may then be the capital which enables the husband to start a small business in migration, a strategy that the geographer Philippe Venier (2011) reports as quite common in the Emirates. The families prospecting for a bride are perfectly aware of these advantages, as are the nurses' families.

For the latter, generally coming from the 'low middle class', as they describe themselves, the price of nursing studies is nevertheless a major stress factor.[7] They often have to borrow money for this, most of the time from a family member, sometimes from a bank, in order to pay for these three years of study. So when parents pay for the nursing study of a daughter, they consider it as an investment that the girl is supposed to largely pay back once she is a single migrant (nowadays during two to three years generally), either by sending money to her parents or by saving for her dowry and by buying in the Gulf – where it is cheaper – the gold that has to be given at the time of the marriage. To say it cynically, the 'burden of having a daughter', as it is often said in India, turns out much lighter if she is able to get a nursing diploma.

Young nurses take an active part in the social mobility strategies that their parents, in the sense of the extended family, are building up, but at the same time their major motivations are more individualistic. Their dreams as 'young modern women' follow a new model in which the traditional joint family has rather limited space. Sonia, a 27-year-old nurse, who has been working for three years in Muscat and got married a year earlier, comments:

> In my native country, it is very difficult to have a personal life and it is worst if you are a woman. Everybody wants to decide for you, everybody knows what is supposed to be better for you. That is not that you have no freedom, but everything has to be discussed with everybody: the way you dress, the way you spend your money, the time you spend with your husband. On everything, not only the family members, but also the neighbours, may give their advice. It is something very hard to bear when you are educated, when you earn your own money and once you have even been able to live alone in a foreign country as I did [. . .] That is why I imagine that it will be difficult for me to come back home one day. Familial solidarity is a good thing that you Westerners have largely forgotten, but it doesn't mean that everything must be shared. I told my husband that there is no way we will live with his parents if we go back one day. I don't feel either that I would be able to live again in a village with the neighbours gossiping because I put on some lipstick or wear high-heel shoes. I also don't want to spend all of our savings to pay for the study of a cousin's son or by contributing to the dowry of an auntie's grandchild. 'Small family is happy

family' as we now say in India: I want to live with my husband, and the children we will have, in a nuclear family. I think that all the decisions which have to be taken about the way we live, the country we live in or any other big decision have to be decided by both of us, with nobody interfering [. . .] Of course, it is easier for a woman to give her voice when the in-laws are not around. That is a big advantage of living abroad, this couple life.

Nurses are not the only ones in Kerala to prefer the idea of a nuclear family. The majority of young Indian people may have the same feeling. Actually, the new model has become a reality for many people, in the cities particularly where the joint family sensu stricto may very well be about to disappear. Yet the 'large family', in the sense of a constant interaction between the different members of a family, be they parents, brothers, sisters, uncles, or cousins, is still the norm; the potential and socially admitted interferences of all these in-laws (among them, in the first place, the mother-in-law) are more and more difficult to bear for young women who wish to get more autonomy and agency. As social pressure to maintain the traditional norms is strong, migration appears as a solution for the young nurses, since by being far away they may partly realise these aspirations without having to fight on a daily basis.

Migration in the Gulf: a changing picture

Bindu, who arrived in Fujairah in 1981, told me:

> It was only possible to bear this life [in the Gulf] by counting the days before coming back home. We had a one or two year contract and most of us were thinking of going back as soon as possible. Yet, as we were not spending a cent on us, we were proud to be able to send so much money to the family. I was earning ten times more than in India, more than my husband and his two brothers put together in their business. I was even able to send some money to my own family [. . .] In India, my salary was just helping. In the Gulf, it could change my entire life. But it has been so hard.

I was told the same story again and again when I interviewed nurses who emigrated before the end of the 1980s. At that time, the migrant nurses were all married women with children, who went alone, leaving their family behind. Their life in the Gulf was strictly confined to the compound of the hospital until, much later, the husbands started to join their wives in migration, following the massive migratory waves of Indians into this area by the middle of the 1980s.

A strict segregation exists in the Gulf countries between the different communities. Outside the professional field, relations between locals and migrants or between migrants of different origins hardly exist at all (Longva 1997). The judgement of Malayalis – and of Indians in general – concerning people in the Gulf is indeed rather severe. If, on the one hand, they feel looked down upon by the locals – as migrants and, moreover, as people coming from a developing country – most Malayalis, on the other hand, despise these locals whom they consider to be uneducated and incompetent. The old Indian tradition of culture is always reminded by my informants, compared to the newly created Gulf States. The migrant nurses share this general opinion about the Gulf and, as women, add a more precise appreciation, taking into account the absence of local nurses: 'Look how they behave with their women. They do not let them work. How many Emirati nurses are there? What are they doing, their women? They just sit a home all day long, idle, their foreign maids taking care of everything. They have no education, they have no ambition' (Beemole, 33 years, who has worked for two years in Saudi Arabia and four years in Abu Dhabi, before migrating to Ireland). Having no personal relation with the locals is thus not considered a problem; indeed, Malayali nurses have also few personal relations with their colleagues from other countries; Filipinos who represent the second higher group of foreign nurses appear, for instance, as having too many cultural differences: 'We do not have the same habits. [. . .] We don't like the smell of their food [. . .] They enjoy partying, some of them even drink alcohol. As Malayali women, we do not consider such behavior as good' (Anita, 26 years, living in Dubai since two years).

While migrant nurses make it clear that they do not like Gulf natives, the evolution of the population structure over the last 20 years has totally changed their way of life in these countries. The mutual dislike of the locals and migrants does not appear to be a daily problem for the nurses who, besides their duty time, live now in a quasi-Malayali environment, allowed by the development of a large diaspora with its neighbourhoods, its shops, churches, schools, etc.

There is thus a huge gap between the rather austere life of the pioneer migrant nurses and the lives of the nurses arriving today. Even the single young women who stay in the hospital hostels may have a social life outside work which includes shopping, meeting friends or family members, or taking part in parish life. In some places, like Dubai, social events may be even more abundant than in Kerala itself with the frequent coming of Indian or Keralese actors or singers, premieres of Indian movies, and other functions. The prevailing liberalism, particularly in the Emirates, but also in Oman or Kuwait, allows people not to change Keralese habits, be it to wear saris, to practise one's religion, or to offer alcohol to male guests. And, anyway, the home country is not very far and very accessible, as is obvious from looking at a map of the air connections between the three international airports in Kerala and all the possible destinations in the Gulf. For those who, like the nurses, have good earnings, going back home for any important occasion is not a problem, even if most of them choose not to go too often in order to save more money.

Gulf versus the West

Academic literature on Indian migration to the Gulf, considering mostly unskilled migrants, tends to stress on exploitation and on the harsh conditions of living that the migrants have to face (Khalaf and Alkobaisi 1999; Rahman 2001). This is particularly true in the literature concerning female migrants who work as housemaids (see, for instance, Varghese and Rajan 2011). Yet, in the Gulf, skilled migrants and successful Indian entrepreneurs can be found, especially Malayali ones (Gardner 2008; Venier 2011). For this category of people – which the nurses belong to – I argue that, in the course of time, the Gulf countries, except perhaps for Saudi Arabia,[8] have become a well appreciated destination and, in a certain way, a more 'comfortable' one than the Western countries, even if they do not offer the same rights to migrants.

In the Gulf, living mostly within one's own community, but far from home, authorises Malayalis to distance themselves somewhat from the social norms of the motherland, without however having to question one's identity, something that nurses particularly appreciate. This is another story when migrants go to a Western country, and more especially to those which have a link with the colonial past (UK, Ireland, Australia). In those places, nurses are well aware that one expects them to adopt the local codes of behaviour and to adopt the local values, particularly regarding gender relations. That is something they are particularly uncomfortable with, a sort of violence towards their own traditions and values. According to K.M. Zentgraf (2002: 639), Salvadorian female migrants that she studied in USA, considered it beneficial to live in a country whose 'sociocultural context was such that women were regarded as valuable and treated with respect'. I argue that in the case of Malayali nurses, their status of female migrant in a Western country leaves them alone to face clichés attached to them as 'coloured women', coming from an ex-colony, where the status of women is notoriously low and whose job, in addition, not so many Western women are willing to do anymore: Says Teresa, 33 years, living in Ireland after working for eight years in Oman:

> My Irish [female] neighbours are nice to me. But they are a little bit too quick to teach me lessons or to give me all sorts of advices, regarding my family life especially. This it is because they consider me as coming from an underdeveloped country. They consider their own culture as superior to our own culture.

It is therefore in terms of gender, class and race (Allan and Larsen 2003; Falquet et al. 2010) that they have to justify their behaviour, a task that they have some difficulty in facing. Actually, if from the beginning of their migratory plans, they were aiming at escaping a social control they felt as too strong, in no case were they engaged in a frontal struggle against the traditional values of Kerala and in no case do they reject all of them: they indeed continue to largely praise the virtues of this social system, particularly when confronted by Western norms that they judge altogether too permissive and lacking familial solidarity. If they take some liberties with tradition, if they have chosen and appreciate a position to do so and if they present themselves as 'modern [Malayali] women', it does not mean that migrant nurses drastically question the social gender relations of their native land. S. George (2005: 122) remarks, for instance, that a group of migrant nurses in USA had chosen, as a philanthropic action, to participate in paying dowry for 'poor young women in Kerala'. As a matter of fact, living in a Western country obliges them to question their own identity in a way which does not exist in the Gulf countries. Often pushed to get rid of the patriarchal norms of their country, in a way that they feel rather humiliating, Malayali nurses may end up having a less comfortable life in the West than in the Gulf.

They also face another problem in the West. In the Gulf, thanks to the development of a large Malayali diaspora, a nurse's husband is almost sure to find a job, whether he has useful qualifications or not, as long as his wife has been able to get a legal entry for him on the territory. If, very often, the wife remains the highest family earner, the husband may also achieve professional success (Venier 2011). On the contrary, in Western labour markets, these men are frequently in a situation of professional de-qualification, when they are not simply 'house husbands' taking care of the young children (Gallo 2006; Percot 2011). It is even more frequent with the last generation of migrant nurses whose husbands are degree-holders, some degrees (masters in social sciences or law, for instance) being more prestigious than useful in the labour market. Therefore, the nurses as main, if not only, breadwinners for sure get some power in the family, but they also have to constantly negotiate with an unsatisfied husband, frustrated by his inability to succeed by himself. This is particularly difficult in a country like Ireland, for instance, where the lack of a Malayali community does not provide space even now for a real masculine sociability, with its arena of distinction and power.

Conclusion

It may not be true for unqualified female migrants or for female migrants who are housewives, but in the case of Malayali migrant nurses, migration is clearly a factor of empowerment: it is indeed chosen as such by the young women from the moment they enter nursing school. As a result, migration is not only a parenthesis in their life as it used to be for the first migrants of the 1970s, but a real strategy in order to escape a too predictable future in their own country. Considering the social milieu the migrant nurses come from, it is surely the easiest way to achieve their individual ambitions. To become a nurse in order to leave has, of course, to do with climbing the social ladder, but it is also a conscious choice of modern values regarding the status of woman. Living abroad is a way to escape a social control felt as too strong, without directly confronting the dominant social model regarding gender norms: to live in a nuclear family, to get rid of pressure from in-laws, to be free from village gossip, or to have more to say in family decisions are benefits of migration that all migrant nurses acknowledge.

Migration to a Western country has for long been considered the best option and when this opportunity was opened for nurses, most of them aimed for countries such as the UK, USA or Australia. Migration to Western countries is still considered more prestigious and it still offers more than the Gulf countries like, for instance, the possibility of getting another citizenship or the possibility of buying a house. Yet, the Gulf countries continue to be the first step of migration for most nurses. However, the evolution that has taken place in the Gulf during the last decades, and especially the development of a Malayali diaspora, has changed these countries into more interesting places to live in and not only places where you have to go as a first possible destination. In addition, having tried both places, more and more nurses – often after getting a new citizenship in the West – consider a resettlement in the Gulf as an interesting option: to be closer to their homeland, to enjoy life in a Malayali environment within the Gulf diaspora, without (as women) having to bear the social pressure existing in their homeland.

Notes

1   Among all the informants, no case has been found where a dowry was not paid (for more details on the dowry system in India, see, for instance, Menski 1998).
2   The National Council Licensure Examination for Registered Nurses (NCLEX-RN) is a compulsory exam in order to work as a nurse in the USA. The USA has stopped recruiting foreign nurses in the last few years, but the new immigration policy of President Obama should open up new recruitments. Many Indian nurses have already passed this exam and are now awaiting migration to the USA.
3   The NCLEX seems difficult, as it is estimated that only 17 per cent of the Indian candidates pass it on the first try.
4   'Contractors' are taking on the job of labour importer; the salaries are then not paid directly to the employees by the societies employing them, but the money is given to the contractor, who deducts his percentage before paying the concerned employees. The contractor's system is obviously less secure for the nurses.
5   Personal interview.
6   Personal interview.
7   This competition is so high that it is now very difficult to enter public nursing schools or colleges which are free, so most of the trainees have to follow their studies in private schools. Parents also have to pay for lodging and boarding when, like in most cases, the school is far from the family home.
8   The lack of religious freedom in particular is a strong problem for the nurses who are mainly Christian and very religious.

References

Allan H. and J.A. Larsen. 2003. *"We Need Respect": Experiences of Internationally Recruited Nurses in the UK*. London: Royal College of Nursing. See http://www.hrhresourcecenter.org/node/449 (accessed on 11 December 2012).

Falquet J., H. Hirata, D. Kergoat, B. Labari, N. Le Feuvre, F. Sow. 2010. *Le sexe de la mondialisation. Genre, classe, race et nouvelle division du travail*. Paris: Presses de Sciences Po.

Gallo, Ester. 2006. 'Italy is not a Good Place for Men: Narratives of Places and Masculinity among Malayali Migrants', *Global Network*, 6(4): 357–72.

Gardner, A. 2008. 'Strategic Transnationalism: The Indian Diasporic Elite in Contemporary Bahrain', *City and Society*, 20(1): 54–78.

George, S.M. 2005. *When Women Come First. Gender and Class in Transnational Migration*. Berkeley: University of California Press.

Khalaf S. and S. Alkobaisi. 1999. 'Migrants' Strategies of Coping and Patterns of Accommodation in the Oil-Rich Gulf Societies: Evidence from the UAE', *British Journal of Middle Eastern Studies*, 26(2): 271–98.

Longva, Ahn Nga. 1997. *Walls Built on Sand. Migration, Exclusion and Society in Kuwait*. Oxford: Westview Press.

Menski, Werner (ed.). 1998. *South Asians and the Dowry Problem*. Stoke-on-Trent and London: Trentham Books.

Percot, M. 2011. 'Masculinity in Transnational Migration: Indian Nurses' Husbands in Ireland', in *Emigrinter*, 9(8): 74–86, http://www.mshs.univ-poitiers.fr/migrinter/e-migrinter/201208/e-migrinter2012_08_074.pdf (accessed on 11 December 2012).

Percot, M. and S. Nair. 2011. 'Transcending Boundaries: Internal and International Migration of Indian Nurses', in S.I. Rajan and M. Percot (eds), *Dynamics of Indian Migration: Historical and Current Perspectives*, pp. 195–223, New Delhi: Routledge.

Rahman A. 2001. *Indian Labour Migration to the Gulf (A Socio-Economic Analysis)*. New Delhi: Rajat Publications.

Varghese V.J. and S.I. Rajan. 2011. 'Governmentality, Social Stigma and Quasi-citizenship: Gender Negotiations of Migrant Women Domestic Workers from Kerala', in S.I. Rajan and M. Percot (eds), *Dynamics of Indian Migration: Historical and Current Perspectives*, pp. 224–48. New Delhi: Routledge.

Venier, Philippe. 2011. 'Development of Entrepreneurial Initiatives in the UAE among Kerala Emigrants', in S.I. Rajan and M. Percot (eds), *Dynamics of Indian Migration: Historical and Current Perspectives*, pp. 164–94. New Delhi: Routledge.

Zachariah, K.C., K.P. Kannan and S.I. Rajan. 2002. *Kerala's Gulf connection. CDS studies on international labour. Migration from Kerala State in India*. Trivandrum: Centre for Development Studies.

Zentgraf, K.M. 2002. 'Immigration and Women's Empowerment: Salvadorans in Los Angeles', *Gender and Society*, 16(5): 625–46.

Labour migration to the Middle East and socio-economic mobility in Pakistan

G.M. Arif

Introduction

Socio-economic mobility is the shifting of an individual, family or some other group from one social class or economic level to another, commonly to a status that is either higher or lower. This mobility can be intergenerational (between parents and children) or intra-generational over the course of a lifetime. In this way, the notion of socio-economic mobility underlines much of the literature on poverty reduction and social change. This change (or mobility) is a long process and comes through several ways, including the diversification of livelihood, better education and building social capital. Migration, internal as well as international, has also been a key channel for socio-economic mobility because it provides an opportunity to earn money at a new place, experience new cultures, gain skills and accumulate wealth.[1]

Pakistan has a long history of labour migration to the Middle East; at present more than 3 million Pakistan are placed in the region. This migration is temporary in nature because migrants have to return home when they complete their contractual jobs at their destination countries. This temporary movement can be a source for socio-economic mobility of migrants and their families at the place of origin through three channels: inflows of remittances and their uses, acquisition of new skills while abroad and successful reintegration of return migrants in the domestic labour market. At the initial stage of migration, better-off people, who can bear the cost of movement, generally go abroad, but as the social network develops over time and the cost of movement reduces to a bearable level, the poor segments of the society take the opportunity and find employment abroad (Mckenzie and Rapoport 2007).

Thus, migration of workers to the Middle East can be a channel for socio-economic mobility of the poor.

Considerable literature has so far been produced to study the different dimensions of migration of Pakistani workers to the Middle East; however, its contribution in socio-economic mobility of Pakistani workers and their families at their place of origin has not been systematically examined. The major objective of this chapter is to develop the nexus between migration to the Middle East and socio-economic mobility in Pakistan.

The rest of this chapter is organised as follows. Section 2 presents the analytical framework used in this chapter, followed by a presentation on the dynamics of Pakistani migration to the Middle East. Section 4 has examined the contribution of remittances in household income while the utilisation pattern of remittances is discussed in Section 5. The change in occupation as a measure of socio-economic mobility is the subject matter of Section 6. Perceived change in social and economic status of migrant families is discussed in Section 7 while the conclusion is given in final section of this chapter.

Analytical framework

This study is exploratory in nature, based on the existing data and literature.[2] It has used the notion of socio-economic mobility as a change in social or economic status of migrants and their families, linked with the movement of their members to the Middle East. The commonly used measures for socio-economic mobility are: change in individual or family income (Colen et al 2006); educational attainment (Wade 2010); change in position of wealth; and change in occupation (Quadrini 1997). Following the literature, this study has used four indicators to examine the role of Middle East migration in socio-economic mobility of migrating workers and their families. First, the share of remittances in the total household income is included in the analysis as a key factor to enable households to transfer money to savings and investment after meeting their basic needs. Second, an analysis of the household consumption expenditure has been carried out; it is probably the most important dimension in a sense that remittances enable the recipient households to have some discretionary resources to buy consumer goods and invest in health, education and housing.

Third, the occupational choices of return migrants can be critical since they, in most labour-sending countries, make a transition to self-employment after their return. The self-employed possess relatively more entrepreneurial ability, as Mckenzie and Rapoport (2007) found that return migrants have the highest entrepreneurship among rural counterparts. This study has examined the occupational choices of return migrants to see the changes, if any, are associated with the experience of overseas migration. Fourth, the perception of migrant households about their economic and social mobility is reviewed. The expectation is that overseas migration has contributed to enhance their socio-economic status through foreign remittances, their uses and occupational choices. Because of these enabling factors, migrants' families may feel that, after migration, they are part of relatively higher economic or social group.

However, the methodological approach as used in this study has several flaws. First, migration is not the only factor that contributes to socio-economic mobility, which is likely to be influenced by other socio-economic developments in the society as well, and these developments have not been examined in this study. For example, socio-economic mobility may come through the process of urbanisation – movements of individuals or groups from a poor, agrarian region to a richer, urban one. Second, it is very difficult to determine pre-migration socio-economic status of migrants. It can be argued that most of the outgoing workers already belong to a high economic and social group, particularly in view of the heavy cost involved in overseas migration. However, this study takes the position that overseas migration, particularly temporary employment in the Middle East, is now more than three decades old. A strong social network, which has developed in the country over time, has given many poor families the opportunity to send their members abroad for temporary employment. Third, education is the other key factor that can contribute in upward socio-economic mobility, which has not been addressed in this chapter. Finally, overseas migration is not a cost-free movement; it involves economic as well as social costs, which have not been examined in this chapter.[3]

Dynamics of Pakistani migration to the Middle East

To put the study in a proper context, this section presents the dynamics of migration of Pakistani workers to the Middle East in terms of their stock, magnitude of return flows, place of origin in Pakistan, change in skill composition, if any, while abroad, and inflows of remittances. The data on the stock of overseas Pakistanis is reported in Table 12.1, which shows that it has increased from 3.97 million in 2004 to 6.7 million in 2012, an annual net increase of about 0.34 million workers. A close look at Table 12.1 reveals that around 85 per cent of overseas Pakistanis are concentrated in seven countries in the following order: Saudi Arabia, United Kingdom (UK), United States of America (USA), United Arab Emirates (UAE), Canada, Oman, and Kuwait. About 3.5 million Pakistanis, which constitutes 50 per cent of the Pakistani diaspora, are presently placed in the Middle East, primarily in Saudi Arabia and the UAE, followed by Oman, Kuwait and Qatar. It indicates the importance of the Middle East labour market for the placement of Pakistani workers. However, it is well documented that the share of Pakistan in the annual placement of Asian workers in the Middle East has gradually declined because of the diversification strategy of the labour-receiving countries of the region. In addition to workers from South Asia, a large number of workers from Indonesia and Philippines are recruited regularly for the Middle East labour market (Skeldon 2012).

The return flows of workers are as important as the stock of overseas workers because they are likely to be the agents of change or socio-economic mobility through both their investment behaviour

Table 12.1 Stock of overseas Pakistanis (in millions) and their share in major destination countries

Destination countries	2004	2009	2012
All countries (million)	3.973	5.500	6.700
Share (%) in the stock	100	100	100
Saudi Arabia	27.7	21.8	25.4
United Kingdom	20.1	21.8	17.9
United States of America	15.1	16.4	13.4
United Arab Emirates	12.9	13.4	17.9
Canada	6.3	5.5	4.5
Oman	N.A.	2.8	3.0
Kuwait	2.5	2.7	2.2
Qatar	N.A.	1.5	N.A.
Others Countries	15.4	14.1	15.7

Source: Amjad, Arif and Irfan (2012).

and their occupational choices. But, unfortunately, there is no source of data on the stock of return migrants. The Overseas Pakistanis Foundation (OPF) in the 1980s and 1990s collected data on return flows and shows that between 1982 and 1995, the annual return flows (permanent) were between 50 and 200 per cent of the annual placement of workers in the Middle East. These percentages reinforce the argument that return migration is part of temporary overseas labour migration; at the expiry of their contracts, migrants need to get these renewed or return home, although the possibility of overstaying without proper documentation exists.

According to the Bureau of Emigration and Overseas Employment (BEOE) data, between 1972 and 2012, more than 10 million Pakistanis have been placed only in the Middle East. During the last three to four years, the annual placement of Pakistani workers in the region is about 400,000. But the stock of Pakistanis in the Middle East, as shown in Table 12.1, is between 3 and 4 million. So the remaining 6–7 million Pakistanis who went to the region for temporary employment during the last 30 years have returned home, although the possibility of re-migration of these returnees cannot be ruled out. Based on these very simple statistics, it appears that not only is the Pakistan diaspora large in size, a large number of returnees have also resettled in the country.

Migrants to the Middle East are not represented evenly from across the country. Pakistan is administratively divided into four provinces and more than a hundred districts. Figure 12.1 shows the breakdown by province/area of origin of the Pakistani workers who went abroad between 1981 and 2012 through the BEOE. The population of Punjab represents 54 per cent of the total population of Pakistan, and 52 per cent of the migrant workers is from Punjab. However, 9 per cent of the workers who went abroad, mainly to the Middle East, between 1981 and 2012, are from Sindh. This proportion is less than half of Sindh's share of the total population of Pakistan. About one-quarter of the migrants who went abroad for employment are from Khyber Pakhtunkhwa, which is twice the proportion of the total population. Balochistan is under-represented; only 1.3 per cent of the migrants are from this province compared to its 5 per cent share of the total population. The BEOE migration data are also available at the district level. More than 60 per cent of the Pakistanis who migrated came from only 20 districts, mainly in northern Punjab and Khyber Pakhtunkhwa, Karachi in Sindh and only 2 districts in southern Punjab. The concentration of

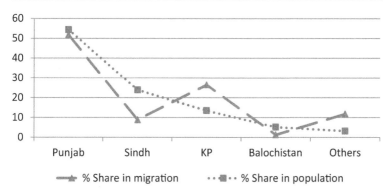

Figure 12.1 Share (%) of provinces/region in the total population and overseas migration

Source: Drawn by authors from the data given in the *Pakistan Economic Survey*, 2012–13 and data files of the BEOE.

migrants in certain regions of the country may restrict the benefits of migration primarily to the population of these regions.

The skill composition of Pakistani workers going to the Middle East has changed very little over the last three and a half decades (BEOE 2007). Figure 12.2 presents the skill composition of Pakistani workers in the Middle East for the period 2004–12. This classification of workers into different skill levels is done by BEOE on the basis of their qualification and the skill requirements of a particular job. For example, the 'highly qualified' and skilled category includes professionals with high levels of education such as doctors and engineers, and occupations that require specialised skills such as technicians and nurses. The jobs that require some training, formal or informal, are included in the 'skilled' and semi-skilled categories. These workers commonly take such jobs as drivers, masons and carpenters. However, it is not easy to draw a clear line between semi-skilled and unskilled workers.

Figure 12.2 shows unskilled and skilled/semi-skilled workers as the dominant categories, while the proportion of highly qualified/ highly skilled workers remained low, around 10 per cent, between 2004 and 2012. It also appears from this figure that the share of skilled/semi-skilled workers in total annual flows of workers to the Middle East has gradually increased since 2009, by lowering the corresponding share of the unskilled workers. Since the 1990s,

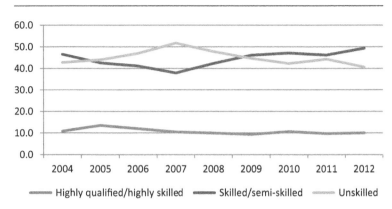

Figure 12.2 Skill composition of Pakistani workers in the Middle East, 2004–12

Source: Drawn by authors from the data files of the BEOE.

there has been a general tendency in the Middle East to hire more professionals and skilled workers as opposed to unskilled and semi-skilled workers. The skill composition of other Asian workers, such as Indians, has changed due to this shift in demand (Srivastava and Sasikumar 2005). The composition of Pakistani workers has not witnessed a major shift towards more skilled workers (Amjad, Irfan and Arif 2013), although a positive trend is found for the recent period.

Table 12.2 presents data on remittances that came through the official sources (banking) from 1998 to 2012. The flows of remittances declined from US$1.5 billion in fiscal year (FY) 1998 to around US$1 billion in FY 2000. The decline can be due to the freezing of foreign currency accounts in Pakistan. Following 9/11, the total official remittance flows doubled from US$1.09 billion in FY 2001 to US$2.4 billion in FY 2002. Since then the annual flows of remittances have steadily increased to a level of US$13 billion in FY 2012 (Table 12.2). This increase has been observed from all major countries where Pakistanis have settled permanently or temporarily including Saudi Arabia and Dubai in the Middle East, UK and USA. Amjad, Arif and Irfan (2012) have estimated that the annual flows of remittances could be more than US$20 billion when the flows from informal sources such as *hundi*[4] are taken into account.

Table 12.2 Remittances (through formal sources) by countries of origin

Countries	FY 1998	FY 1999	FY 2000	FY 2001	FY 2002
All countries	1489.55	1060.19	988.73	1086.57	2389.05
Saudi Arabia	474.76	318.49	309.85	304.43	376.34
UAE	207.70	125.09	147.75	190.04	469.41
Dubai	(101.01)	(70.57)	(87.04)	(129.69)	(331.47)
Abu Dhabi	(75.53)	(38.07)	(47.30)	(48.11)	(103.72)
Other GEC countries	160.85	197.28	224.32	198.75	224.29
US	166.29	81.95	79.96	134.81	778.98
UK	98.83	73.59	73.27	81.39	151.93
Other EU countries	35.87	26.48	24.06	21.50	28.80
Other countries	66.38	34.03	35.38	67.71	256.24
Encashment FEBCs	251.87	184.64	70.24	64.98	48.26
	FY 2003	FY 2004	FY 2005	FY 2006	FY 2007
Total	4236.85	3871.58	4168.79	4600.12	5493.65
Saudi Arabia	580.76	565.29	627.19	750.44	1023.56
UAE	837.87	597.48	712.61	716.30	866.49
Dubai	(581.09)	(447.49)	(532.93)	(540.24)	(635.60)
Abu Dhabi	(212.37)	(114.92)	(152.51)	(147.89)	(200.40)
Other GEC countries	474.02	451.54	512.14	596.46	757.33
US	1237.52	1225.09	1294.08	1242.49	1459.64
UK	273.83	333.94	371.86	438.65	430.04
Other EU countries	53.53	74.51	101.51	119.62	149.00
Other countries	658.05	497.14	417.25	573.31	642.11
Encashment FEBCs	46.12	45.42	16.25	12.09	2.68
	FY 2008	FY 2009	FY 2010	FY 2011	FY 2012
Total	6451.24	7810.95	8905.90	11200.97	13186.58
Saudi Arabia	1251.32	1559.56	1917.66	2670.07	3687.00
UAE	1090.30	1688.59	2039.59	2597.74	2848.86
Dubai	(761.24)	(970.42)	(851.54)	(1201.15)	(1411.26)
Abu Dhabi	(298.80)	(669.40)	(1130.33)	(1328.82)	(1367.62)
Other GEC countries	983.39	1202.65	1237.86	1306.18	1495.00
US	1762.03	1735.87	1771.19	2068.67	2334.47
UK	458.87	605.59	876.38	1199.67	1521.10
Other EU countries	176.64	247.66	252.21	354.76	364.79
Other countries	530.39	609.00	577.37	653.26	562.14
Encashment FEBCs	2.40	0.48	1.02	0.07	13186.58

Source: Amjad, Arif and Irfan (2012).

This brief review of the dynamics of migration to the Middle East shows the importance of such movement in terms of the stock of both emigrants and return migrants and the volume of remittances. Although the data show a geographical concentration of migrants, it seems to have influenced a large part of the country's population.

Contribution of remittances in household income

Change in family income is a commonly used measure for socio-economic mobility. It is crucial to see the contribution of remittances in household income. Based on the household survey data, recent studies have shown that migrants remit home, on average, Rs 200,000 per annum (Ahmed 2012; Arif 2009). This amount is more than double the average monthly wages of unskilled workers, if they were employed throughout a year. These remittances have enabled households to diversify their sources of income. This diversification has been a major factor, particularly in rural areas, where employment opportunities are limited, to enhance the socio-economic status of the respective households. For example, the relatively better-off position of rural households in northern Punjab compared to households of other regions is commonly linked to the diversification of their incomes from employment in urban areas as well as overseas employment.

The data presented in Table 12.3 support this view and show the importance of remittances in migrants' household income, based on a survey of more than 500 households in rural and urban areas of Pakistan. Remittances constituted 41 per cent of the average

Table 12.3 Sources of monthly household income by occupation

Sources of income	All	Professional workers	Clerical/sales workers	Skilled workers	Unskilled workers
Salaries	17.23	16.00	15.59	19.33	16.53
Businesses	20.6	21.01	11.23	20.79	18.73
Agriculture/livestock	16.98	13.56	13.81	17.57	21.41
Remittances	40.59	48.15	42.55	37.99	36.22
Other sources	4.56	1.27	5.82	4.32	7.10
All	100	100	100	100	100

Source: Arif (2009).

Table 12.4 Remittances as proportion of income of international and internal migrants by rural–urban origin

Region of origin	International migrants			Internal migrants			Ratio of foreign remittances to remittances
	Foreign remittances (Pakistani rupees)	Annual income (Pakistani rupees)	Remittances as % of income	Domestic remittances (Pakistani rupees)	Annual income (Pakistani rupees)	Remittances as % of income	
	1	2	3 (1/2*100)	4	5	6 (4/5* 100)	7 (1/4)
Urban	238,367	424,872	56.1	105,241	127,289	82.68	2.26
Rural	219,965	436,672	50.37	54,351	104,620	51.95	4.05
Total	223,174	434,356	51.38	60,568	107,577	56.3	3.68

Source: Ahmed (2012).

monthly income of the households surveyed. However, it varies across the occupation of migrants while abroad, from 48 per cent for professional workers to 36 per cent for unskilled workers. The other sources of household income include the salaries of family members in Pakistan, businesses and agriculture/livestock. Ahmed (2012) has recently calculated the share of foreign remittances in migrants' household income as 51 per cent; 56 per cent in urban areas and 50 per cent in rural areas. For internal migrants, the corresponding share is only 4 per cent (Table 12.4).

It is worth noting that income from non-remittance sources constitutes approximately 60 per cent of the total household monthly income (Table 12.4). Based on these statistics, Arif (2009) has argued that, on the one hand, the larger share of non-remittance income shows the ability of households to save or invest part of their remittances after meeting daily needs with non-remittance incomes. One the other hand, this shows less dependency on remittances, which are not the permanent source of income. He argues that it is likely that when a migrant returns home permanently he may be able to start a new business or be active in the existing one, thus generating an alternative source of permanent household income. From this very simple statistics, it is argued that the diversification of household sources of income, primarily through foreign remittances, sets the ground for socio-economic mobility of such households.

Uses of remittances

The utilisation pattern of remittances determines the mechanism through which migrant households succeed in improving their socio-economic status. The uses of remittances are discussed in this section in three ways: (a) what are the changes that overseas migration and remittance flows have brought in the total household consumption expenditure when compared to pre-migration expenditure, which has been shown in Table 12.5, by quintile; (b) how are the remittances used, or have the households been able to get some discretionary income from remittances to spend on non-food items such as consumer durables, health and education; and (c) what proportion or how much remittance money has been used for investment to sustain the positive change associated with overseas migration.

The data presented in Table 12.5 show that the overall monthly expenditure of migrant households increased by 158 per cent in

Table 12.5 Mean duration of stay abroad and change in household consumption expenditures by quintile

Quintile	Mean duration of stay abroad (years)	Average monthly household consumption expenditure before migration (Pakistani rupees)	Average monthly household consumption expenditure at the time of survey (Pakistani rupees)	Change (%)
First quintile	7.69	1,167.92	2,283.42	95.5
Second quintile	8.71	1,586.99	3,036.09	91.3
Third quintile	7.56	2,222.91	4,317.71	94.2
Fourth quintile	6.86	2,078.65	5,445.36	162.0
Fifth quintile	6.72	3,727.99	11,622.46	211.8
Total	7.56	2,080.59	5,362.17	157.7

Note: US$1 = PKR 78.88

Source: Arif (2009).

nominal terms during the average stay of seven years abroad. The greatest increase was observed for the fifth quintile (wealthiest). Even the lowest quintile households were able to increase their monthly expenditure by more than 90 per cent after migration.

With respect to the uses of remittances, the prevailing view in the literature on the subject is that the share of remittances channelled towards consumption is generally very high. However, the decision on how much of the remittances to invest and how much to consume depends upon many factors including the pre-migration economic position of households, the life cycle stages of migrants, access to household non-remittance income, particularly during the migration phase, and length of stay abroad (Arif 2009).

Table 12.6 presents data on the uses of total amount of remittances received since the migrants went abroad. The three most common uses, for which more than half of the total remittances were used, were: real estate and agricultural machinery (22 per cent), marriages (17 per cent) and savings (14 per cent). Of the total remittances received, only 18 per cent was spent on providing the family with food. Poorer families in Pakistan generally spend more than half of their total expenditures on food items. The purchase of durable items (8 per cent), loan repayments (5.5 per cent) and donations (3.7 per cent) were other important uses of remittances.

Table 12.6 Uses of remittances received (%)

Uses of remittances	Total	Urban	Rural	Punjab	Sindh	Others
Food	17.75	14.83	22.06	13.76	18.02	28.30
Health	3.56	3.81	3.28	3.41	4.27	3.86
Education	4.51	4.21	5.00	3.06	4.50	7.90
Real estate and agricultural machinery	22.12	23.75	20.34	25.39	16.22	22.05
Durable items	8.06	8.82	7.13	9.06	10.17	5.62
Marriage	17.14	17.31	17.61	16.31	14.96	16.48
Loan repayments	5.52	4.84	6.52	5.81	6.17	3.87
Savings	14.08	15.18	10.70	15.3	20.55	4.40
Donations	3.65	4.40	2.58	5.24	3.17	1.35
Others	3.61	2.85	4.78	2.66	1.96	6.16
Total	100.00	100.00	100.00	100.0	100.00	100.00

Source: Arif (2009).

Approximately 8 per cent of the total remittances were used for education and health services for household members. It appears that food, real estate savings and marriage were important areas for the use of remittances for both rural and urban households. Ahmed (2012), based on the Pakistan Panel Household Survey 2010, has examined migrants household preferences for the use of foreign remittances. The identified four priority areas are: food, health, education, and housing (Table 12.7).

Based on these statistics, it appears that households spend the remittances according to their needs and priorities. A considerable proportion of the remittances received has been used for education, health services and housing. So, the overseas migration gives respective households a substantial discretionary income to spend on these sectors. According to the Pakistan Socio-economic Living Standard Measurement Survey (PSLM) data, the share of food in the total household expenditure is around 50 per cent, which is much larger than the share of remittances used for food consumption. It seems that migrant households meet their food needs from non-remittance sources of income.

It is well documented in recent studies that, on average, the sampled migrant households were able to direct more than Rs 200,000 to investments and savings (Arif 2009; Irfan 2012). This amount increases to an average of Rs 369,000 when households with no investments or savings are excluded. In the local context this

Table 12.7 Percentage distribution of international migrant households by their preferences regarding use of remittances

Preferences for use of remittances	1st preference	2nd preference	3rd preference
Food	66.51	3.77	1.42
Health	0.94	59.91	3.30
Education	0.47	2.83	35.38
Housing	0.00	3.77	11.79
Purchase of land	0.00	0.00	0.47
Saving	0.47	0.47	2.83
Business	0.00	0.00	0.00
Marriages	0.94	0.00	0.00
Loan return	3.30	2.36	5.66
Others	0.00	0.47	11.32
No information	27.36	26.42	27.83
Total	100.00	100.00	100.00

Source: Ahmed (2012).

investment can be considered an amount likely to have lasting positive effects on upward socio-economic mobility. Arif (2009) found a positive relationship between the remittances and the amount invested. The greater the amount of remittances received, the more likely the household is to direct remittances to investments. A higher proportion of overseas earnings went into productive investments, probably because the household's day-to-day sustenance was drawn from other income sources. It short, remittances have not only enabled the recipient households to enhance their consumption level but also to have some money for health care, education and housing.

Migration and occupational change

Change in occupation is other commonly used measure of socio-economic mobility. Workers' original (pre-migration) occupational backgrounds compared to their post-migration jobs measure the impact of migration on occupational shifts after migration. To learn more about the occupational shifts over time, occupations held by returnees during their stay in the Middle East are also included in the analysis. However, this type of data is not available for the recent period. This study has relied on the survey data produced in the 1980s, but supplemented by the experience of migrants in three Maghreb countries – Algeria, Morocco and Tunisia.

Table 12.8 shows a concentration of workers in the production-service sector before going to the Middle East. Approximately two-thirds of the migrants from urban areas and more than half from rural areas were in this sector before migration. In rural areas, 29 per cent were engaged in the agriculture sector, while, as expected, the shares of professional clerical workers were higher among the urban sample than among the rural sample. During migration, production-service sector employment increased substantially: from 60 per cent before migration to 91 per cent while in the Middle East (Table 12.8).This indicates a substantial mismatch between the pre-migration and during migration occupations of return migrants. A transition matrix for movement from pre-migration occupations to occupations while in the Middle East shows that about 21 per cent of those who were professional workers before migration were production workers in the Middle East. In the case of migrants who were clerical workers before migration, 15 per cent were skilled workers and 26 per cent were unskilled workers abroad. More than two-thirds of agricultural workers switched to unskilled jobs in the Middle East.

After migration, Table 12.9 shows that production-service sector employment for all migrants declined substantially: from 60 per cent before migration and 91 per cent during migration to only 37 per cent after return. The share of unskilled workers declined from 21 per cent before migration and 39 per cent while in the Middle East to only 10 per cent after return. In turn, business sector

Table 12.8 Percentage distribution of return migrants by pre-migration and post-return occupation, controlling for geographical location

Occupation	Urban			Rural		
	Pre-migration	During migration	Post-return	Pre-migration	During migration	Post-return
Professional/clerical workers	8.8	10.9	6.7	5.8	2.8	3.3
Agriculture workers	11.7	1.5	3.5	28.5	1.4	39.3
Business workers	14.7	2.3	42.3	8.6	1.4	26.4
Production/service workers	64.8	85.3	47.5	57.1	94.4	31.0
All	100	100	100	100	100	100

Source: Arif and Irfan (1997).

Table 12.9 Employment status of return migrants before migration, after migration and today (Algeria, Morocco and Tunisia)

Employment status	Algeria			Morocco			Tunisia			All		
	Before	After	Today	Before	After	Today	Before	After	Today	Before	After	Today
Waged	37.5	25.3	25.9	19.0	21.3	21.6	36.6	25.8	26.7	31.3	24.2	24.8
Employer	1.8	9.3	11.1	0.7	11.9	15.9	1.2	23.4	28.2	1.3	14.9	18.4
Self-employed	15.1	14.2	15.4	15.1	16.6	17.5	14.6	12.0	13.8	14.9	14.2	15.5
Seasonal worker	12.4	0.9	0.3	9.8	7.5	8.6	15.8	3.7	1.8	12.7	4.0	3.5
Family worker	2.1	0.0	0.0	5.6	0.6	0.6	3.4	1.8	2.1	3.7	0.8	0.9
Unemployed	17.2	13.0	11.1	9.8	18.8	14.9	9.9	10.5	6.4	12.4	14.0	10.8
Retired	0.3	31.3	31.3	0.3	5.3	5.7	0.0	15.4	16.9	0.2	17.5	18.2
Student	10.3	2.1	0.9	28.9	2.2	0.6	12.7	1.5	0.3	17.0	1.9	0.6
Inactive	3.3	3.9	3.9	1.0	3.4	3.2	4.3	2.8	2.1	2.9	3.4	3.1
Other	0.0	0.0	0.0	9.8	12.2	11.4	1.12	3.1	1.5	3.5	5.0	4.2

Source: Gubert and Nordman (2011).

employment increased from 32 per cent before migration to 60 per cent after return. In rural areas, the concentration of migrants shifted to agriculture work, while in urban areas the importance of business occupation increased substantially.

The findings of Gubert and Nordman (2011) regarding the labour-exporting countries in Maghreb are not different. They have examined the changes in three periods by employment status; employer and self-employed are used as separate categories (Table 12.9).

Employer and self-employed match the business category of occupation discussed above in the case of Pakistan. The proportion of employers rose from 1 per cent to 15 per cent of the whole sample between the pre-migration and post-return periods. This increase arises largely because some of those individuals who were wage workers prior to migration (31 per cent of the whole sample prior to migration) became employers. This shift in employment status is particularly pronounced in the case of Tunisia, where the percentage of employers rose from 1 per cent to 23 per cent between the pre-migration and post-return periods. Another study of Tunisian return migrants by Mesnard (2004) also found that self-employment has increased among return migrants. Workers who are self-employed after return have accumulated much large amounts of savings during migration. They stayed abroad on average larger than other workers. The evidence from other countries, like China and India, is similar (Czaika and Varella 2012; Demurger and HuiXUnd, n.d.).

In short, the occupational choices of return migrants in Pakistan as well as other labour-exporting countries are in the expected direction – a transition from wage employment to self-employment. Although return migrants' job as a self-employed worker may not match with their overseas work experience, remittances and a desire to earn a better livelihood may have a major effect on the choice of post-return occupation, leading to socio-economic mobility.

Socio-economic mobility: perception of migrant families

In a recent study on migration of Pakistani workers to Saudi Arabia, left-behind families of migrants were asked to rank separately the economic and social status of their household prior to migration and after migration (Arif 2009). This ranking shows the perception of the respondents regarding their overall economic and social status relative to that of the other households of the community. The ranking was done using a scale of 1 to 10, where 1 represented the highest status and 10 the lowest status. The percentage distributions of households by perceived economic status prior to migration and at the time of the survey are shown in Figures 12.3 through 12.5. There is a marked difference between perceived pre- and post-migration economic status. The majority of respondents selected numbers between 6 and 9 when referring to their perceived economic status before migration, showing a

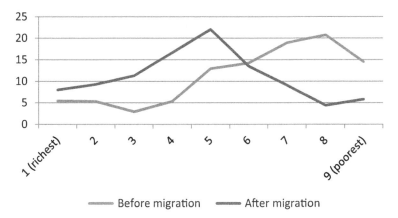

Figure 12.3 Economic status before and after migration (total sample)

Source: Arif (2009).

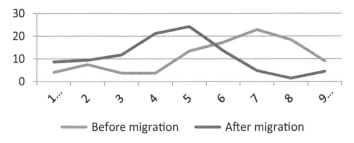

Figure 12.4 Economic status before and after migration (urban areas)

Source: Arif (2009).

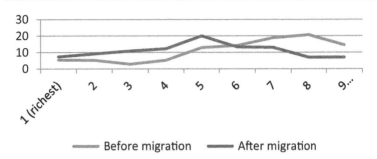

Figure 12.5 Economic status before and after migration (rural areas)

Source: Arif (2009).

relatively low pre-migration economic status. Regarding economic status at the time of the survey, most responses were between 3 and 5, indicating an improvement in status. For pre-migration economic status, the lowest number given (9) was selected by 15 per cent of the respondents; for status at the time of the survey, only 5 per cent of the respondents selected this number. This change can also be observed in both rural and urban areas (Figures 12.3 and 12.4). Almost all households with professional or educated workers abroad enjoyed better status after migration. There is no major change, however, for those household who selected numbers 1 and 2 for their pre-migration household status; their status at the time of the survey remained the same. So, these are the pre-migration low-economic status migrants and their families who have been able to improve their status after migration.

More than one-third of the sampled households reported that poverty was the main push factor. The data on the perceived economic status at the time of the survey shows that both the overseas work experience and the remittances had improved the economic status of households. Keeping in mind that perceived poverty was one of the major reasons for both migration and the perceived low economic status prior to migration, the improvement in the economic status of households after migration shows the great contribution of remittances to improving the overall well-being of migrant households.

Poverty levels among households of high migration districts are considerably lower than poverty levels among households from low-migration districts in Sindh and southern Punjab (Amjad, Arif and Mustafa 2008). In areas where agricultural incomes are low, households resort to migration as one way of improving their economic conditions. Migrants to the Gulf region include a significant number of unskilled workers from rural areas who would otherwise work in low-paid jobs in the informal sector in Pakistan. If temporary migration overseas is considered to be a strategy to alleviate poverty, Pakistan needs to ensure more migration opportunities for households in those provinces and districts that have benefited less from migration to the Middle East.

The migrant households were also asked to rank their social status in the community prior to migration and at the time of the survey. The ranking was done using a score of 1 to 10, with 1 representing the highest status and 10 representing the lowest status. As shown in Figures 12.6 through 12.8, there is a marked difference

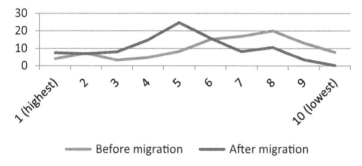

Figure 12.6 Social status before and after migration (both rural and urban areas)

Source: Arif (2009).

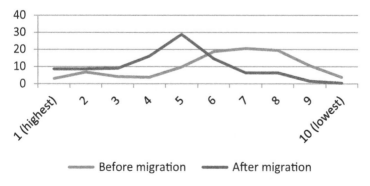

Figure 12.7 Social status before and after migration (urban areas only)

Source: Arif (2009).

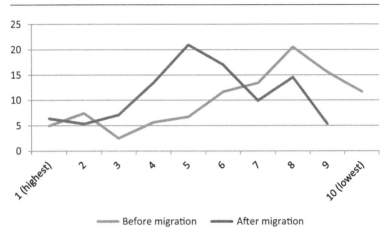

Figure 12.8 Social status before and after migration (rural areas only)

Source: Arif (2009).

between pre- and post-migration social status for most households. The majority of respondents selected numbers between 6 and 9 when referring to their social status before migration, showing a relatively low perceived pre-migration social status (Figure 12.6) among respondents. For perceived social status after migration the majority of respondents selected numbers between 3 and 5. This change is observed in both rural and urban areas (Figures 12.7 and 12.8). Almost all households with professional and educated workers abroad perceived a high social status after migration. However, there is no major change between the time periods for those who had selected numbers 1 or 2. A social change associated with overseas migration is also witnessed in other countries like Bangladesh (Dannecker 2011).

In short, migration and remittances appear to have a positive social impact on the remittance-receiving households. Remittances have contributed to improving the quality of children's education, improving access to better health facilities, and providing good quality housing. The overall economic and social status of the households has shown a marked improvement in both rural and urban areas.

8. Conclusions

This study has shown that migration of Pakistani labour to the Middle East is likely to have contributed in socio-economic mobility of migrants and their families in the following ways: first, migration has provided the households an opportunity to diversify their sources of income through the inflows of remittances. The value of these remittances is much larger than what migrants, particularly unskilled worked, would have earned in Pakistan had they not found employment in the Middle East. Remittances surely have increased the financial resources available to households. Second, about half of the foreign remittances received by the migrant households are used to buy consumer goods, to improve housing quality and to invest in health and children's education. This pattern of consumption indicates a visible improvement in living standard of migrant families. Third, a large number of migrants, probably around 7–8 million, have resettled in the country after the completion of overseas employment. The empirical evidence from Pakistan and elsewhere shows that they are at an advantage, because of both remittance-induced savings and overseas experience, to start their own businesses after returning to the home country. This promotes entrepreneurship in the country. The business activities are likely to provide resources to households to sustain their consumption expenditure after migration. For migrants, the change in occupation or movement to self-employment shows a shift from a lower to a relatively better economic and social status. Similarly, based on the perception of migrant families, there is a movement from lower status to higher economic and social status. These families consider themselves as part of the middle economic and social groups.

However, based on the simple analysis carried out in this study, it is not possible to claim that all of the migrants and their families have been upwardly mobile. There could be cases of failure because of short duration of stay abroad, inefficient use of remittances and poor working conditions while abroad. To make migration more useful for the poor, it is recommended that:

- The opportunity to migrate to the Middle East be extended to the populations of the poor regions such as rural Sindh and southern Punjab through awareness on job opportunities in the region and through the provision of better and affordable recruitment services in these regions.
- Return migration should not be considered a burden for the economy. Instead, the tendency of return migrants to lean towards self-employment should be encouraged to boost entrepreneurship in the country.

- The role of the diaspora in different economic and social activities should be increased through their involvement in community projects to bring economic and social stability in the country.

Notes

1 https://en.wikipedia.org/wiki/socio-economic-mobility.
2 The major findings of this study are drawn from the previous work of the author, particularly Arif (2009), Amjad Arif and Irfan (2012) and Arif and Irfan (2007).
3 For details on the social cost of migration, see UN Women (2013).
4 "Hundi" refers to a system for remitting money to Pakistan from overseas through non-banking sources. In this system, the money (foreign currency) given to a dealer abroad is transferred in Pakistani rupees to the family of the sender by an agent.

References

Ahmed, Irfan. 2012. 'Determinants of Remittances and their utilization at the Household Level', Unpublished MA Thesis, Pakistan Institute of Development Economics, Islamabad.

Amjad, R., G. M. Arif and U. Mustafa. 2008. 'Does the Labor Market Structure Explain Differences in Poverty in Rural Punjab?', *The Lahore Journal of Economics* (Special Edition): 139–62.

Amjad, Rashid, G. M. Arif and M. Irfan. 2012. 'Preliminary Study: Explaining the Ten-fold Increase in Remittances to Pakistan 2001–2012', PIDE Working Papers 2012, Pakistan Institute of Development Economics, Islamabad, p. 86.

Amjad, Rashid, M. Irfan and G. M. Arif. 2013. 'An Analysis of the Remittances Market in Pakistan', Post-1, January 06, 2014, Lahore School of Economics, Lahore, pp. 345–74.

Arif, G. M. 2009. *Economic and Social Impacts of Remittances on Households: The Case of Pakistani Migrants in Saudi Arabia.* Islamabad: International Organization for Migration, PIDE.

Arif, G. M. and M. Irfan. 1997. 'Return Migration and Occupational Change: The Case of Pakistani Migrants Returned from the Middle East', *The Pakistan Development Review*, 36(1):1–37.

Bureau of Emigration and Overseas Employment (BEOE). 2007. Unpublished data on the placement of Pakistani migrants abroad, BEOE, Islamabad.

Colen, Cnythia G., Arline T. Geronimus, John Bound and Sherman A. James. 2006. 'Maternal Upward Socio-economic Mobility and Black-White Disparities in Infant Birth Weight', *American Journal of Public health*, 96(11): 2032–39.

Czaika, Mathias and Maria Villores Varella. 2012. 'Labour Market Activity, Occupational Change and Length of Stay in the Gulf', DEMIG Project Paper No. 12, International Migration Institute, University of Oxford.

Dannecker, Petra. 2011. *Beyond Economic Transformation: Return Migration and Social Change in Bangladesh, Rethinking Development in an Age of Scarcity and Uncertainty: New Values, Voices and Alliances for Increased Resilience.* Heslington, England: EADI/DSA, University of York.

Demurger, Sylvie and Hui Xu. n.d. *Return Migration and Occupational Change in Rural China: A Case Study of Wuwei Country,* Grouped' Analyse et de Theorie Economique (GATE), Ecully Codes, France.

Government of Pakistan. 2013. Pakistan Economic Survey 2013–2013, Economic Advisor's Wing, Finance Division, Government of Pakistan, Islamabad.

Gubert, Flore and Christophe J. Nordman. 2011. 'Return Migration and Small Enterprise Development in the Maghreb', in Sonia Plaza and Dilip Ratha (eds), *Diaspora for Development in Africa.* Washington, DC: The World Bank.

Mckenzie, David and Hillel Rapoport. 2007. 'Network Effects and the Dynamics of Migration and Inequality: Theory and Evidence from Mexico', *Journal of Development Studies,* 84: 1–24.

Mesnard, Alice. 2004. 'Temporary Migration and Self-Employment: Evidence from Tunisia', *Brussels Economic Review – Cahiers Economiques De Bruxelles,* 47(1): 120–38.

Quadrini, Vincenzo. 1997. 'Entrepreneurship, Saving and Social Mobility', Discussion paper 116, Institute for Empirical Macroeconomics Federal Reserve Bank of Minneapolis.

Skeldon, Ronald. 2012. 'Migration and Asia Reflections on Continuities and Change', *Asia-Pacific Population Journal,* 27(1): 103–18.

Srivastava, R. and S.K. Sasikumar. 2005. 'Migration and the poor in India: an overview of recent trends, issues and policies', in T. Siddiqui (ed.), *Migration and Development Pro-Poor Policy Choices.* University Press, Dhaka.

United Nations Entry for Gender Equality and the Empowerment of Women (UN Women). 2013. 'Valuing the Social Cost of Migration: An Exploratory Study', pp. 1–167, Bangkok: UN Women Regional Office for Asia and the Pacific.

Wade, Lisa. 2010. 'Comparing Socio-economic Mobility across OECD Countries', Sociological Images, 18 February, http://thesocietypages.org/socimages/2010/02/18/comparing-socioeconomic-mobility-across-oecd-countries/.

The financial crisis in the Gulf and its impact on South Asian migrant workers

S. Irudaya Rajan and D. Narayana

Introduction

The financial crisis had its origins in the United States of America (USA) in 2008, spread to Europe, and then to Japan. The effect of the crisis has been slow to manifest in the six Gulf Co-operation Council (GCC) countries.[1] Their basic strengths – a public funded banking sector and huge trade surplus due to the export of oil, the price of which saw unprecedented increase in a span of six months in 2008 – shielded the GCC economies from the adverse impact during the initial days of the crisis. This, coupled with significant inward foreign direct investments (FDIs) to all GCC countries, except Kuwait, also had a beneficial impact (ESCWA 2008).

The GCC economies, however, began to feel the impact of the global crisis since the last quarter of 2008. The most significant indicator was the slowdown in the gross domestic product (GDP) growth rate in 2008 and the negative growth rate in 2009 in some of these economies. In the financial sector, the stock markets in all the GCC countries recorded a decline owing to the withdrawal of foreign institutional investors. A number of private funded domestic and international projects in the Gulf region had reportedly been cancelled or abandoned, leading to a large number of lay-offs or retrenchment of the workforce. Countries that are more exposed to global capital, investment and consumption demand face a greater risk of being affected by the crisis than others. For instance, Dubai in the UAE, which depends heavily on international capital, tourism and real estate, seems to be more adversely affected than other countries. On the other hand, Saudi Arabia, which has only 25 per cent foreign workers compared to much higher proportions in the other GCC economies, might be much less affected than the others

(Zachariah and Rajan 2009). The slowdown in the growth rates of the GCC economies has particular significance for South Asian expatriates who are the main migrant labour in GCC countries. This would, it was expected, affect the flow of migration and cause unexpected large-scale return emigration and falling remittances (Kapiszewski 2006).

In this context, the following research issues become important:

- How has the crisis affected the demand for South Asian migrant workers in the Gulf countries?
- What strategies did the emigrants adopt to cope with the situation at their place of work (countries of destination) and what is the likely impact of the crisis on the home country in terms of decline in remittances, if any?
- Did countries in South Asia see large-scale return emigration? Did they find a decline in the outflow of emigrant labour to Gulf countries, and inward remittances from them?

The chapter is a modest attempt at analysing these issues in some depth.

Approach and methodology

Following an assessment of the trends in expatriate workers and employment structure in the GCC countries based on the published data and mapping the trends and patterns of international migration, the preferred countries of destination and trends in remittances over a long period of time is attempted. In addition to the macro assessment of the situation, the study is based on two surveys: (a) return emigrants in the countries of origin who lost their jobs in the countries of destination due to the financial crisis and (b) return migrants who come back as per the terms of contract migration.

Return emigrant survey

This survey was conducted among emigrants who had lost their jobs and were forced to return home because of the financial crisis in the Gulf. It also aimed to examine their coping mechanism after their return to their home country. The survey was canvassed among 50 return emigrants, each in the four countries of South Asia – Pakistan, Bangladesh, Nepal, and Sri Lanka. In India, the survey was canvassed among 250 return emigrants in five states of India, selecting 50 each in Andhra Pradesh, Tamil Nadu, Kerala, Maharashtra, and Punjab. Thus the total number of return emigrants surveyed was 450 among the five countries of origin in South Asia. However, we confess that it was difficult to locate the emigrants who lost their jobs in the countries of destination and returned to the countries of origin. The return emigrant survey collected information on household details, the profile of return emigrants, household economic assets, employment, remittances and their utilisation, household expenditure pattern, reasons for return, adaptation and coping mechanisms.

Return migrant resurvey, 2009

Return migration from the Gulf is the normal process of contract migration. Migrants from South Asia go on contract work to the destination countries; and once the contract ends, they, in the normal course, return to the countries of their origin. As of now, we have no estimate of return emigration from the Gulf to South Asia. However, the Centre for Development Studies (CDS) has completed four large-scale migration surveys (1998, 2003, 2007 and 2008) over the last decade. One of the research objectives of this project is to assess the flow of forced return emigration, or return emigrants before the expiry of contract from the Gulf region to South Asia. To assess both regular return migrants and the crisis-led return emigrants from the Gulf, we revisited emigrant households from the 15,000 households of the 2008 Kerala migration survey. We estimated the extent of crisis-led return emigrants to Kerala after the revisit. In a later section of this chapter we apply the same methodology and project the figures to estimate the number of return emigrants from the Gulf to South Asia. In addition, the return migration resurvey 2009 also estimates the number of emigrants who lost their jobs in the Gulf, but had chosen to remain there without returning to their countries of origin. This is new information ('lost job, but have not returned') which will also be generated for South Asia.

3. Financial crisis and growth in the Gulf[2]

The global crisis originating in the USA, spreading to Europe and to Japan, has affected the Middle East through a large fall in price of oil, reversal of capital inflows, depression of property and equity markets, and losses in sovereign wealth funds. The effect of the crisis varied across countries depending upon each country's characteristics, such as high share of oil exports in total exports, large quantum of re-exports, sizeable share of services in GDP, especially transportation, trade, hotel and restaurants. In the region as a whole, growth declined from 5.1 per cent in 2008 to 2.4 per cent in 2009. Among the oil-producing countries, the sharpest slowdown was in the UAE, where the exit of external funds contributed to a large contraction in liquidity, a sizeable fall in property and equity prices, and substantial pressure in the banking system. At the other end of the spectrum is Qatar, which grew by about 9 per cent in 2009 (Table 13.1).

Interestingly, the comparison for the countries in Table 13.1 of growth forecasted for 2009 and the realised growth shows some important patterns. For the developed countries, the contraction that was forecast and realised hardly showed much difference, but the recovery is expected to be quicker. For the South Asian countries as a whole, realised growth is much better than the forecasts and recovery is also rapid. The GCC countries show a mixed pattern: both UAE and Kuwait witnessed contractions more than the forecasts, the rest of the countries except for Qatar reported growth rates higher than the forecasts; the growth recovery in 2010 and 2011 is along expected lines (Table 13.1).

Gulf economies: population and GDP growth

The population of the GCC countries has increased by 8.39 million between 2000 and 2008, an increase which is almost the size of the GCC region, excluding Saudi Arabia, in 2000. The large increase in populations of almost all the Gulf countries is spawned by the high average growth of GDP between 2000 and 2009. Only Kuwait showed a large increase in population with a relatively low increase in GDP (Table 13.2). Along with population growth, the proportion of expatriates in the population has shown an increase. In Qatar and UAE, expatriates constitute over 80 per cent of the total population, and in Kuwait they account for close to 70 per cent of the total population. While in Saudi Arabia and Oman, expatriates constitute slightly over a quarter of the population, Bahrain has over 40 per cent of non- nationals in the total population. The proportion of expatriates in the labour force moves with

Table 13.1 Selected economies: real GDP growth rates (annual % change)

	2001	2002	2003	2004	2005	2006	2007	2008	2009	2010	2011
Country of destination											
Bahrain	4.62	5.19	7.25	5.64	7.85	6.65	8.07 (8.38)	6.12 (6.31)	2.64 (3.11)	3.47 (3.96)	3.94 (4.50)
Kuwait	0.22	3.01	17.33	10.24	10.62	5.14	2.51 (4.46)	6.33 (5.53)	–1.14 (–4.82)	2.39 (2.33)	4.34 (4.44)
Oman	7.51	2.57	2.01	5.33	6.02	6.79	6.38 (6.81)	6.18 (12.84)	3.02 (3.59)	3.80 (4.72)	6.00 (4.68)
Qatar	6.32	3.20	6.32	17.72	9.24	15.03	15.35 (26.76)	16.40 (25.42)	17.99 (8.65)	16.37 (15.96)	8.90 (18.58)
Saudi Arabia	0.55	0.13	7.66	5.27	5.55	3.03	3.52 (2.02)	4.63 (4.23)	–0.91 (0.60)	2.90 (3.42)	4.40 (4.51)
United Arab Emirates	1.70	2.65	11.89	9.69	8.19	9.39	6.34 (6.06)	7.41 (5.14)	–0.60 (–2.47)	1.55 (2.43)	3.29 (3.18)
Country of origin											
Bangladesh	4.83	4.85	5.78	6.11	6.30	6.53	6.32 (6.31)	5.59 (5.96)	5.00 (5.64)	5.38 (5.78)	6.01 (6.26)
India	3.89	4.56	6.85	7.90	9.21	9.82	9.30 (9.89)	7.29 (6.40)	4.52 (5.68)	5.61 (9.67)	6.89 (8.37)
Nepal	5.63	0.12	3.95	4.68	3.12	3.72	3.19 (3.41)	4.70 (6.10)	3.60 (4.86)	3.25 (2.98)	4.81 (4.01)

Pakistan	1.98	3.22	4.85	7.37	7.67	6.18	6.02 (5.64)	5.95 (1.64)	2.50 (3.37)	3.50 (4.79)	4.50 (2.75)
Sri Lanka	−1.55	3.96	5.94	5.45	6.24	7.67	6.80 (6.80)	5.95 (5.95)	2.20 (3.54)	3.59 (7.0)	4.98 (7.0)
Major developed countries											
Japan	0.184	0.262	1.414	2.744	1.934	2.039	2.392 (2.36)	−0.641 (−1.20)	−6.197 (−5.22)	0.515 (2.82)	2.168 (1.50)
United States	0.751	1.599	2.51	3.637	2.939	2.779	2.028 (1.95)	1.111 (0)	−2.751 (−2.63)	−0.049 (2.64)	3.53 (2.31)
United Kingdom	2.462	2.097	2.818	2.758	2.058	2.838	3.022 (2.69)	0.707 (−0.07)	−4.086 (−4.89)	−0.396 (1.70)	2.121 (2.02)

Note: Figures within brackets are from IMF (2010); data for 2009–11 and 2010–11 are forecasts in the IMF (2009) and IMF (2010), respectively.

Source: IMF (2009, 2010) 2010.

Table 13.2 Growth of population and GDP in GCC countries

Country	Population (million)				GDP Growth 2000–08 (%)
	2000	*2009*	*Increase*	*Increase (%)*	
Kuwait	2.217	3.443	1.226	55.30	6.68
Qatar	0.606	1.098	0.492	81.19	11.17
Saudi Arabia	20.474	24.897	4.423	21.60	3.91
UAE	2.995	4.764	1.769	59.07	7.74
Bahrain	0.670	0.779	0.109	16.27	6.29
Oman	2.402	2.769	0.367	15.28	5.36
Total	29.364	37.750	8.386	28.56	–

Source: IMF (2009).

Table 13.3 Profile of expatriates in the Gulf, 2009

Country	Population ('000s)	% Expatriates to total population	% of South Asian expatriates to total expatriates	% of Expatriates in the labour force
Kuwait	3,443	68.8	52.8	83.9
Qatar	1,098	86.5	68.4	92.5
Saudi Arabia	24,897	27.8	54.9	55.8
UAE	4,764	81.0	68.7	89.8
Bahrain	779	43.0	95.1	58.3
Oman	2,769	28.4	89.0	64.3
GCC	37,750	40.3	61.8	–

Sources: Compiled from various sources such as the country reports prepared by the CDS team.

the proportion in the population. Over 60 per cent of the expatriates are from South Asia and in some countries, such as Oman and Bahrain, they account for over 90 per cent of the expatriates (Table 13.3). Overall, the flow of South Asian migrants to the GCC countries is a function of GDP growth in the latter.

Reported figures from the respective embassies in the Gulf and from Kapiszewski (2006), Shah (2009), Taattolo (2006), UN (2009).

Employment structure in the GCC countries

In the GCC countries, over 50 per cent of the workforce is employed in manufacturing, trade and construction. Kuwait and Saudi Arabia are the exceptions, where the share of public administration and defence is rather high (Table 13.4). The share of construction in

Table 13.4 Share of employment (%) across economic activities in GCC countries, 2007

Activity	Bahrain	Oman	Kuwait	Qatar	Saudi Arabia	UAE
Agriculture, hunting & forestry	0.47	9.09	2.60	1.92	4.69	5.0
Fishing	0.01	0.44	0.08	0.43	*	*
Mining & quarrying	0.49	1.96	1.90	5.27	1.32	1.3
Manufacturing	17.54	10.77	4.43	8.69	7.28	13.0
Electricity, gas & water supply	0.13	0.33	0.01	0.66	0.96	1.2
Construction	29.86	34.68	14.23	37.14	10.22	20.6
Wholesale, retail trade & car repairs	24.62	16.18	14.03	12.28	16.10	20.0
Hotels & restaurants	6.55	5.97	2.89	1.96	3.20	4.2
Transport, storage & communication	4.20	1.30	3.85	4.33	4.42	6.2
Financial intermediaries	3.46	0.29	1.21	1.09	1.08	1.4
Real estate & renting services	7.54	1.77	5.59	3.43	3.22	3.3
Public administration and defence	0.01		14.75	6.35	18.03	10.8
Education	1.24	0.76	5.23	3.16	11.96	**
Health & social work	0.24	1.91	2.40	2.55	4.33	**
Community & personal services	2.11	1.08	4.18	1.54	2.26	4.5
Domestic services	0.06	9.96	21.86	8.79	10.79	8.4
Extra-territorial org. & bodies	0.21	2.59	0.11	0.21	0.13	–
Not classified by economic activity	0.30	0.90	0.66	0.18	0.01	0.01
Total	100	100	100	100	100	100

Notes: For Bahrain and UAE, the figures show paid employment by economic activity. For Oman, the figures show expatriate workers in the private sector. Figures for Kuwait are for the year 2005.

*Fishing is included in Agriculture, Hunting and Forestry.
**Education and Health and Social Work are included in Public Administration and Defence.
Source: Rajan and Narayana (2012).

total employment increased rapidly during 2001–08 in some GCC countries. For instance, in UAE, the share of construction sector employment increased by 5 percentage points during the period. In Saudi Arabia, the increase in employment in the construction sector during the period was of the order of 300,000.

As construction is one of the major sectors attracting expatriate labour, it is important to analyse the effect of the crisis on this sector. Project finance and utilities have taken a severe beat-ing along with finance institutions in the current crisis. A survey of projects (worth at least $10 million) in mid-2009 reported 10–30 per cent cancellations or orders put on hold in the GCC countries (Table 13.5). Dubai, which has about 60 per cent of all projects in the GCC region, has taken the largest hit, which in turn has affected the GCC region as a whole. Interestingly, the crisis has affected all sub-sectors – from commercial projects to residential properties – as the illustration from UAE shows (Table 13.6).

While no new projects are being started in the UAE, there is continuing high level of activity in ongoing projects that would be

Table 13.5 Projects affected by the crisis in the GCC region

Country	Projects and finances involved			
	Projects under construction	Projects cancelled/ on hold	Total project worth (billion $)*	% Cancellation
Kuwait	90	18	114	17
Qatar	124	7	42	–
Saudi Arabia	442	106	387	19
UAE	1372	566	900	29
Bahrain	148	54	36	27
Oman	95	8	38	8

Note: *All projects including cancelled/on hold.

Source: Rajan and Narayana (2012).

Table 13.6 Projects affected by sub-sectors, UAE

Sub-sector	Projects under construction	Total number of projects	% Cancellation
Commercial projects	340	487	147 (30)
Hospitality business	288	406	118 (29)
Residential properties	495	712	217 (30)
Retail projects	249	333	84 (25)
Total	1372	1938	566

Source: http://www.gulfbase.com/site/interface/NewsArchiveDetails.aspx?n=110724 (accessed 14 November 2009).

'the envy of many' elsewhere in the world. There is evidence of increased construction activity in Abu Dhabi, Sharjah and Ajman.

Gulf crisis and South Asian labour: the links

The link between economic growth and labour flow is through the growth in manufacturing, trade and construction. Construction, in particular, attracts large numbers of expatriate labour from South Asia. Any of the factors adversely affecting construction would affect labour. The quick rebound of oil prices by mid-2009 and the not too depressing current account and budget balances have made the governments of the GCC countries bolder and induced them to continue major infrastructure investments. The increase in government expenditures (as percentage of GDP) was close to 10 points in most countries (Table 13.7), except Bahrain and Qatar. Fiscal policy has played a crucial role in cushioning the impact of the global crisis in the GCC countries.

The interventions in the banking sectors have also been decisive. A further boost has been the albeit lower but healthy GDP growth in the whole of South Asia in 2009 and the forecast of higher growth rates in 2010. South Asia and China have emerged as the major trading partners of GCC economies and the trade outlook does not look very depressing.

However, the continuing adverse factors have been the depressed real estate market and equity prices in the GCC countries, in particular in Dubai. The recovery would remain fragile as long as private investment does not stimulate growth. FDI, which had played a major role in the high growth of the pre-crisis days, fell drastically in 2009 in almost all GCC countries except Oman, Qatar and Saudi

Table 13.7 Government expenditure in the GCC countries, 2006–11 (% GDP)

Country	2006	2007	2008	2009	2010	2011
Kuwait	31.83	29.94	40.15	47.36	43.22	44.28
Qatar	26.42	25.37	24.52	26.66	23.22	22.47
Saudi Arabia	31.96	34.36	30.81	44.54	42.80	40.75
UAE	18.39	18.98	21.22	32.11	28.34	23.07
Bahrain	28.48	28.70	28.00	31.42	30.83	29.53
Oman	34.44	35.33	29.42	38.73	37.38	37.02

Source: IMF (2010).

Arabia. The fall in UAE is from \$13.7 billion in 2008 to \$4 billion in 2009 (UNCTAD 2009). It is unlikely that the situation would improve till the Dubai World[3] crisis is resolved.

Impact of the crisis on South Asian migrant workers

This section is devoted to an assessment of the impact of the crisis: on the South Asian migrant workers in terms of return emigration; flows of labour emigration from Asia to the Gulf; and inward remittances to South Asia. The assessment is based on the summary results of the emigrant household surveys and survey of return emigrants carried out to understand the coping mechanisms of individuals and families in times of crisis.

Return migration to South Asia from the Gulf, 2009

All agencies working on migration and remittances in the South Asian countries and the Gulf region predicted an exodus of return emigrants from the Gulf to their countries of origin following the crisis. CDS, in Kerala, which has undertaken four large-scale migration surveys in Kerala during the last 10 years to estimate the number of emigrants, return emigrants and remittances, revisited the households of the 2008 survey in 2009[4] to arrive at reliable estimates of return emigrants. All those in the original sample who had returned were asked to cite the reasons for returning to Kerala. The questionnaire provided 10 possible reasons for return, among which the following three could be attributed to recession: job loss and return due to financial crisis, expiry of contract (renewal of contract did not take place as expected due to recession), and compulsory expatriation. The estimates of return migrants due to the crisis are provided in Table 13.8.

If we deduce that out of the stock of 2.19 million emigrants from Kerala, about 61,036 crisis-led migrants returned, then what could be the number of return emigrants from the Gulf to South Asia? According to the database available from various sources (both formal and informal), we arrived at a figure of 9.5 million South Asian emigrants in the Gulf; and the projected return emigrants from the Gulf region to South Asia at about 263,660[5]. The country-wise estimates of return emigrants are provided in Table 13.9. One can also estimate the number of return emigrants from the countries

Table 13.8 Number of return emigrants to Kerala due to recession in 2009

	Sample	Kerala
Total emigrants in 2008 based on 2008 Kerala migration survey	3,953	2,193,412
Return emigrants among emigrants of 2008 in return migration survey in 2009	304	168,681
Return emigrants to Kerala due to financial crisis and recession	110	61,036

Source: Zachariah and Rajan (2009).

Table 13.9 Estimates of return emigrants to South Asia from the Gulf due to financial crisis, 2009

Country	Stock of emigrants	Return emigrants due to crisis
Kerala	2,193,412	61,036
India	5,050,000	140,526
Pakistan	2,300,000	64,002
Bangladesh	900,000	25,044
Nepal	250,000	6,957
Sri Lanka	975,000	27,131
South Asia	9,475,000	263,660

of destination in the Gulf to countries in South Asia. For instance, India had a stock of 1.7 million migrants settled in the UAE; and in the projected number of return emigrants from the UAE, there were 47,000 Indians.

Why is the number so small compared to the numerous prediction? We postulate two important features of Gulf migration from South Asia as responsible for this: (i) the cost of migration to the Gulf and (ii) the peculiarities of the channel of migration. South Asians incur huge costs to migrate to the Gulf. According to the Kerala Migration Survey 2008, the cost of migration to the Gulf varied between Rs 53,951 for Kuwait to Rs 74, 606 for Saudi Arabia – between US$1,200 and US$1,660 at an exchange rate of Rs 45 per US dollar (see Table 13.10). This applies to all the South Asian countries (also see Rajan and Prakash 2009; UN 2009; Zachariah

Table 13.10 Average cost of emigration for different migration corridors from Kerala, 2008

Countries	Average cost (Rupees)
Kerala-Bahrain	57,172
Kerala-Kuwait	53,951
Kerala-Oman	56,840
Kerala-Qatar	66,316
Kerala-Saudi Arabia	74,606
Kerala-UAE	61,308
Kerala-UK	56,589
Kerala-USA	42,080

Table 13.11 Channels of migration by emigrants, 2007

Channel	Male	Female	Total	Male	Female	Total
Friends and relatives	330	185	515	74.2	88.52	78.7
Government agency	3	0	3	0.7	0.00	0.5
Foreign employer	41	7	48	9.2	3.35	7.3
Private recruitment agencies	71	17	88	16.01	8.1	13.5
Total	445	209	654	100.0	100.0	100.0

Source: Rajan, Varghese and Jayakumar (2009).

and Rajan 2009). The high cost of migration to the Gulf caused many emigrants to borrow from various financial sources. Under such conditions, even if the expatriates lost their jobs in the Gulf, they would prefer not to return home fearing their inability to repay the debt already contracted there. They would rather accept any job at a lower wage and send home remittances to repay their loans even during a crisis in the destination country.

Another characteristic of South Asian migration to the Gulf is the part played by the social network, which consists of friends and relatives, who perform a major role in the channel of migration flows by arranging visas and other requirements for the emigration process. For instance, an all-India survey conducted by CDS for the International Labour Organization (ILO) and the Ministry of Overseas Indian Affairs revealed that close to 80 per cent of Indian emigrants utilised their friends and relatives as an important channel for migration (Table 13.11). This also ensured that in the event of a job loss, they could rely on someone to provide them temporary support.

Lost jobs in the Gulf and have not returned to the country of origin

So there is a category of migrants, termed 'lost jobs in the gulf and have not returned to the country of origin', who remain unemployed in the destination country and continue to look for jobs in sectors that are less or not affected by the crisis, at lower wages and poorer working conditions. The Return Emigrant Survey 2009 conducted in Kerala offered a unique opportunity to estimate the number of those who lost their jobs in the Gulf countries due to the crisis there. According to the estimate made by the authors, of the 2.2 million stock of emigrants from Kerala, about 39,396 persons lost their jobs between 2008 and 2009 but have not returned to their country of origin (Zachariah and Rajan 2009). Applying the same methodology to estimate the number of South Asian migrants who lost their jobs in the Gulf yields the number 170,181 (Table 13.12).

Outflow of workers from South Asia to the Gulf, 2009

As there was no official data to show the extent of outflow from South Asia to the Gulf, we estimated the possible trends using reasonably well-managed databases from these countries. All the countries in South Asia, except Sri Lanka, reported decline in the flow of workers to the Gulf. The projected decline for India is huge – about 280,000 – followed by Pakistan with just 12,000 (See Table 13.13).

Table 13.12 Estimates of emigrants who lost jobs in the Gulf but have not returned, 2009

Country	Stock of emigrants	Number lost job but did not return
Kerala	2,193,412	39,396
India	5,050,000	90,703
Pakistan	2,300,000	41,310
Bangladesh	900,000	16,165
Nepal	250,000	4,490
Sri Lanka	975,000	17,512
South Asia	9,475,000	170,181

Table 13.13 Outflow of migrant workers from South Asia to the Gulf, 2005–09

	India	Pakistan	Bangladesh	Nepal	Sri Lanka
2005	454,628	127,810	207,089	88,230	192,004
2006	618,286	172,837	307,620	128,306	170,049
2007	770,510	278,631	483,757	182,870	188,365
2008	818,315	419,842	643,424	169,510	215,793
2009	538,090	407,077	N.A.	152,272	226,299

Source: This table is based on the country papers prepared by the respective country team at the countries of origin for this project.

With regard to destination, the decline was large for UAE, which has been more severely affected by the crisis than the other countries in the Gulf. But this was more than compensated by the increase in the number who left for Saudi Arabia. This pattern holds for India, Pakistan, Sri Lanka, and Nepal. Thus, the crisis has changed the migration and demographic dynamics of South Asian workers in the Gulf region.

Inward remittances to South Asia, 2009

The money that migrants send home is important not only to their families, but also to their country's balance of payments. In many developing countries, remittances represent a significant proportion of the GDP as well as foreign exchange receipts. In *Doing Business 2010* (International Finance Corporation 2009) among the South Asian countries, India was ranked number one in terms of the volume of remittances with US$52 billion in 2008 (4.2 per cent of GDP). Bangladesh was ranked eighth and Pakistan ranked 11th in terms of remittances. On the other hand, Nepal is listed as one of the top 10 countries with the highest share of remittances to the GDP at 22 per cent. When the crisis hit in 2008, the World Bank (2008) stated, 'The outlook for remittances for the rest of 2008 and 2009–10 remains as uncertain as the outlook for global growth, oil and non-oil commodity prices, and currency exchange rates'. After several years of strong growth, remittance flows to developing countries began to slow down significantly in the third quarter of 2008 in response to a deepening global financial crisis.

In late 2008, on request from the Government of Kerala, CDS prepared a report on the 'Global Financial Crisis and Kerala

Table 13.14 Inward remittances to South Asian countries from migrant workers, 2000–09

	India	Pakistan	Bangladesh	Nepal	Sri Lanka
	US$ millions				
2000	12,890	1,075	1,968	111	1,166
2001	14,273	1,461	2,105	147	1,185
2002	15,736	3,554	2,858	678	1,309
2003	20,999	3,964	3,192	771	1,438
2004	18,750	3,945	3,584	823	1,590
2005	22,125	4,280	4,314	1,212	1,991
2006	28,334	5,121	5,428	1,453	2,185
2007	37,217	5,998	6,562	1,734	2,527
2008	51,581	7,039	8,995	2,727	2,947
2009 *	47,000	8,619	10,431	3,010	2,892
2009 +	53,227	8,856	10,525	2,812	3,308
	Percentage change				
2000–01	10.73	35.91	6.96	32.43	1.63
2001–02	10.25	143.26	35.77	361.22	10.46
2002–03	33.45	11.54	11.69	13.72	9.85
2003–04	−10.71	−0.48	12.28	6.74	10.57
2004–05	18.00	8.49	20.37	47.27	25.22
2005–06	28.06	19.65	25.82	19.88	9.74
2006–07	31.35	17.13	20.89	19.34	15.65
2007–08	38.60	17.36	37.08	57.27	16.62
2008–09 *	−8.88	22.45	15.96	10.38	−1.87
2008–09 +	**3.19**	**25.81**	**17.01**	**3.12**	**12.25**

Notes: * World Bank Estimates; + Our estimates

Source: World Bank and the country reports prepared by the research team for this project from five countries of South Asia.

Economy: Impact and Mitigation Measures' (CDS, 2008). The report predicted that the remittances to Kerala were expected to increase from Rs 30.122 crore in 2007 to Rs 42.917 crore in 2008. Both the World Bank and CDS reports predicted that the inflows of remittances to South Asia and Kerala were likely to continue, when the general expectation was that it would fall drastically.

Our estimates based on the simple average of remittances for the available months from the country reports prepared by the teams suggests that all the countries of South Asia are resilient to the crisis in terms of remittances (Table 13.14). Our estimates put the growth in remittances to India at 3 per cent, from US$52 billion in 2008 to US$53 billion in 2009. The World Bank (2009b) report 'Migration and Remittance Trends 2009' confirmed our estimates and said that the outcomes were better than expected, but that there were significant risks ahead.

Why did remittances not decline in South Asia? From our study, the following six observations can be made: (a) the debts contracted to meet the high cost incurred during their migration kept the emigrants from returning to the countries of origin in spite of the lay-offs; (b) the predictions of a large exodus of return emigrants from the Gulf did not come true; (c) though the outflow declined in the first half of 2009, it has still not significantly affected the stock of South Asian migrants in the Gulf; (d) the appreciation of the US dollar vis-à-vis South Asian currencies; (e) continuous rise in oil prices generating more income in the Gulf; and (f) 'reverse migration' of the crisis-led return emigrants back to the Gulf.

Conclusions

The unravelling of the impact of the crisis on output and employment in the US had generated anticipation of large-scale retrenchment of expatriate labourers in the Gulf region. The anticipated misery and the need for rehabilitation did get some governments in South Asia thinking about plans for the returning migrants. We find that the dimensions of the impact were not as large as was feared earlier. For a stock of approximately 9.5 million South Asian emigrants in the Gulf, the number who returned due to the crisis was about 264,000 (just around 2.78 per cent) and the number who lost jobs but who continued to stay in the Gulf was about 170, 000 (1.80 per cent). Overall, less than 5 per cent of the South Asian emigrants had lost their jobs owing to the crisis. But such an impact had not adversely affected the yearly flow of out-migrants from South Asia.

With regard to remittances (in US$), the annual percentage increase since 2004–05 has been over 20 per cent for the South Asian countries, except for Sri Lanka. The magnitude of the increase has taken a hit all over South Asia, except Pakistan from where the outflow of migrants had been increasing at around 50 per cent every year since 2005. But remittances have not fallen following the crisis. As most South Asian currencies have depreciated against the US$ (to which the GCC currencies are pegged) since late 2007, remittances in terms of domestic currencies would have shown an increase. A survey of migrant households in South Asia confirmed these estimates as 94 per cent of households reported regular remittances during the crisis period also (as in previous years) and no significant change in the use of remittances.

Overall, less than 5 per cent of the stock of South Asian migrants in the Gulf had lost jobs and either returned or were struggling to continue in the Gulf. The flow of workers from South Asia to the Gulf had also not been affected to any significant extent, but there were changes in the origin (in favour of Pakistan) and the destination (in favour of Saudi Arabia) of the flow. The volume of remittances into South Asia had also not fallen to any significant extent.

In sum, the crisis of 2008–09 is a blip on the radar of labour migration to the GCC countries from South Asia. A few thousands lost their jobs and had to come back but the number migrating to the Gulf has hardly fallen. With the modest economic recovery since 2010, both the outward flow of labour and inward flow of remittances are on the increase.

Notes

1   The GCC countries are: United Arab Emirates (UAE), Saudi Arabia, Qatar, Bahrain, Kuwait, and Oman.
2   This section is based on the six country reports prepared by the research teams at CDS. Most of the members of the research team have already visited the Gulf to assess the situation on the ground by talking to several stakeholders; additional research is done by the authors of this report.
3   Dubai World, a holding company owned by the Government of Dubai, manages about 90 entities, was asked to delay for six months payment on a $26 billion debt thus shaking the confidence of investors holding the government's debt.
4   Return Emigrant Survey 2009 was conducted at CDS and sponsored by the Department of Non-Resident Keralite Affairs, Government of Kerala (for more details of the survey report, see Zachariah and Rajan 2009a). The fieldwork was carried out from 16 June to 7 September 2009.
5   These could be underestimates as the composition of migrants from Kerala would have a lower proportion of unskilled workers.

References

Centre for Development Studies (CDS). 2008. Global Financial Crisis and Kerala Economy: Impact and Mitigation Measures. Report submitted to the Government of Kerala.

Economic and Social Commission for Western Asia (ESCWA). 2008. 'Foreign Direct Investment Report', E/ESCWA/EDGD/2008/Technical Paper.1, 3 September, United Nations, New York.

International Finance Corporation. 2009. *Doing Business 2010: Reforming through Difficult Times*. The International Bank for Reconstruction and Development and The World Bank, Washington, DC.

International Monetary Fund (IMF). 2009. *World Economic Outlook Database*, April 2009 edition, https://www.imf.org/external/pubs/ft/weo/2009/01/weodata/index.aspx (last accessed on 10 February 2015).

International Monetary Fund (IMF). 2010. *World Economic Outlook Database*, October 2010 edition, https://www.imf.org/external/pubs/ft/weo/2010/01/weodata/index.aspx (last accessed on 10 February 2015).

Kapiszewski, Andrzej. 2006. Arab versus Asian Migrant Workers in the GCC Countries, UN Expert Group Meeting on International Migration and Development in the Arab region, UN/POP/EGM/2006/02.

Rajan, S. I. and B. A. Prakash. 2009. 'Migration and Development Linkages Re-Examined in the Context of the Global Economic Crisis', invited paper for the Civil Society Days of the 3rd Global Forum on Migration and Development, 2–3 November, Athens.

Rajan, S. I., V. J. Varghese and M. S. Jayakumar. 2009. Overseas Recruitment Practices in India: A Critical Assessment. Report submitted to the International Labour Organization (Thailand) and Ministry of Overseas Indian Affairs, Government of India, New Delhi.

Rajan, S. I., V. J. Varghese and M. S. Jayakumar. 2012. *Dreaming Mobility and Buying Vulnerability: Overseas Recruitment Practices and Its Discontents in India*. New Delhi: Routledge.

Ratha, Dilip, Sanket Mohapatra and Zhimei Xu. 2008. Outlook for Remittance Flows 2008–2010: Growth Expected to Moderate Significantly, but Flows to Remain Resilient. Migration and Development Brief, Migration and Remittances Team, Development Prospects Group, The World Bank, November 11.

Ratha, Dilip, Sanket Mohapatra and Ani Silwal. 2009. Outlook for Remittance Flows 2009–2011: Remittances Expected to Fall by 7–10 per cent in 2009. Migration and Development Brief 10, World Bank, July.

Shah, Nasra M. 2009. 'Trends and Policies for Contract Worker Mobility of Asian to the Gulf Cooperation Council Countries', Paper presented at the IUSSP Conference in Marrakech, Morocco, 27 September–2 October, Session 603 on International Migration organised by Ayman Zohry.

Taattolo, Givonni. 2006. *Arab Labor Migration to The GCC States*, Project on Arab Labour Migration.

United Nations (UN). 2009. *International Migration 2009*. New York: Department of Economic and Social Affairs, Population Division.

United Nations Conference on Trade and Development (UNCTAD). 2009. World Investment Report. Transnational Corporations, Agricultural Production and Development, UNCTAD, New York.

World Bank. 2008. *Migration and Development Brief 8. Outlook for Remittance Flows 2008–2010: Growth Expected to Moderate Significantly, but Flows to Remain Resilient.* Washington, DC: World Bank.

World Bank. 2009. *Migration and Development Brief 11. Migration and Remittance Trends 2009: A Better-than-Expected Outcome So Far, but Significant Risks Ahead.* Washington, DC: World Bank.

Zachariah, K. C. and S. Irudaya Rajan. 2009. *Migration and Development: The Kerala Experience.* New Delhi: Daanish Publishers.

For Product Safety Concerns and Information please contact our EU representative GPSR@taylorandfrancis.com Taylor & Francis Verlag GmbH, Kaufingerstraße 24, 80331 München, Germany

Printed and bound by CPI Group (UK) Ltd, Croydon, CR0 4YY

08/05/2025

01864331-0001